The Role of Brands in an Era of Over-Information

Ricardo Fontes Correia
Polytechnic Institute of Bragança, Portugal

Dominyka Venciūtė
ISM University of Management and Economics, Lithuania

Bruno Miguel Sousa
Polytechnic Institute of Cávado and Ave, Portugal

A volume in the Advances in
Marketing, Customer Relationship
Management, and E-Services
(AMCRMES) Book Series

Published in the United States of America by
    IGI Global
    Business Science Reference (an imprint of IGI Global)
    701 E. Chocolate Avenue
    Hershey PA, USA 17033
    Tel: 717-533-8845
    Fax: 717-533-8661
    E-mail: cust@igi-global.com
    Web site: http://www.igi-global.com

Library of Congress Cataloging-in-Publication Data

Names: Correia, Ricardo Fontes, 1978- editor. | Venciūtė, Dominyka, 1990-
    editor. | Sousa, Bruno Miguel, 1983- editor.
Title: The role of brands in an era of over-information / edited by Ricardo
    Fontes Correia, Dominyka Venciūtė, and Bruno Miguel Sousa.
Description: Hershey, PA : Business Science Reference, [2023] | Includes
    bibliographical references and index. | Summary: "This book intends to
    provide knowledge and skills so the readers could understand the digital
    branding process, and its implications in choosing products, services or
    organizations. It is also intended that the book contribute to the
    development and consolidation of recent concepts linked with branding
    and over-information, providing also practical cases where these
    concepts show their relevance"-- Provided by publisher.
Identifiers: LCCN 2023008209 (print) | LCCN 2023008210 (ebook) | ISBN
    9781668483510 (hardcover) | ISBN 9781668483527 (paperback) | ISBN
    9781668483534 (ebook)
Subjects: LCSH: Branding (Marketing) | Marketing--Technological
    innovations. | Information overload.
Classification: LCC HF5415.1255 .R556 2023 (print) | LCC HF5415.1255
    (ebook) | DDC 658.8/27--dc23/eng/20230310
LC record available at https://lccn.loc.gov/2023008209
LC ebook record available at https://lccn.loc.gov/2023008210

This book is published in the IGI Global book series Advances in Marketing, Customer Relationship Management, and E-Services (AMCRMES) (ISSN: 2327-5502; eISSN: 2327-5529)

British Cataloguing in Publication Data
A Cataloguing in Publication record for this book is available from the British Library.

All work contributed to this book is new, previously-unpublished material.
The views expressed in this book are those of the authors, but not necessarily of the publisher.

For electronic access to this publication, please contact: eresources@igi-global.com.

Advances in Marketing, Customer Relationship Management, and E-Services (AMCRMES) Book Series

ISSN:2327-5502
EISSN:2327-5529

Editor-in-Chief: Eldon Y. Li, National Chengchi University, Taiwan

MISSION

Business processes, services, and communications are important factors in the management of good customer relationship, which is the foundation of any well organized business. Technology continues to play a vital role in the organization and automation of business processes for marketing, sales, and customer service. These features aid in the attraction of new clients and maintaining existing relationships.

The Advances in Marketing, Customer Relationship Management, and E-Services (AMCRMES) Book Series addresses success factors for customer relationship management, marketing, and electronic services and its performance outcomes. This collection of reference source covers aspects of consumer behavior and marketing business strategies aiming towards researchers, scholars, and practitioners in the fields of marketing management.

COVERAGE

- Mobile Services
- B2B marketing
- Telemarketing
- Ethical Considerations in E-Marketing
- CRM strategies
- Data mining and marketing
- Online Community Management and Behavior
- Mobile CRM
- Cases on Electronic Services
- Customer Relationship Management

IGI Global is currently accepting manuscripts for publication within this series. To submit a proposal for a volume in this series, please contact our Acquisition Editors at Acquisitions@igi-global.com or visit: http://www.igi-global.com/publish/.

Titles in this Series

For a list of additional titles in this series, please visit:
http://www.igi-global.com/book-series/advances-marketing-customer-relationship-management/37150

Influences of Social Media on Consumer Decision-Making Processes in the Food and Grocery Industry
Theodore Tarnanidis (International Hellenic University, Greece) Maro Vlachopoulou (University of Macedonia, Greece) and Jason Papathanasiou (University of Macedonia, Greece)
Business Science Reference • © 2023 • 317pp • H/C (ISBN: 9781668488683) • US $250.00

Contemporary Approaches of Digital Marketing and the Role of Machine Intelligence
Afzal Sayed Munna (University of Sunderland in London, UK) Md Sadeque Imam Shaikh (University of Wales Trinity Saint David, UK) and Baha Uddin Kazi (Humber Institute of Technology and Advanced Learning, Canada)
Business Science Reference • © 2023 • 260pp • H/C (ISBN: 9781668477359) • US $250.00

Social Media and Online Consumer Decision Making in the Fashion Industry
Theodore Tarnanidis (International Hellenic University, Greece) Eyridiki Papachristou (International Hellenic University, Greece) Michail Karypidis (International Hellenic University, Greece) and Vasileios Ismyrlis (Hellenic Open University, Greece & Hellenic Statistical Authority, Greece)
Business Science Reference • © 2023 • 393pp • H/C (ISBN: 9781668487532) • US $250.00

Management and Marketing for Improved Retail Competitiveness and Performance
José Duarte Santos (Accounting and Business School, Polytechnic of Porto, Portugal) Inês Veiga Pereira (Accounting and Business School, Polytechnic of Porto, Portugal) and Paulo Botelho Pires (Centre for Organizational and Social Studies, Polytechnic of Porto, Portugal)
Business Science Reference • © 2023 • 457pp • H/C (ISBN: 9781668485743) • US $325.00

Global Developments in Nation Branding and Promotion Theoretical and Practical Approaches
Andreas Masouras (Neapolis University, Cyprus) Sofia Daskou (Neapolis University, Cyprus) Victoria Pistikou (Democritus University of Thrace, Greece) Dimitrios Dimitriou (Democritus University of Thrace, Greece) and Tim Friesner (University of Winchester, UK)
Information Science Reference • © 2023 • 324pp • H/C (ISBN: 9781668459027) • US $240.00

701 East Chocolate Avenue, Hershey, PA 17033, USA
Tel: 717-533-8845 x100 • Fax: 717-533-8661
E-Mail: cust@igi-global.com • www.igi-global.com

Table of Contents

Detailed Table of Contents

    Maria Randers, ISM University of Management and Economics, Lithuania
    Ricardo Correia, Polytechnic Institute of Bragança, Portugal
    Dominyka Venciute, ISM University of Management and Economics,
       Lithuania
    Ruta Fontes, Aveiro University, Portugal

This study explores the factors that influence followers' trust in influencer marketing in the Baltic countries and provides practical recommendations for agencies and influencers. Through a comprehensive literature review, the study emphasizes the significance of influencer credibility, encompassing elements such as expertise, image congruence, branded content labeling, and the influencer-follower relationship. The research employs a mixed-methods approach, combining quantitative data collection through a survey targeting social media users and qualitative data collection through interviews with influencer marketing experts. The findings reveal that followers are more likely to trust influencers who exhibit expertise in the specific field being advertised, while incoherence between regular content and advertisements decreases credibility. The outcomes provide valuable insights, offering practical recommendations for agencies and influencers to establish trust and credibility in their advertising efforts.

Chapter 2

Ana Pinto Borges, ISAG-European Business School, Portugal &
Research Center in Business Sciences and Tourism (CICET-
FCVC), Portugal & Research Centre in Organizations, Markets and
Industrial Management (COMEGI), Portugal
Elvira Vieira, ISAG-European Business School, Portugal & Research
Center in Business Sciences and Tourism (CICET-FCVC), Portugal
& Polytechnic Institute of Viana do Castelo (IPVC), Portugal &
Applied Management Research Unit (UNIAG), Portugal
Paula Rodrigues, Lusíada University and Research Centre in Organizations,
Markets and Industrial Management (COMEGI), Portugal
Ana Isabel Canavarro, Universidade Europeia - Ipam, Porto, Portugal

The authors explore the degree of consumer trust regarding the various brands of Covid-19 vaccines made available by laboratories in Portugal. This chapter aims to fill a gap in the literature, since brands of COVID-19 vaccines have never been analysed from a brand trust perspective. The results show that the level of trust differs significantly between vaccine brands, with BioNtech - Pfizer, Moderna - National Institute of Health and Oxford -AstraZeneca inspiring the highest levels of trust among respondents. Other vaccine brands - Sanofi GSK, Janssen Pharmaceutica NV, and CureVac - showed lower levels of trust or respondents had no opinion whatsoever. Gender, age, family net monthly income, educational qualifications, and being a health professional were also found to influence the level of trust towards vaccine brands differently. The results may serve as strategic orientations for the pharmaceutical industry brands, but they may also be the object of reflection for public organisms when making purchasing and implementation decisions in the country.

Chapter 3

Edna Mngusughun Denga, American University of Nigeria, Nigeria

Consumers assess the credibility of a brand by examining its brand narrative, which is crafted to distinguish it from other brands. Marketing professionals create narratives to promote their brands. Brand narratives emerge when there is a consistent and recurring set of meanings associated with a brand, portraying its place in the world. These narratives play a crucial role in reinforcing brand awareness, promotion, and positioning. Brands must effectively convey unique stories that enhance and deepen consumer relationships. As social creatures, people connect with narratives, making a robust brand narrative a powerful tool for interacting, listening to, and engaging with customers. While brand narratives are not a novel concept, social media has transformed the way they are executed. It serves as a form of content marketing, intriguing audiences without overtly promoting products or businesses.

Chapter 4

Nihan Tomris Küçün, BILDAM Cognitive and Behavioral Research and Applications Centre, Turkey

Neuromarketing, which involves the application of neuroscience techniques to investigate the cognitive mechanisms of consumers, independent of their subjective self-reports, has gained significant traction among both commercial entities contending with a diverse target audience and scholars actively involved in associated inquiries. However, it is important to determine the potential and limitations of the techniques, to define the outputs that can be put into practice with research examples, and to create a methodological and ethical framework. In line with these priorities, in this section, neuromarketing instruments are explained and the integration with other methods is discussed. Then, it is detailed which components that effectuate consumer behavior can be monitored and to what extent they can be interpreted with neuromarketing methods. Finally, the criticisms within the framework of scientific ethics are evaluated and suggestions developed for both researchers and brands in the field in order to reach the targeted sustainable benefit.

Chapter 5

Sebastiano Mereu, Sports Business Research Academy, Switzerland

This empirical research examines how motivational factors for sport consumption affect the intention to watch the National Women's Soccer League (NWSL) in the USA. The motivation scale for sport consumption (MSSC) was adopted to collect quantitative data through an online questionnaire from a convenience sample of 302 spectators in the USA who follow the NWSL. The hypothesized relationships were tested via structural equation modeling (SEM). The results indicate that aesthetics, social interaction, escape, and physical skill of the performing athletes have a significant and positive influence on consumption intention or consumption frequency for watching NWSL matches. This study contributes to the body of knowledge for the business of women's sports with an empirical examination on motives for watching the NWSL, a popular women's football league, and explores possible marketing communications tactics necessary to promote the sports brand and encourage people to consume the sports product offered by the NWSL.

Chapter 6

Francesco Pacchera, Tuscia Univeristy, Italy
Chiara Cagnetti, Tuscia University, Italy
Mariagrazia Provenzano, Tuscia University, Italy
Tommaso Gallo, Tuscia University, Italy
Cecilia Silvestri, Tuscia University, Italy

Digital transformation (DT) affects companies' competitiveness mainly in terms of innovation, efficiency, and cost reduction and affects global value chains in specialization, geographic scope, governance, and upgrading. In food, digital tools can improve competitive advantage by supporting companies in ensuring food quality and safety. However, many companies still struggle to respond adequately to DT challenges by adopting new technology concepts as a trend and not a real company imperative, misallocating internal resources and capabilities around technology, and expecting good results. There are no studies in the literature that consider both the adoption of digital technologies and consumer perception in the olive oil sector at the same time. This study has two purposes. The first is to analyse the use of digital technologies by companies in the olive oil sector, and the second is to understand consumer perceptions of the use of digital technologies in traceability.

Chapter 7

Liu Xinyu, Universidade Católica Portuguesa, Portugal
Liu Minghui, Guangzhou College of Technology and Business, China

The rapid growing of social media has created many live-influencers and playing an important role to leading consumer for new brand cognition in competitive market. This chapter examines the influence factors of experience sharing, skill teaching and value perception by live-influencer for a new brand enter into a competitive market. The result shows that the live-influencer's experience sharing (H1a), skill teaching (H1b), and value perception (H1c) are positive influences to customer loyalty; the live-influencer are negative influences to consumer brand satisfaction (H2); the live-influencer's customer loyalty are positive influences to consumer brand satisfaction (H3), which indicates that the live-influencer become a new mediation model and playing important role for new brand in consumer loyalty and consumer satisfaction.

The 21st-century marketplace and its consumers are connected digitally as an innovative and inquisitive technique of information gathering. In the first two decades of this millennium, the proliferation of digital media and increasingly mobile Internet connectivity have undoubtedly had a significant influence on brands and brand management. Innovations have ushered in a brand-new epoch known as "the digital era." This golden age has fostered a few unique challenges that aim to approach branding in novel and interesting ways. Brands are attempting to create a digital identity for their business in today's technology-driven economy to sustain consumer awareness. Maintaining an online presence is essential for businesses to continue being successful and relevant considering the increasing amount of time that customers are spending on digital platforms nowadays.

Chapter 9

In an era of highly polarized public opinion, organizations all over the world are now facing a great dilemma, as brand activism and CSR strategies have a stronger influence on consumer behaviors than the traditional marketing campaigns. With marketing changing from purpose to action, and consumers becoming more belief driven, companies are being asked to take a stand, and choose a side on controversial sociopolitical issues. Advertising, the spearhead of organizational communication, which has always appropriated the social codes in force in society to persuade its target audience to carry out certain actions, nowadays, can no longer be dissociated from the moral concerns of consumers who increasingly demand corporate responsibility from organizations. This chapter explores the evolution of advertising's role, in a historical and contextual approach, analyzed from the new relationship model that citizens and consumers demand from companies and the reflection that it has on the advertising message.

Preface

In today's rapidly evolving digital landscape, consumers embark on their journeys with a multitude of information at their fingertips. The digital branding processes and their implications for consumer behavior have become vital areas of study for marketers, academics, and researchers alike. As the sources of information continue to proliferate, the challenge of processing this vast array of content becomes increasingly daunting.

Led by the surge of social networks and user-generated content, the market is flooded with an overwhelming number of posts. Micro-segmentation has become the norm, resulting in numerous variations of core products, presenting consumers with an abundance of choices. In the midst of this information overload, brands play a crucial role by serving as mental shortcuts, enabling consumers to navigate through the complexities and make decisions that align with their preferences and values.

However, as brands strive to stand out and differentiate themselves, they also face the dilemma of finding unique and distinctive signals that resonate with consumers. Concepts like sustainability, inclusivity, and eco-friendliness have now become common claims made by brands, but their effectiveness in aiding consumer decisions is a subject of inquiry. Do these signals genuinely assist consumers in making better choices, or have they become so commonplace that they are merely ignored?

This edited reference book endeavors to explore and address such pressing questions, focusing on brand management and the emerging trends that foster customer-centric approaches, adding significant value and relevance to brands. Our aim is to equip readers with the knowledge and skills necessary to comprehend the digital branding process and its impact on product, service, and organizational choices. Additionally, we seek to contribute to the development and consolidation of recent branding concepts in the context of over-information, illustrating their practical relevance through insightful case studies.

The book's audience primarily comprises three groups. First and foremost, marketing academics and their students, both at the undergraduate and graduate levels, will find value in strengthening or mastering new concepts concerning brands and branding. Secondly, researchers seeking to stay updated on conceptual advancements and explore real-world case studies will discover meaningful insights within these pages. Lastly, marketers, driven by the need to optimize the potential of brands and marketing strategies, will gain valuable knowledge and skills to thrive in this dynamic era of over-information.

ORGANIZATION OF THE BOOK

Chapter 1: This chapter delves into the factors influencing followers' trust in influencer marketing within the Baltic countries. Drawing upon a comprehensive literature review, the study highlights the importance of influencer credibility, including expertise, image congruence, branded content labeling, and the influencer-follower relationship. Employing a mixed-methods approach, combining quantitative data from a social media user survey and qualitative insights from interviews with influencer marketing experts, the research reveals valuable insights. Followers are more likely to trust influencers displaying expertise in the advertised field, while inconsistency between regular content and advertisements diminishes credibility. Practical recommendations for agencies and influencers are presented to establish trust and credibility in their advertising endeavors.

Chapter 2: This chapter addresses the degree of consumer trust concerning various COVID-19 vaccine brands available in Portugal. Filling a literature gap, it adopts a brand trust perspective to analyze COVID-19 vaccine brands. The results reveal differing levels of trust among vaccine brands, with certain brands inspiring higher levels of trust, while others receive lower levels or remain neutral among respondents. Factors such as gender, age, family net monthly income, educational qualifications, and being a health professional influence trust towards vaccine brands differently. The findings offer strategic guidance for pharmaceutical industry brands and serve as points of reflection for public organizations when making purchasing and implementation decisions in the country.

Chapter 3: This chapter explores how consumers evaluate a brand's credibility through its brand narrative, a compelling tool to differentiate it from competitors. Brand professionals craft narratives to promote their brands, depicting their position in the world consistently. Effective brand narratives reinforce brand awareness, promotion, and positioning, forging deeper connections with consumers. While brand narratives are not new, social media has revolutionized their execution, acting as content marketing to captivate audiences without overtly promoting products. This chapter examines the power of brand narratives and their transformation in the digital era.

Chapter 4: Examining the application of neuroscience techniques in consumer behavior, this chapter explores neuromarketing's potential and limitations. It outlines the integration of neuromarketing with other methods, monitoring components affecting consumer behavior and their interpretability through neuromarketing methods. Ethical considerations within the scientific framework are evaluated, offering suggestions for researchers and brands to achieve sustainable benefits. Neuromarketing's growing significance for commercial entities and scholars is highlighted, emphasizing its role in understanding consumer cognition beyond subjective self-reports.

Chapter 5: This empirical research focuses on the motivational factors influencing the intention to watch the National Women's Soccer League (NWSL) in the USA. Utilizing the Motivation Scale for Sport Consumption (MSSC), the study gathers quantitative data through an online questionnaire from NWSL spectators. Structural equation modeling (SEM) is employed to test the hypothesized relationships. Results indicate that aesthetics, social interaction, escape, and athletes' physical skill significantly influence consumption intention for watching NWSL matches. The findings contribute to understanding motives for watching women's sport and offer marketing communications tactics to promote the NWSL sports brand.

Chapter 6: This chapter examines the impact of digital transformation (DT) on companies' competitiveness and global value chains in the olive oil sector. Digital tools can enhance competitive advantage by ensuring food quality and safety. However, many companies struggle to respond to DT challenges effectively. This study analyzes the adoption of digital technologies by olive oil companies and explores consumer perceptions of digital technologies in traceability. By fulfilling this dual purpose, the chapter provides insights into the potential benefits of DT in the olive oil industry.

Chapter 7: The chapter investigates the influence of live-influencers on consumer brand loyalty and satisfaction. Examining experience sharing, skill teaching, and value perception by live-influencers for new brands entering competitive markets, the study reveals their positive impact on customer loyalty. Surprisingly, live-influencers show negative effects on consumer brand satisfaction. The research establishes a new mediation model, highlighting the significance of live-influencers in driving consumer loyalty and satisfaction for new brands.

Chapter 8: In this chapter, the editor discusses the transformative influence of digital media and mobile Internet connectivity on brands and brand management in the 21st century. Termed "the digital era," this new epoch presents unique branding challenges. Brands must establish a digital identity to maintain relevance in a technology-driven economy where customers spend increasing amounts of time on digital platforms. The chapter emphasizes the importance of sustaining an online presence to sustain consumer awareness and success in today's competitive market.

Chapter 9: The final chapter delves into the evolving role of advertising in an era of polarized public opinion. As brand activism and corporate social responsibility gain prominence, advertising plays a pivotal role in reflecting consumers' moral concerns and demands for corporate responsibility. The chapter provides historical and contextual analysis of advertising's new relationship model, where brands are asked to take a stand on controversial sociopolitical issues. Brands must adapt their messaging to resonate with belief-driven consumers seeking responsible and ethical practices from organizations.

By delving into these subjects, we hope to shed light on the pivotal role of brands amidst the ever-expanding realm of information and assist readers in navigating this complex landscape effectively. As editors, we extend our gratitude to the contributing authors for their valuable insights and expertise, which have made this book possible. It is our sincere belief that this collective effort will enrich the knowledge base and inspire further exploration into the fascinating world of brands and their significance in an era defined by over-information.

Ricardo Correia
Polytechnic Institute of Bragança, Portugal

Dominyka Venciute
ISM - University of Management and Economics, Lithuania

Bruno Sousa
Polytechnic Institute of Cávado and Ave, Portugal

Chapter 1
Trust in Influencer Marketing:
Factors Influencing Followers' Perceptions in the Baltic Countries

Maria Randers
ISM University of Management and Economics, Lithuania

Dominyka Venciute
ISM University of Management and Economics, Lithuania

Ricardo Correia
ⓘ https://orcid.org/0000-0002-0132-4002
Polytechnic Institute of Bragança, Portugal

Ruta Fontes
ⓘ https://orcid.org/0000-0001-8697-1323
Aveiro University, Portugal

ABSTRACT

This study explores the factors that influence followers' trust in influencer marketing in the Baltic countries and provides practical recommendations for agencies and influencers. Through a comprehensive literature review, the study emphasizes the significance of influencer credibility, encompassing elements such as expertise, image congruence, branded content labeling, and the influencer-follower relationship. The research employs a mixed-methods approach, combining quantitative data collection through a survey targeting social media users and qualitative data collection through interviews with influencer marketing experts. The findings reveal that followers are more likely to trust influencers who exhibit expertise in the specific field being advertised, while incoherence between regular content and advertisements decreases credibility. The outcomes provide valuable insights, offering practical recommendations for agencies and influencers to establish trust and credibility in their advertising efforts.

DOI: 10.4018/978-1-6684-8351-0.ch001

1. INTRODUCTION

Over the past decade, the entire concept of advertising has changed due to the growing popularity of social media platforms such as Instagram, Snapchat, TikTok, etc. People got an opportunity to freely share information, recommendations, and opinions. Eventually, such individuals were called influencers, and now it is a profession successfully used for advertising. The entire influencer marketing field exploded in 2013 when Instagram introduced a sponsored advertisement function (Goel & Ember, 2015). Consequentially, influencer marketing organizations sprung up one after another, whereas more and more businesses and potential buyers flocked to social media platforms.

However, since influencer advertising has become so widespread, it is only natural there has been a backlash. The followers have become less trusting and more unaffected by anything the influencers say, hence creating a growing issue for the influencer marketing agencies and influencers themselves (Venciute et al., 2023). The agencies must achieve the client's objectives, which is very difficult to do without knowing how people will react to the content created by a specific person. Meanwhile, Influencers who do not produce good results become irrelevant and unappealing for future orders. Therefore, to survive in this market and keep the competitive advantage both as an agency and as an influencer, it is critical to understand the main factors affecting influencer marketing reliability leading to positive customer intentions.

Based on empirical research, this chapter intends to identify and analyze the main factors affecting followers' trust in influencer marketing in Baltic countries suggesting practical recommendations both for agencies and influencers.

2. LITERATURE REVIEW

One of the main issues that influencer marketing agencies are dealing with these days is the credibility that the chosen influencer conveys (Sokolova and Kefi, 2020). Some credibility level is crucial for developing favorable attitudes and intentions toward the influencer to maintain relevance and the overall influencer capacity (Belanche et al., 2021). Credibility refers to the consumer's view of the source of information, with people more inclined to choose a reputable source (Kerstetter and Cho, 2004). Analyzing the literature on the subject revealed that expertise and similarity of the product and the influencer, branded content labeling, and a bond between the follower and the influencer are the key elements that affect the credibility of influencer marketing.

2.1 Influencers' Expertise and Image

Expertise is described as the degree a person is regarded to have the necessary knowledge and experience on a specific product or service (Van der Waldt et al., 2011). Followers tend to value the influencer's recommendations more if the influencer has any expertise and experience in that specific topic (De Veirman et al., 2017). Moreover, when an influencer's image fits with the promoted products, the credibility and attitude toward further possible intentions improve. The more the product is congruent with the influencer's style, the more positive effects it might bring (Belanche et al., 2021). However, influencers are frequently persuaded to make advertisements that do not correspond to the represented image for a higher payment, resulting in negative short and long-term consequences. Followers can judge such publications for the absence of coherence between the product advertised and the influencer's typical content (Kim and Kim, 2021). Therefore, influencers should think wisely before doing such collaborations and incorporating them into the personal narrative (Casaló et al., 2020). There is a good example of this case when influencer Chriselle Lim, that usually covers beauty and fashion topics, posted a component of a new Volvo car consequentially, both the brand and the influencer received negative feedback and poor advertisement results. On the contrary, when Danielle Bernstein who is associated with a healthy lifestyle posted a workout video with Fiji water – the advertisement brought very positive reactions and success to both sides (Hesterberg, 2019).

2.2 Branded Content Label

The branded content label indicates that the creator has been rewarded, either financially or with something else of value by a business partner. Collaborations between the influencers and the brands are not as frequent as influencers posting general content. Therefore, it is only natural that the labeled content has a critical nature since it may not be so closely related to the usually covered topics (Castillo and Fernández, 2019). Moreover, direct monetary incentives to influencers in exchange for recommending the product to the followers are regarded the same as a purchased article, thus the influencer is considered to be selling the gathered follower's trust (Hsu and Tsou, 2011). Following that it was stated that an influencer's credibility suffers when followers believe the influencer has been paid to participate in any promotional activities (Belanche, et al., 2021). However, the product samples and discount codes may help the situation as the customers perceive this as a product trial opportunity and would respond to this type of advertisement more positively (Hsu and Tsou, 2011).

2.3 Relationship With the Followers

Previous research has shown that when the influencer-follower relationship is weak, followers are less likely to trust and behave positively (Anongdeth and Barre, 2019). Therefore, it can be argued that the success of influencers on social media is heavily dependent on the relationship between the influencer and the follower. People frequently follow influencers who share a common interest in a particular field to obtain advice and useful information on which the influencer is considered to be an expert. As a result, communities of special interests are forming, and influencers may achieve even better results by generating greater affinity (Casaló et al., 2020). Since followers make daily decisions affecting the influencer through simple click-based behaviors, influencers typically seek to form deeper links with their followers to establish long-term relationships that would improve overall performance (Tafesse and Wood, 2021). Therefore, each publication is very important because, collectively, it should foster a community in which consistent and relevant content is discussed (Casaló et al., 2020). If the publication does not correspond to the influencer's regular content, it may negatively impact future influencer growth and influencer marketing results (Kim and Kim, 2021).

3. METHODOLOGY

The purpose of this study is to identify and analyze the main factors affecting followers' trust in influencer marketing in Baltic countries suggesting practical recommendations both for agencies and influencers. Both quantitative and qualitative data collection methods were used to gather the information for the research. A survey of social media users was used to clarify how to improve influencer marketing credibility in the Baltic states. Additionally, 5 interviews were conducted with influencer marketing experts working for agencies for more detailed insights to substantiate the arguments gathered in quantitative data collection.

3.1 Description of Sampling and Data Collection Process

The target population for the quantitative research was social media users in Lithuania, Latvia, and Estonia that follows at least one influencer on their social media. For this data collection, a mix of non-probability sampling techniques, such as convenience internet and snowball sampling were used. The population consists of an estimated 2.04 million social media users in Lithuania (Kemp, 2021), 1.55 million users in Latvia (Statista, 2022), and 1.05 million users in Estonia (Kemp, 2022), for a total population of 4,64 million social media users in the Baltic states. The intended sample size of the research is 1040. The sampling frame for the survey is Instagram story frame sharing on influencer accounts and Facebook groups that consists of people living in Latvia and Estonia. The survey data was collected from the 30th of October till the 3rd of November 2022. The Five semi-structured interviews with specialized influencer marketing specialists were also conducted to delve deeper into the findings (Table 1). The interview data took place from the 24th to the 28th of October 2022.

Table 1. Semi-structured interviews

Name	Position	Agency	Company Description
Simona Sesickaitė	General Manager	Bmedia	Bmedia it's a boutique digital marketing agency specialized in influence marketing, located in Vilnius Lithuania.
Laura Daugelevičiūtė	Digital Project Manager	INK	INK agency was founded in 2005 and is an integrated creative communications agency Located in Vilnius Lithuania. It operates with several brands in Lithuania, Latvia, and Estonia
Andrius Minsevičius	CEO	SwaY	Sway is a specialized influencer marketing agency located in Lithuania's capital Vilnius. It began to operate in 2019 with an attitude that these days everyone can influence.
Paulina Diržiūtė	Project manager		
Vaiva Gasiūnaitė	Influencer marketing specialist		

From Table 2, it can be seen that a large majority of the respondents (70%) are from Lithuania, with significantly fewer participants coming from other Baltic states. This was expected but with a slightly smaller proportion difference. Furthermore, the rest 14% (166 out of 1182 surveyed) of respondents are not residents of Lithuania, Latvia, or Estonia, indicating that the intended target population was not met. Such participants were directed to the survey's end. Meanwhile, all the interviewees were Lithuanians from Lithuanian agencies operating in all three Baltic countries.

Then participants were asked to identify which social media accounts they use. The greater part of the survey respondents (1007 out of 1016 surveyed) has an Instagram account, with Facebook being slightly behind. Meanwhile, the least used social media platform is Twitter. This highlights the most popular social media platforms in the Baltic states, which businesses should consider when displaying advertisements.

Table 2. Sample profile and demographics

Item		Frequency	Percentage (%)
Gender	Male	61	5
	Female	1121	95
	Total	1182	100
Age	Under 18	118	10
	18-24	461	39
	25-34	319	27
	35-44	213	18
	45-54	71	6
Residence	Lithuania	827	70
	Latvia	130	11
	Estonia	59	5
	Other	166	14

Table 3. Social media accounts

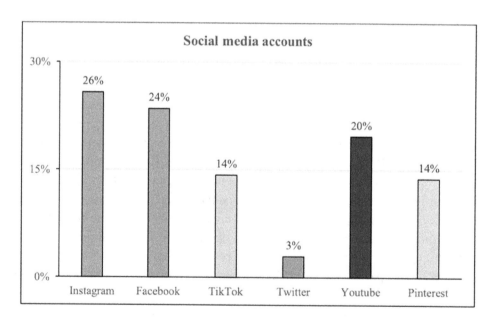

Survey participants were asked to indicate what encourages them to follow influencers (Table 4).

Table 4. Following factors

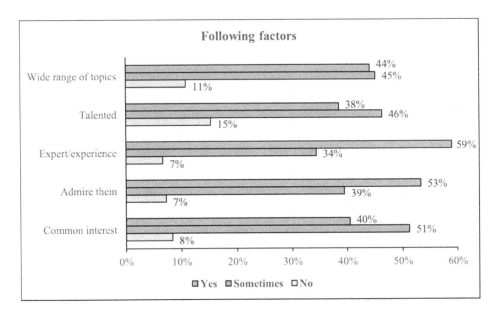

More than half of survey participants answered that they follow influencers who are experts or have experience in a specific topic that interests them. Not far behind is the admiration factor. Furthermore, watching people with some kind of talent was the least preferred following factor. All in all, looking at the results, it can be said that most followers are attracted by niche accounts led by specialists in their field, rather than overall talented personalities.

This was also highlighted in the interview with Simona from the Bmedia agency. She emphasized the importance of considering how a person grew their social media following when choosing an influencer. She supported this statement with the observation that famous people known from television or other places produce significantly worse advertising results than influencers who have gathered followers through their hard work specifically on social media.

Survey participants were asked if they had ever searched for a recommendation on social media before purchasing a specific product or service (Table 5).

The survey displays that two-thirds of respondents (607 out of 1016) stated they do or have previously looked for product recommendations on social media

Table 5. Recommendation searching

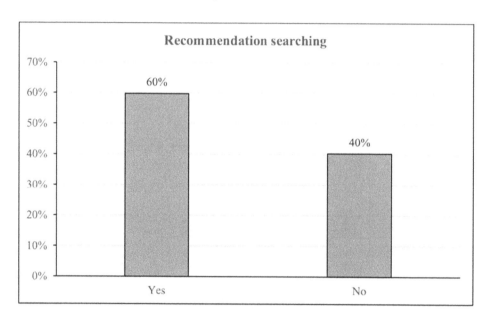

before purchasing. While the remaining 40% argued they do not engage with social media advertisements before making a purchase decision. The key finding from this question perceives the strength of word-of-mouth marketing on social media. Respondents displayed the impact influencer marketing has on purchase intent. Therefore, influencers have a special role in the virtual community and companies have to carefully search for influencers who can differentiate their content from traditional paid endorsements/advertisements and generate genuine interest and impact purchase intention.

Respondents to the survey were asked if they had ever purchased anything after seeing an influencer advertisement on social media (Table 6)

More than 80% (842 out of 1016 surveyed) replied that they had purchased a product or service after seeing an influencer advertisement on social media. This study confirms once again that influencer media marketing is very effective, and there is a high probability that people will purchase a product or service after seeing an advertisement from a specific person on social media.

During an interview with Simona from Bmedia, who previously worked in TV marketing, it was noted that old marketing forms, such as TV, have passed their prime and no longer produce the same strong results. She was certain that it had been intercepted by social media influencers.

Table 6. Purchasing after ad

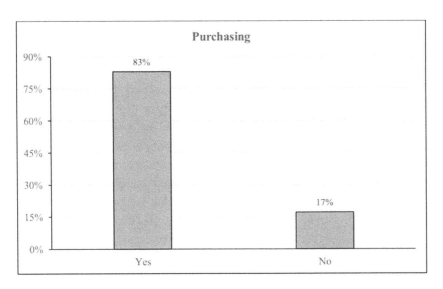

Survey participants were asked to rate how credible they thought influencers were in general (Table 7)

The survey responses ranged more between the averages. The majority of the respondents (374 out of 1016 surveyed) considered influencers were somewhat credible,

Table 7. Influencer credibility level

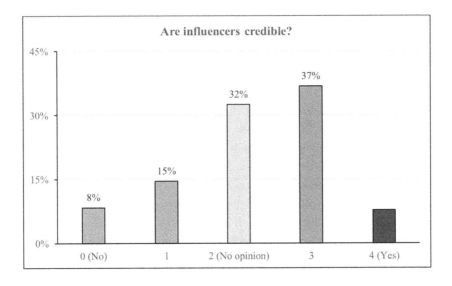

meanwhile, only the minority of the participants (79 out of 1016 surveyed) believed that the influencers were truly credible. The remaining 55% of the participants indicated that they had no opinion or believed that the influencers were rather not trustworthy. This demonstrated that people are unsure whether influencers can be trusted, which is a problem for both influencers and specialized influencer marketing agencies.

All of the interviewees denied this issue and argued that based on previous campaign results - people do trust influencers. Even though influencers face a lot of backlash and criticism for "selling their soul" for money, Vaiva from SwaY agency believed that influencer marketing provides the most benefits to the clients. According to Vaiva, influencer trends are increasing since more and more businesses are beginning to use them, which is the best argument for claiming that influencer marketing is reliable and effective. On the other hand, Laura from the INK agency stated that everything is heavily dependent on the specific influencer. It appears that consumer confidence and trust levels vary depending on who is delivering the advertisement. This was also confirmed by Audrius, the CEO of SwaY agency, who stated that there are various types of influencers in the industry, but self-respecting businesses that have invested a significant amount of time and effort into the reputation and brand development should not risk working with influencers who are fake and pretends to use its services or products. All in all, even though the survey results did not show that people believe influencers are credible, it was demonstrated during the interviews that they are credible when compared to other marketing methods. Although Simona from Bmedia mentioned that she noticed a difference in perception in Latvia, implying that people are not as trusting as in other Baltic states, the impact of influencers in this country is still greater than other forms of marketing.

Survey participants were asked to rank factors to better understand what makes influencer advertisements credible (Table 8).

According to the findings of this survey, influencer advertising is held most reliable when the influencer is an expert in the subject area. Moreover, another critical factor that affects ad reliability is the overall influencer credibility level, which impacts the positive or negative end-user perception of the advertisement and most probably brand itself. Meanwhile, the least popular factor that increases the trustworthiness of influencer marketing is when the advertisement does not correspond to the usual person's content. On the contrary, this factor received the most disagreements (21% "disagree" and 21% "strongly disagree") from respondents, implying that a lack of content coherence would not increase, but rather decrease, the credibility of such influencers' advertisements. The remaining factors such as admiration and influencer-follower bond received an approximately similar distribution of agreement and disagreement between the defendants.

Moving on to the interviews, when questioned about the potential impact of influencer knowledge or experience on the advertised subject, Laura from INK

Table 8. Credibility factors

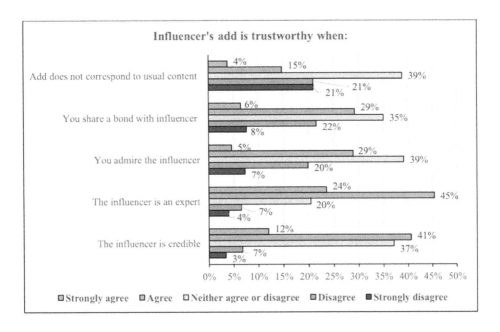

agency stated that people would undoubtedly trust an influencer more if his/her profession or entire activity is related to the advertised product. Paulina from the SwaY agency agreed to that, saying that in such a case, the influencer would be more honest about the promotion. It would not be as promotional or staged, but on the contrary - the influencer would be able to provide some personal advice, further encouraging followers to buy or use the service. Furthermore, Audrius from the SwaY agency added that influencers with subject knowledge can use much stronger arguments and answer questions straight off, which is much more effective and convincing. Meanwhile, Simona from Bmedia only partially agreed to it saying that expertise might increase the credibility level of the advertisement, but much greater results come from those influencers who have a strong authority among people. She argued that even if the influencer has no knowledge of that specific field but is a strong person whom people look up to, they will blindly trust him/her. A similar thing was mentioned in the interview with Laura from INK, where she emphasized that there is a type of influencer who can sell everything very well and nobody knows why because there are no measurable indicators that explain it. Finally, Vaiva from the SwaY agency did not believe that influencer expertise would affect user perception, stating that one does not need to be a hairdresser to recommend a good shampoo. People would believe an influencer with beautiful hair if she said that a certain hair product is good.

The influencer content and ad coherence factor were also discussed during the interviews. The majority of those interviewed agreed with the survey respondents that the lack of coherence would not make the ad trustworthy, however, there were some exceptions. Audrius, the CEO of SwaY, and Laura from INK agency both agreed that such advertising would fail because the focus would be on the influencer's unusual behavior rather than the product or brand itself. Besides, such communication could spark a lot of controversies and follower dissatisfaction, potentially harming the influencer's reputation and even the image of the advertised brand. Furthermore, even though Vaiva from the SwaY agency agreed that a lack of coherence between the advertisement and the usual content would, in most cases, harm the advertisement's reach and make it irrelevant, both Vaiva and Paulina mentioned some instances when such content could improve the results. According to these two interviewees, bold and unusual advertising can garner much more attention and success, even if the advertised product is completely unrelated to the influencer. It was emphasized that content with a dash of humor works particularly well in the Lithuanian market, thus, the influencers should be encouraged to be creative.

Survey participants were asked if the paid partnership label influenced their level of trust in the recommendation.

According to the survey, more than half of the respondents (542 out of 1016 surveyed) answered that the paid partnership label reduces their trust and willingness

Table 9. Branded content

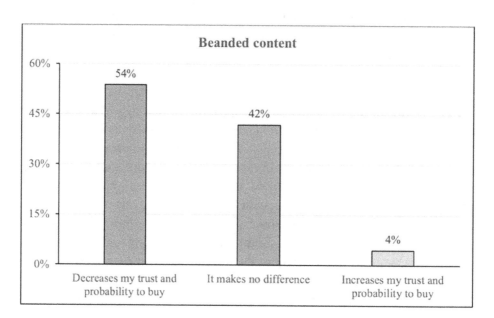

to buy. Meanwhile, only 4% of the participants (45 out of 1016 surveyed) indicated that they would trust the influencer recommendation more if the content was labeled. This finding demonstrates that influencers are distrusted when people believe they were compensated for sharing a product or service on social media.

However, there were a variety of viewpoints expressed during the interviews. Simona from Bmedia claimed that ad labels negatively impact people's reactions and overall ad performance. It makes no difference whether the influencer is honest or not when people realize it is an advertisement - some of them will reject it immediately. Moreover, Vaiva from the SwaY agency agreed to it saying that people are simply inclined, perhaps out of rage and hatred, to avoid such content that influencers advertise and profit from. However, the reach of Latvians and Estonians, even with fewer followers, is always greater than that of Lithuanians, so Lithuanians may react to the word "advertising" a bit worse than others. The remaining interviewees believed that ad labels did not affect people's reactions towards the influencer recommendations since it is already a kind of standard practice because influencer marketing has been around for a long time and people are used to it.

Survey respondents were asked to indicate if they would be more likely to buy a product advertised by the influencer if there was an incentive such as a discount code, two for the price of one, or something else offered (Table 10).

Table 10. Purchase incentives

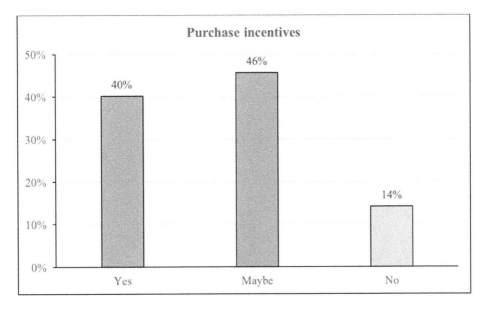

The survey displays that when incentives are offered in the advertisement, people's purchase intentions increase. 40% of the respondents (408 out of 1016 surveyed) indicated that they would be more likely to buy the advertised product or service if a discount code or other sales promotion was offered, while 46% (465 out of 1016 surveyed) answered "Maybe".

All of the interviewees agreed that when there are special promotions, people tend to buy more. Audrius, the CEO of SwaY, stated that it immediately gives a call to action and creates the impression that this offer will only be valid for a limited time, ensuring sales right now, not in the future. Regarding discount codes, Simona from Bmedia stated that her company does not recommend using influencer name-related codes (f.e. "SIMONA20") because it gives the impression that it is a direct advertisement made by a person. However, if it is a general discount code, people in Baltic countries appreciate gifts, discounts, and other low-cost offers and it will increase the purchase results. Furthermore, Vaiva from the SwaY agency stated that when it comes to any giveaways (gifts) from influencer accounts, it does not matter if the product is suitable for the followers or not - people will still participate because they always want to get something for free. Overall, these findings highlight the significance of purchase incentives in social media influencer advertisements if the primary goal is to sell.

Survey participants were asked if they would trust the influencer more if he/she developed a closer bond with the followers (Table 11)

Table 11. Influencer-follower bond

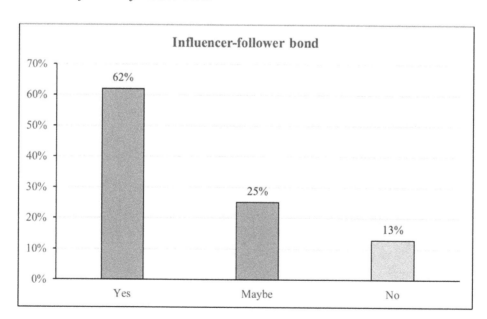

The majority of respondents (629 out of 1016 surveyed) replayed that they trust the influencer more if he or she has a stronger bond with them. Simultaneously, only 13% (131 out of 1016 surveyed) believe that engaging with followers does not increase the influencer's overall credibility. This demonstrates the importance of maintaining constant communication with the followers to improve the overall performance of the influencer and its advertisements.

The impact of the influencer-follower bond was also emphasized in the interviews. All respondents agreed that maintaining a positive relationship with their followers is critical, emphasizing that an influencer should be a friend, albeit behind the screen. Simona from Bmedia noticed that, while closer bonds are not as important in other countries, it is critical in the Baltic states. That was further explained by Paulina from the SwaY agency, who stated that content creators that involve followers in his/her daily life activities receive a lot more attention and admiration. When people are genuinely interested in that person, it encourages people to watch the advertisements, believe them, and buy the advertised product.

4. CONCLUSION

According to the interviews with marketing agencies experts companies frequently choose prominent celebrities or completely wrong influencers to promote their brand due to admiration or a large following, without considering any other valuable factors. However, based on the findings of this study, to achieve the desired advertisement performance, it is critical to connect the product or service with the right influencer. When conducting the quantitative research, it was discovered that most people follow influencers because they are experts in the field that followers are interested in. This was also evident when respondents were asked to identify the factors that increase their trust in the influencer recommendations, with the results indicating that people trust influencers the most when they have knowledge or experience in the advertised field. On the contrary, the lack of coherence between regular influencer content and the displayed advertisement was identified as the least favorable factor, which would rather lower the credibility of influencer advertisements. This was expected, considering that the same factors were emphasized in the literature review as well. Moreover, it is important to note that according to the research, people are least attracted to talented individuals, as argued by Simona from Bmedia agency, who shared her observations that famous people known from television or other places produce significantly worse advertising results than influencers who have gathered followers through their hard work on social media. In such cases, it is critical to discuss this possibility and consider whether paying more for the "name" in social media advertising is worthwhile if it does not produce results. Furthermore, survey results revealed that a growing amount of people search for product recommendations on social media before purchasing, so it would be wise for the agencies to propose such influencer marketing content units that would remain on the profile indefinitely and be easily discovered later by protentional future customers. By carefully considering all of these steps, the agencies are very likely to generate excellent exposure and achieve high standards of advertising reliability and overall performance in the Baltic region. All in all, even though this may change quickly, agencies should prioritize Instagram and Facebook for the time being before releasing ads on other platforms. Then, the agency must thoroughly assess the product's features and determine which category it falls into before selecting an influencer for promotion. Finally, it is necessary to look for influencers who are skilled or have any experience in that determined category to better reflect the desired message. Based on the study, this will foster a stronger bond and level of credibility between the target audience and the influencer.

Finally, throughout the data-gathering process, it was discovered that the level of the bond the influencer has with his or her followers affects the credibility people perceive. This means that the more time the influencer spends communicating with his or her followers, answering messages, doing Q&A's (Instagram Question and Answers function), and so on, the more views, responses, and trust the content generated on that platform attracts because followers see the influencer as a friend. The importance of the influencer-follower connection was also emphasized in the interviews, as it was stated that content creators who involve followers in their daily lives receive a lot more attention and admiration. As a result, people are more likely to see advertisements and believe them. Considering all of this, perhaps it would be beneficial to develop a marketing plan that includes not only informing customers through influencers but also interacting with them.

5. MANAGERIAL IMPLICATIONS

Previous studies have shown that influencer marketing already has a direct impact on sales (Somppi, 2017). However, when businesses use influencers as a marketing strategy and their primary goal is to increase sales, they must find a way to encourage people not only to be engaged but also to buy the advertised product. One of the most used alternatives is competing on pricing when businesses position themselves as a more appealing option. During the quantitative research, it was discovered that if a sales promotion was offered, people would be more likely to purchase that specific advertised product or service. This was emphasized in the interviews as well, revealing that discount codes are considered important as an immediate call to action that creates the impression that the offer is only valid for a limited time, ensuring sales at that exact moment. It can be safely stated that these days, discount codes are the most commonly used promotion since they not only attract buyers but also assist marketing firms in calculating the true advertisement provided worth. However, it was suggested that instead of using name-related codes, which gives the immediate impression that this is a direct advertisement, general codes be displayed. Furthermore, there are some other ways to persuade people to take action and buy the product such as giveaways, two-for-one pricing, additional gifts, and some kind of product-winning contests. During the empirical research, it was identified that people, especially in the Baltic countries, appreciate gifts, discounts, and other low-cost offers and will most likely take advantage of such opportunities, even if they do not need that product or service.

On the other hand, it was stated in the interviews that regularly organizing giveaways for comments, follows, or likes may harm that influencer's marketing because some of his/her followers gathered to win something rather than because they genuinely like that person, and thus do not intend to buy the product advertised by the influencer in the future, thereby harming the influencer's advertising results. Considering this, influencers and businesses should not overuse it to maintain a real engagement circle and only occasionally reward the followers.

During the interviews, it was revealed that brands rarely retain the same influencer for advertising and are continuously searching for new people to reach new customers, resulting in the brand remaining in a constant introduction faze. However, in the quantitative research, a large portion of people surveyed stated that frequently switching brands harms the credibility of influencer advertising as well as customer-brand loyalty more than it helps it. By encouraging clients to pursue long-term ambassadorships, the agencies could develop additional strategies with the same influencer that go beyond simply presenting the product to followers. Consequentially, being regularly reminded of the brand, informed about developments and promotions, and guided by a feeling of community, followers may purchase the product more than once.

Nonetheless, shorter campaigns should not be dismissed because they provide the agency with a better judgment of which influencers can be hired on a long-term basis depending on the kind of engagement they generate. short campaigns to run special holiday offers or create some hype with mega influencers may be a great alternative that requires less influencer budget allocation whilst also having a higher chance of getting noticed and bringing in some additional purchases. All in all, based on the findings of this study, to encourage repeat purchases and brand loyalty, influencer marketing agencies should encourage clients to select one or more influencers with whom to form long-term ambassadorships rather than frequently changing influencers to improve follower reactions, credibility level, and overall advertising results in the Baltic states.

6. LIMITATIONS AND SUGGESTIONS FOR FURTHER RESEARCH

This study has several limitations that should be considered when interpreting the findings. Firstly, it is important to note that the research was conducted specifically in the Baltic countries (Lithuania, Latvia, and Estonia), and therefore, caution should be exercised in generalizing the results to other regions or cultures. Secondly, the sampling technique used convenience internet and snowball sampling, which may introduce biases and limit the representativeness of the sample. Lastly, the reliance on self-reported data through surveys and interviews introduces the possibility of biases. Participants' responses may be influenced by factors such as social desirability bias, which can impact the accuracy of the findings.

To expand our knowledge of influencer marketing credibility and trust, there are several avenues for future research worth exploring. Conducting cross-cultural comparisons would provide valuable insights into the variations in trust in influencer marketing across different cultural contexts. Longitudinal studies could be conducted to examine the dynamics of influencer-follower relationships over time and investigate the long-term effects of trust on consumer behavior. Experimental designs could be employed to establish causal relationships between influencer credibility factors and followers' trust.

REFERENCES

Anongdeh, A., & Barre, H. I. (2019). Instagram profile's effect on influencer credibility. *Jönköping International Business School.* https://hj.diva- portal.org/smash/get/diva2:1321148/FULLTEXT01.pdf

Belanche, D., Casaló, L. V., Flavián, M., & Ibáñez-Sánchez, S. (2021, July). Building influencers' credibility on Instagram: Effects on followers' attitudes and behavioral responses toward the influencer. *Journal of Retailing and Consumer Services, 61,* 102585. doi:10.1016/j.jretconser.2021.102585

Casaló, L. V., Flavián, C., & Ibáñez-Sánchez, S. (2020). Influencers on Instagram: Antecedents and consequences of opinion leadership. *Journal of Business Research, 117,* 510–519. doi:10.1016/j.jbusres.2018.07.005

Castillo, D., & Fernández, R. (2019). The role of digital influencers in brand recommendation: Examining their impact on engagement, expected value and purchase intention. *International Journal of Information Management, 49,* 366–376. doi:10.1016/j.ijinfomgt.2019.07.009

De Veirman, M., Cauberghe, V., & Hudders, L. (2017, July 14). Marketing through Instagram influencers: The impact of number of followers and product divergence on brand attitude. *International Journal of Advertising*, *36*(5), 798–828. doi:10.10 80/02650487.2017.1348035

Goel, V., & Ember, S. (2015). Instagram to Open Its Photo Feed to Ads. *New York Times*. https://www.nytimes.com/2015/06/03/technology/instagram-to-announce-plans- to-expand-advertising.html

Hesterberg, K. (2022, July 13). *13 Influencer Marketing Campaigns to Inspire and Get You Started With Your Own*. Hubspot. https://blog.hubspot.com/marketing/examples-of-influencer-marketing- campaigns

Hsu, H. Y., & Tsou, H. T. (2011). Understanding customer experiences in online blog environments. *International Journal of Information Management*, *31*(6), 510–523. doi:10.1016/j.ijinfomgt.2011.05.003

Kemp, S. (2021, February 11). *Digital in Lithuania: All the Statistics You Need in 2021*. DataReportal – Global Digital Insights. https://datareportal.com/reports/digital-2021-lithuania

Kemp, S. (2022, February 15). *Digital 2022: Estonia*. DataReportal – Global Digital Insights. https://datareportal.com/reports/digital-2022- estonia

Kerstetter, D., & Cho, M. H. (2004, October). Prior knowledge, credibility and information search. *Annals of Tourism Research*, *31*(4), 961–985. doi:10.1016/j.annals.2004.04.002

Kim, D. Y., & Kim, H. Y. (2021). Influencer advertising on social media: The multiple inference model on influencer-product congruence and sponsorship disclosure. *Journal of Business Research*, *130*, 405–415. doi:10.1016/j.jbusres.2020.02.020

Sokolova, K., & Kefi, H. (2020, March). Instagram and YouTube bloggers promote it, why should I buy? How credibility and parasocial interaction influence purchase intentions. *Journal of Retailing and Consumer Services*, *53*, 101742. doi:10.1016/j.jretconser.2019.01.011

Somppi, S. (2017, November 16). *RESEARCH: Instagram Influencer Marketing in Finland*. Annalect. https://www.annalect.fi/research-instagram-influencer-marketing-finland/

Statista. (2022, June 15). *Latvia number of social media users 2017-2026*. Statista. https://www.statista.com/statistics/568969/predicted-number-of- social-network-users-in-latvia/

Tafesse, W., & Wood, B. P. (2021). Followers' engagement with instagram influencers: The role of influencers' content and engagement strategy. *Journal of Retailing and Consumer Services*, *58*, 102303. doi:10.1016/j.jretconser.2020.102303

Van der Waldt, D. M., van Loggerenberg, M., & Wehmeyer, L. (2011, August 12). Celebrity endorsements versus created spokespersons in advertising: A survey among students. *Suid-Afrikaanse Tydskrif vir Ekonomiese en Bestuurswetenskappe*, *12*(1), 100–114. doi:10.4102ajems.v12i1.263

Venciute, D., Kazukauskaite, M., Correia, R., Kuslys, M., & Vaiciukynas, E. (2023). The effect of cause-related marketing on the green consumption attitude–behaviour gap in the cosmetics industry. *Journal of Contemporary Marketing Science*, *6*(1), 22–45. doi:10.1108/JCMARS-08-2022-0019

Chapter 2
Factors Influencing the Level of Trust in Vaccines

Ana Pinto Borges

(iD) https://orcid.org/0000-0002-4942-079X
*ISAG-European Business School,
Portugal & Research Center in Business
Sciences and Tourism (CICET-FCVC),
Portugal & Research Centre in
Organizations, Markets and Industrial
Management (COMEGI), Portugal*

Elvira Vieira

(iD) https://orcid.org/0000-0002-9296-3896
*ISAG-European Business School, Portugal
& Research Center in Business Sciences
and Tourism (CICET-FCVC), Portugal &
Polytechnic Institute of Viana do Castelo
(IPVC), Portugal & Applied Management
Research Unit (UNIAG), Portugal*

Paula Rodrigues

(iD) https://orcid.org/0000-0003-2967-2583
*Lusíada University and Research Centre
in Organizations, Markets and Industrial
Management (COMEGI), Portugal*

Ana Isabel Canavarro

(iD) https://orcid.org/0000-0001-9249-6864
*Universidade Europeia - Ipam, Porto,
Portugal*

ABSTRACT

The authors explore the degree of consumer trust regarding the various brands of Covid-19 vaccines made available by laboratories in Portugal. This chapter aims to fill a gap in the literature, since brands of COVID-19 vaccines have never been analysed from a brand trust perspective. The results show that the level of trust differs significantly between vaccine brands, with BioNtech - Pfizer, Moderna - National Institute of Health and Oxford -AstraZeneca inspiring the highest levels of trust among respondents. Other vaccine brands - Sanofi GSK, Janssen Pharmaceutica NV, and CureVac - showed lower levels of trust or respondents had no opinion whatsoever. Gender, age, family net monthly income, educational qualifications, and being a health professional were also found to influence the level of trust towards vaccine brands differently. The results may serve as strategic orientations for the pharmaceutical industry brands, but they may also be the object of reflection for public organisms when making purchasing and implementation decisions in the country.

DOI: 10.4018/978-1-6684-8351-0.ch002

INTRODUCTION

Vaccines constitute one of the greatest success stories in the health sector. They are part of a multifaceted public health response to the emergence of pandemics (Hussein et al., 2015). Indeed, the history of vaccines is long, having started with Hippocrates (400 BC) and his description of diseases such as mumps and diphtheria. No further discoveries were recorded until 1100 (AD) when the smallpox vaccine was identified (idem, ibid). Currently, under COVID-19, the global market size of the respective vaccines is projected to reach over 5 billion by 2024 (Reportlinker, 2021).

On 11 March 2020, COVID-19 (a disease caused by the novel coronavirus) was characterized by the World Health Organization (WHO) as a pandemic. The term "pandemic" refers to the geographical distribution of a disease, not its severity. The designation recognizes that outbreaks of COVID-19 exist in several countries and regions of the world (PAHO, 2020). As of 19 February 2022, 61.9% of the world's population has received at least one dose of a COVID-19 vaccine. 10.42 billion doses have been administered globally and 30.92 million are administered every day. However, only 10.6% of people in low-income countries have received at least one dose (Hannah et al., 2020).

Vaccines are a technology that humanity has always relied on in the past to reduce the number of deaths from infectious diseases (Andre et al. 2008).

Methods of growing viruses in the laboratory led to rapid discoveries and innovations, including the creation of polio vaccines. Other childhood diseases were in the scientists' sights such as measles, mumps and rubella, and vaccines for these diseases considerably reduced their negative effects.

Less than 12 months after the beginning of the pandemic, several research teams around the world have taken up the challenge and developed vaccines to protect against SARS-CoV-2. As of 13 August 2021, there were 21 COVID-19 vaccines from different sources approved worldwide for emergency use (Rahman et al., 2022).

Effectively, preference for a particular brand is built up over time, taking into account the associations and expectations that users make, which may be positive or negative. In the case of vaccine brands, some factors to be considered by users are the characteristics of the brand itself, such as its effectiveness, type of regulation, approval, manufacturing origin, public trust and professional trust (i.e. by physicians) (Quintanilla, 2021).

In this sense, it was considered important in this research to provide a theoretical and practical reflection related to concepts intrinsic to the brand, understood as a promise of certain tangible and intangible benefits and, as such, producer of various meanings, perceptions, and associations in the minds of their publics (not forgetting the specific situation of brands, in the context of the pharmaceutical industry in particular). In this sense, it is intended with the current study to answer the following research question: What factors influence the level of brand trust of the vaccines against COVID-19?

LITERATURE REVIEW

Brand: Promise and Value

A product offers certain tangible benefits, but a brand offers additional benefits, which are both tangible and intangible. A brand can, in this sense, be considered as the added value of investment made in a certain product (Kapferer, 1992).

Aaker (1991) defines brand value as a set of assets and liabilities linked to a brand, its name and symbol, which add or subtract to the value provided by a product or service, to a company and/or its customers. In turn, Keller (1993) defines consumer-based brand equity (CBBE) as the differential effect that brand awareness has on consumer response to brand marketing.

A long tradition of scientific research shows that brand names act as risk reducers for the consumer's purchase of a product or service (Montgomery & Wernerfelt, 1992).

Interpreting brands as promises is a way for companies to improve their credibility by making a binding commitment. Thus, if a company interprets its brand as a promise, then it is likely to make clear what the brand promise is and link it directly to the organization. Keeping that brand promise before the public will result in greater credibility for the organization (Abela, 2003).

In the 21st century, brand promise requires moving away from just thinking about positioning perceptions with potential customers of the brand and making the brand real from within (21st century brand knowledge, 2000). In this scope, the three core constructs are P*T: P = Brand Promise; T = Brand Trust; * = The web and net information communities that, as an integrated whole, make the relationship of a brand promise truly reliable (Editorial, 2000).

Although brand equity can be seen as an evolution of three different perspectives, in general, it can be classified into two broad categories: the financial perspectives, for example, firm-based brand equity (FBBE) and consumer-based brand equity (CBBE) (Keller, 1993).

According to Shahin (2018), the most influential factor on the overall brand equity is brand loyalty.

Brand Loyalty: Trust, Affection and Performance

Two aspects of brand loyalty - purchase loyalty and attitudinal loyalty - are variables in the chain of effects of brand trust, brand affection, and brand performance - market share and relative price (Chaudhuri & Holbrook, 2001; Aureliano-Silva et al., 2022).

Despite managers' emphasis on customer loyalty, it remains one of the most challenging issues facing firms in the modern business era, which is characterized by intense competition (Macit et al., 2016).

When product and brand-level variables are controlled, brand trust and brand affection combine to determine purchase loyalty and attitudinal loyalty. Purchase loyalty, in turn, leads to higher market share, and attitudinal loyalty leads to a higher relative price for the brand (Chaudhuri & Holbrook, 2001).

Trust has been one of the essential elements of long-term and reliable connections between people (Akoglu & Özbek, 2022; Atulkar, 2020; Aureliano-Silva et al., 2022). Personal relationships were often employed as a comparison when describing the connection between the brand and the purchaser (Fournier, 1998).

Brand trust is considered the main ingredient to generate an intense bond between consumer and brand (Elliott & Yannopoulou, 2007). Trust is considered as a basic expectation that a customer has about the reliability of the brand (brand reliability). Brand trust reflecting this one-dimensional perspective is often considered as a consumer's belief in the technical characteristics of the brand (Chaudhuri & Holbrook, 2001; Kwon et al., 2021).

However, the notion of brand trust has evolved over the years and, as such, is not exclusively influenced by expectations about product attributes or performance, but also encompasses emotional evaluations (Becerra & Badrinarayanan, 2013). In this regard, Ballester and Aleman (2001) argued that brand trust is a multidimensional concept comprising two main components, namely brand reliability and brand intentionality.

The relationship between brand trust and brand loyalty has been widely studied. Most studies argue that brand trust is an antecedent of brand loyalty (Akoglu & Özbek, 2022; Aureliano-Silva et al., 2022; Samarah, et al., 2022).

Atulkar (2020) in his study shows that brand loyalty is directly and indirectly influenced by brand trust. But there are also studies that evaluate the moderating effect of brand trust on brand loyalty (Huang, 2017). Chaudhuri and Holbrook (2001) provided support for the substantial impact of brand trust on both attitudinal and repurchase loyalty, based on the commitment-trust theory of brand commitment (Morgan & Hunt, 1994). According to this theory, trust plays a crucial role in building strong and valuable exchange relationships that foster greater levels of loyalty (Kwon et al., 2021). Morgan and Hunt (1994) also emphasized the significance of trust in this context.

Brand loyal consumers may be willing to pay more for a brand because they perceive a unique value in the brand that no alternative can provide (Jacoby & Chestnut 1978; Pessemier 1959; Reichheld, 1996). This uniqueness may derive from greater confidence in a brand's reliability (brand reliability) or a more favorable effect when customers use the brand (Chaudhuri & Holbrook, 2001).

Customers now have more opportunities to choose goods in a competitive and fluctuating business context (Choi et al., 2020).

Three studies have led to the development of brand trust scales. In line with research on trust, these studies conceptualize brand trust as multidimensional. First, the development of the scale by Hess (1995) comprises three dimensions of brand trust: altruism, honesty, and trustworthiness. Second, Delgado-Ballester et al. (2003) developed a measurement scale based on two dimensions: trustworthiness and intentions. Third, Li et al. (2008) conceptualized brand trust as a second-order construct with two indicators: competence and benevolence.

However, there have always been gaps and controversies concerning these scales, given the limitations of the studies. The scale that has been most widely applied is that of Chauduri and Holbrook (2001). However, this scale is not based on a formal development process.

Koschate-Fischer & Gartner (2015) provided empirical evidence for a new scale measuring brand trust that is unidimensional and focuses on the performance dimension (performance). They thus provide empirical support to Chaudhuri and Holbrook's (2001) conceptualization and do not make this new scale dependent on whether consumers perceive a brand as an active relational partner or not. However, the study is limited to fast moving consumer goods (FMCG) brands. As such, Koschate-Fischer & Gartner (2015) suggest conducting additional research to further validate the brand trust scale by applying it to other product categories. For example, for several high involvement products, the product brand equals the corporate brand, and, in these situations, consumers may more easily perceive a company as an active relational partner. But, indeed, it is important to reinforce that brand trust is distinct from closely related brand concepts such as brand attitude, brand affect, brand attachment and brand love (Aureliano-Silva et al., 2022; Gecti & Zengin, 2013).

In addition, the growth in popularity of the Internet has long been exposing the shortcomings of brands, providing greater opportunities for brand weaknesses to be exposed (Chen & Qasim, 2021; Abela, 2003).

Branded products and media companies used to have a virtual monopoly over mass media, whereas now they are forced to compete with the voice of individuals who publish messages freely, impacting hundreds of millions of people around the world (Levine et al., 2000; Prahalad and Ramaswamy, 2002).

The internet and its technologies have thus disrupted the information asymmetry that for so many years worked in favor of brand managers (Dwivedi et al., 2019). Consumers are empowered to interact with brands and other consumers, but also to create their own content, leading to a more participatory approach to branding (Christodoulides, 2009).

It is argued that due to the greater involvement of the brand community on the Internet, a new form of control is needed, placing greater emphasis on brand management as value management, while considering how this involvement can be used to coproduce greater value (Chernatony, 2001).

Ebrahim (2019) emphasized the importance of social media marketing on brand equity and brand loyalty. These authors sustain that companies should use social media and other online applications to provide consumers with the latest, relevant, and freshly information. The positive effects of these depend on the customers' degree of confidence or trust in the published online content. This is a major factor in brand building and in the creation of long-term customer relationships.

In the same line of though, Haudi, et al. (2022) sustain social media marketing activities that have been carried out on Instagram can affect consumer confidence in brands, consumer views on equity brands and affect consumer loyalty to the brand. Instagram can effectively generate brand trust by social media users.

Brands in the Pharmaceutical Industry

The branding activity came relatively late to the pharmaceutical industry. The success of this industry was fundamentally based on the following aspects: strong research and development of new products (R&D); an aggressive defense of patents; the use of the powerful tool of the sales force (Schuiling & Moss, 2004).

Progressively, with successful brands like Lipitor by Pfizer, Advair by GlaxoSmithKline, Nexium by AstraZeneca and many others, the pharmaceutical industry has demonstrated its expertise in building strong product brands (Angelmar & Kane, 2007).

This industry has relied heavily on the ability of marketers to market new (complex) products more effectively. However, a more simplified marketing approach can help meet customer needs and alleviate the pressure on pharmaceutical companies to discover successful new drugs (Rao, 2002). Indeed, to maintain double-digit growth rates, a pharmaceutical company would need to launch at least four new drugs each year - a difficult task. To meet these challenges, the use of new and current medicines needs to be increased (Rao, 2002).

The consequences of extending existing brands are much more complex in the pharmaceutical industry than for the so-called fast moving consumer goods (FMCG). There is always the risk of confusion and misuse of medicines (Schuiling & Moss 2004).

As Kejariwal and Bhat (2022) posit, in the new hybrid world with the broad use of digital technologies, the number of datasets being collected is constantly increasing. As a result, there is a greater availability of data for determining the preferences of physicians on certain illnesses, degrees of patient engagement, preferred forms of communication, and aggregate subtleties that vary according to the area of specialization and geographic region.

Brand Loyalty and Trust in the Pharmaceutical Industry

The competition among companies in the pharmaceutical industry is high. Therefore, pharmaceutical companies have to develop strategies to achieve competitive advantage. Brand loyalty is a powerful tool in the development of pharmaceutical brands (Macit et al., 2016). "From the physicians' standpoint belief in brand is crucial for the creation of brand loyalty and the key for building up trust is the scientific data regarding the effectiveness and safety of the drug obtained from large-scale clinical trials." (Macit et al., 2016, p.5).

In order to increase customer loyalty, an organization can work on brand awareness among its customers. Therefore, it is important to increase brand awareness, since the perception and recognition of the brand among current and potential customers will contribute positively to customer loyalty and, consequently, to the achievement of better business results. In addition, this brand recognition also contributes to the brand's respect in the highly competitive pharmaceutical market (Dlacic & Kezman, 2014).

By maintaining continuous satisfaction and a high level of brand equity, customers express the intention to assure the long-term purchase of the product and their choice extends to other products in the organisation's portfolio (Dlacic & Kezman, 2014). If a customer does not trust the brand efficiently for problem solving, he will not be prepared to buy it again (Dlacic & Kezman, 2014).

According to McCarthy (2019), public distrust in the pharmaceutical industry has increased in United States (U.S), mainly due to perceptions of pharmaceutical manufacturers as profit seeking and also due to pharmaceutical manufacturers practices, including off-label marketing, overcharging government programs, and concealing data.

This weak level of trust translates into skepticism about using pharmaceutical products, thus leading to new patient behaviors ranging from poor adherence to strong rejection of health policies, such as vaccine campaigns (Pahus et al., 2020).

In this sense, Singh et al. (2023) concluded that approximately 60% of individuals at high risk for cardiovascular disease did not trust pharmaceutical manufacturers. This lack of trust was higher among certain profiles - those in poor health or without an usual source of care, raising concerns that vulnerable populations have experiences where trust has been broken.

Plessis et. al (2017) defend a need for change in the mindset of pharmaceutical industry. A change from a "brand focus to a patient-value focus which requires leadership from the top and drives the need to redefine strategy, organizational structure and processes, and capabilities to focus on transparency, credibility, and value for the patient."

Regarding Covid 19 vaccines, a study conducted by Wang et al. (2022) suggests that vaccine hesitancy exists among participants in Taiwan, the United States, the Netherlands, and Haiti. This same study outlines that building trust in the COVID-19 vaccine, cultivating vaccine literacy, clarifying misinformation and rumors regarding COVID-19 vaccines, and providing verified information are critical for increasing public acceptance of getting a COVID-19 vaccine.

Another study conducted by Szilagyi et al. (2021) concluded that building trust in the vaccine approval/development processes is an essential step, addressing vaccine hesitancy, and ensuring the future success of any national vaccination program.

METHOD, QUESTIONNAIRE DESCRIPTION, AND DATA ANALYSIS

Data collection was carried out through an online survey and was available (and promoted) on various social networks between February and March 2021. In total, 1057 valid responses were obtained. Before the application, the questionnaire was validated by a group composed by 30 individuals with different age, academic qualifications, and professions. This procedure avoided biases related to questionnaire structure and wording.

In order to answer the research question, the following parts of the questionnaire were used: i) the sociodemographic characteristics of the respondent - gender, age, family net monthly income, educational qualifications and professional activity, if the respondents were health professionals and ii) measuring trust towards brands - (1) I do not trust, (2) trust, (3) I fully trust and (4) I have no opinion.

Data Analysis

In the data analysis technique, firstly we describe the samples through descriptive statistics. After that, it was performed the differences between the sociodemographic characteristics of the respondents and the confidence level of vaccines against COVID-19, through the analysis of the non-parametric Chi-Square test. This test was applied because the data was measured using the nominal or ordinal scale. In this sense, it was possible to determine the relationship between categorical variables using a chi-square statistic. After that, we run a multinomial logistic regression considering the four categories (I do not trust, trust, I fully trust, and I have no opinion) and the sociodemographic characteristics of the respondents as independent variables.

RESULTS

Sample Description

In the analysis of the collected sample, we found a slight predominance of female respondents (60%) aged between 26-40 years old (35.6%) and over 40 years old 17.1%. Most respondents completed at least one higher education course (64.0%) and the most common households' net monthly income is between 1001 EUR and 2000 EUR (44%). In relation to being a health professional, 9% indicated that they exercise one of the professions in this sector.

Table 1. Sample description, n=1057

Variable	Description	%
Gender	1- Female	60,0%
	0- Male	38,2%
	2- Prefer not to say	1,8%
Age	1 - Inferior 15 years old	1,1%
	2 - Between 16 - 25 years old	46,3%
	3 - Between 26 - 40 years old	35,6%
	4 - Between 41 - 55 years old	12,8%
	5 - Superior 55 years old	4,2%
Family net monthly income	1- Less than or equal 1000 EUR	26,9%
	2 - Between 1001 - 2000 EUR	44,5%
	3 - Between 2001 - 3000 EUR	19,2%
	4 - Superior 3000 EUR	9,5%
Educational qualifications	1 - Elementary studies	8,8%
	2 - Secondary studies	27,2%
	3 – Degree or Master's/PhD degree	64,0%
Are you a healthcare professional?	1 – Yes	9,0%
	0 - No	91,0%

Source: Own elaboration.

The vaccine brands that most inspire confidence to the respondents are BioNtech -Pfizer (22,6% fully trust and 45,6% trust), Moderna - National Institute of Health (13,6% fully trust and 46.5% trust) and Oxford- AstraZeneca (12,3% fully trust and 48,0% trust).

The brands Sanofi GSK, Janssen Pharmaceutica NV, and CureVac seem to be little known among respondents, considering that the majority of respondents had no opinion (57,1%, 54,4% and 58,3%, respectively).

Table 2. Description of the level of trust in the vaccine brand, n=1057

Vaccines Brand	I do not trust	Trust	I fully trust	I have no opinion
BioNTech - Pfizer	5,6%	45,6%	22,6%	26,2%
Oxford - AstraZeneca	9,1%	48,0%	12,3%	30,7%
Moderna - National Institute of Health	6,1%	46,5%	13,6%	33,8%
Sanofi - GSK	11,8%	25,4%	5,6%	57,1%
Janssen Pharmaceutics NV	11,2%	26,5%	7,9%	54,4%
CureVac	12,9%	23,3%	5,6%	58,3%

Source: Own elaboration.

The analysis of the sociodemographic characteristics shows that gender has an influence on the level of trust for the brands BioNTech - Pfizer, Sanofi - GSK, Janssen Pharmaceutica NV and CureVac. Specifically, women showed higher levels of trust for the BioNTech - Pfizer brand, and for the other brands they showed the highest percentage for the "I have no opinion" option.

Age does not present significant levels for any brand, with the exception of the brand Janssen Pharmaceutics NV where the highest percentage is for the "I have no opinion" option for age groups between 16 and 25 years old and 26 and 40 years old.

The monthly income level assumed statistical strength for brands BioNTech - Pfizer, Oxford - AstraZeneca and Moderna - National Institute of Health, with income levels below 1000 EUR and between 1001 EUR and 2000 EUR exhibiting higher confidence levels.

The level of education was statistically significant for all brands, with the exception of the Janssen Pharmaceutics NV brand, leading to the conclusion that respondents with higher educational levels (bachelor's, master's or doctoral degrees) show higher levels of trust comparing to respondents with lower educational levels.

Regarding the respondent being a health professional, it was observed that it always assumed statistical significance. Specifically for the brands BioNTech - Pfizer, Oxford - AstraZeneca and Moderna - National Institute of Health, respondents who are not health professionals present a higher level of confidence in relation to health professionals. For the remaining brands, non-professional respondents were more prevalent in having no opinion than health professionals.

Through the results in Table 4, it can be seen that gender presented significant results for the fully trust, for vaccines BioNTech – Pfizer, Sanofi – GSK and CureVac. Thus, for example, the relative probability of fully trusting rather than not trusting the BioNTech - Pfizer vaccine is 39,0% higher for women than for men with the same age, income, level of education and whether or not they have a profession in health sector. The impact of the level of income presents a level of significance in most of the confidence levels of the brands, and reinforces the results previously shown. More concretely, higher levels of income are less likely to have confidence in vaccine brands when compared to lower income of individuals. For higher education levels (Degree, Master's or PhD) the trust level increases in relation to lower educational levels. The relative probability of trusting versus not trusting vaccine brands is higher for respondents with a higher educational level than for those without an academic degree, with the remnant sociodemographic characteristics remaining constant. In relation to being a healthcare professional with the same sociodemographic profile, the relative probability increases in fully trusting compared to not trusting the brands Oxford – AstraZeneca, Sanofi - GSK and CureVac.

DISCUSSION AND CONCLUSION

Less than 12 months after the start of the pandemic, several research teams around the world have taken up the challenge and developed vaccines to protect against the SARS-CoV-2 virus. As of 13 August 2021, there were at least 21 approved COVID-19 vaccines from different sources.

A consumer's preference for a particular brand is built over time, with all the associations and expectations that the receivers of the brand's message develop in their minds, which can be positive or negative. Specifically, in the 21st century, it is also imperative to consider the power of web and liquid information communities that make it necessary to make brands truly real from the inside, given the exposure and scrutiny to which they are subjected by people.

In the case of vaccine brands (high-risk products and, as such, requiring high consumer involvement), some factors to be taken into account by users will be the characteristics of the brand itself, such as its efficacy, type of regulation, approval, manufacturing origin, public trust and professional trust (i.e. by doctors).

As further explored, brand trust can be understood as a multidimensional concept comprising two main components: brand reliability and brand intentionality (Ballester & Aleman, 2001).

Table 3. Respondent segmentation considering the sociodemographic characteristics and the confidence level of vaccines, Chi-Square test

Vaccines Brand	Level of trust	Gender			Age					Family net monthly income (EUR)				Educational qualifications			Healthcare Professional	
		Male	Female	Prefer not to say	< 15	16-25	26-40	41-55	> 55	≤ 1000	Between 1001 - 2000	Between 2001 - 3000	> 3000	Elementary studies	Secondary studies	Degree or Master's/ PhD degree	No	Yes
BioNTech - Pfizer	I do not trust	2,3%	3,1%	0,2%	0,0%	2,4%	2,4%	0,8%	0,1%	1,6%	2,2%	1,0%	0,8%	0,7%	2,4%	2,6%	5,2%	,4%
	Trust	17,2%	27,7%	0,7%	0,6%	21,1%	15,9%	5,8%	2,3%	12,4%	19,6%	9,4%	4,3%	4,1%	11,4%	30,1%	41,8%	3,8%
	I fully trust	10,5%	11,9%	0,2%	0,2%	11,0%	8,2%	2,7%	0,5%	5,1%	9,3%	5,2%	3,0%	0,8%	6,3%	15,5%	19,2%	3,4%
	I have no opinion	8,2%	17,2%	0,8%	0,4%	11,8%	9,1%	3,5%	1,4%	7,8%	13,4%	3,6%	1,4%	3,3%	7,1%	15,8%	24,8%	1,4%
Chi-Square test (sig.)		15,751 (0,015)***			7,815 (0,799)					23,017 (0,006)***				23,925 (0,001)***			15,737 (0,001)***	
Oxford - AstraZeneca	I do not trust	4,1%	4,7%	0,3%	0,0%	3,9%	3,4%	1,4%	0,4%	1,4%	4,0%	2,4%	1,3%	1,0%	3,0%	5,0%	8,4%	0,7%
	Trust	18,6%	28,7%	0,7%	0,6%	22,5%	16,7%	6,0%	2,2%	14,3%	19,4%	9,6%	4,6%	3,8%	12,5%	31,7%	43,5%	4,4%
	I fully trust	4,9%	7,3%	0,1%	0,2%	6,1%	4,4%	1,4%	0,3%	2,6%	5,4%	2,9%	1,4%	0,5%	2,6%	9,2%	10,2%	2,1%
	I have no opinion	10,6%	19,3%	0,8%	0,4%	13,8%	11,1%	4,0%	1,4%	8,6%	15,7%	4,3%	2,1%	3,5%	9,1%	18,1%	28,9%	1,8%
Chi-Square test (sig.)		6,881 (0,332)			4,350 (0,976)					27,816 (0,001)***				16,294 (0,012)**			14,259 (0,003)***	
Moderna - National Institute of Health	I do not trust	2,4%	3,7%	0,1%	0,0%	2,8%	2,4%	0,8%	0,2%	1,5%	2,2%	1,6%	0,9%	0,6%	2,5%	3,1%	5,5%	0,7%
	Trust	18,1%	27,6%	0,8%	0,5%	21,1%	16,7%	6,3%	1,8%	11,2%	20,5%	10,3%	4,4%	3,8%	11,6%	31,0%	42,3%	4,2%
	I fully trust	6,1%	7,3%	0,2%	0,0%	6,8%	5,0%	1,0%	0,8%	3,6%	5,7%	2,5%	1,9%	0,6%	3,8%	9,3%	11,4%	2,2%
	I have no opinion	11,6%	21,4%	0,8%	0,7%	15,5%	11,4%	4,6%	1,5%	10,6%	16,1%	4,8%	2,3%	3,9%	9,4%	20,5%	31,8%	2,0%
Chi-Square test (sig.)		5,511 (0,480)			10,150 (0,603)					22,231 (0,008)***				14,814 (0,022)**			13,049 (0,005)***	

continued on following page

Table 3. Continued

Vaccines Brand	Level of trust	Gender			Age					Family net monthly income (EUR)				Educational qualifications			Healthcare Professional	
		Male	Female	Prefer not to say	< 15	16-25	26-40	41-55	> 55	≤ 1000	Between 1001 - 2000	Between 2001 - 3000	> 3000	Elementary studies	Secondary studies	Degree or Master's/ PhD degree	No	Yes
Sanofi - GSK	I do not trust	4.8%	6.6%	0.4%	0.0%	4.6%	4.4%	2.3%	0.5%	2.6%	5.3%	2.7%	1.2%	1.3%	4.4%	6.1%	10.7%	1.1%
	Trust	10.7%	14.4%	0.4%	0.4%	10.6%	10.2%	3.3%	0.9%	8.1%	9.9%	4.9%	2.5%	2.3%	6.3%	16.8%	22.2%	3.2%
	I fully trust	3.0%	2.6%	0.0%	0.0%	2.7%	2.3%	0.5%	0.1%	1.4%	2.2%	1.1%	0.9%	0.2%	1.7%	3.7%	3.9%	1.7%
	I have no opinion	19.7%	36.4%	1.0%	0.8%	28.3%	18.6%	6.7%	2.7%	14.8%	27.1%	10.4%	4.9%	5.0%	14.9%	37.3%	54.2%	2.9%
Chi-Square test (sig.)		14,308 (0,026)**			17,219 (0,142)					11,580 (0,238)				11,288 (0,080)*			48,823 (0,000)***	
Janssen Pharmaceutics NV	I do not trust	4.6%	6.4%	0.1%	0.0%	4.3%	4.7%	1.8%	0.4%	2.6%	5.1%	2.0%	1.4%	1.2%	4.0%	6.0%	9.6%	1.5%
	Trust	11.7%	14.5%	0.3%	0.4%	11.0%	9.6%	4.4%	1.1%	7.9%	10.5%	5.0%	3.0%	2.5%	7.1%	16.9%	23.8%	2.6%
	I fully trust	3.8%	4.0%	0.2%	0.0%	3.8%	3.3%	0.5%	0.4%	1.9%	3.2%	2.0%	0.9%	0.4%	2.1%	5.5%	6.3%	1.6%
	I have no opinion	18.1%	35.1%	1.2%	0.8%	27.2%	18.0%	6.1%	2.4%	14.4%	25.6%	10.2%	4.2%	4.7%	14.1%	35.6%	51.2%	3.2%
Chi-Square test (sig.)		15,810 (0,015)**			20,350 (0,061)*					10,763 (0,292)				8,332 (0,215)			23,009 (0,000)***	
CureVac	I do not trust	5.3%	7.2%	0.4%	0.2%	4.7%	4.8%	2.5%	0.7%	2.7%	6.3%	2.3%	1.5%	1.6%	4.7%	6.5%	11.3%	1.6%
	Trust	10.4%	12.7%	0.2%	0.4%	10.2%	8.8%	2.9%	0.9%	8.0%	8.9%	4.2%	2.2%	2.2%	5.6%	15.5%	20.6%	2.6%
	I fully trust	3.0%	2.6%	0.0%	0.0%	3.3%	1.7%	0.5%	0.1%	1.3%	2.4%	1.1%	0.8%	0.2%	1.9%	3.5%	4.4%	1.2%
	I have no opinion	19.5%	37.6%	1.2%	0.6%	28.0%	20.2%	6.9%	2.6%	14.8%	26.9%	11.6%	5.0%	4.8%	15.0%	38.4%	54.8%	3.5%
Chi-Square test (sig.)		20,042 (0,003)***			14,812 (0,252)					13,937 (0,125)				15,641 (0,016)**			22,745 (0,000)***	

Source: Own elaboration. Note: Significant at: * $p < 0.10$ level ;** $p < 0.05$ level; *** $p < 0.01$.

Brand loyalty implies that consumers may be willing to pay more for that brand, given the perception of a unique value in the brand that no alternative can match. This will result from greater confidence in the reliability of the brand (brand reliability).

Several scales on this brand trust concept have been developed, all of them with some limitations. For example, for several high involvement products, the product

Table 4. Econometric model to explain the level of trust, multinomial logistic regression

Level of trust	Variable	Relative Odds[a,b,c] (%)					
		BioNTech - Pfizer	Oxford – AstraZeneca	Moderna - National Institute of Health	Sanofi - GSK	Janssen Pharmaceutics NV	CureVac
Trust	**Gender (base=male)**						
	Female	-	-	-	-	-	-
	Prefer not to say	-	-	-	-	-	-
	Age						
	16-25	-	-	-	-	-	-
	26-40	-	-	-	-	-	-
	42-55	-	-	-	-	-	-
	> 55	-	-	-	-	-	-
	Family net monthly income (EUR) (base = ≤ 1000)						
	1001-2000	-	55,3%*	-	46,1%**	38,9%*	59,3%***
	2001-3000	-	-69,4%***	-	-59,4%***	-	-57,3%**
	> 3000	-	-75,2%***	-	-54,9%*	-	-65,7%***
	Educational qualifications (base = elementary studies)						
	Secondary studies	-	-	-	-	-	-
	Degree or Master's/ PhD degree	74,5%***	89,9%**	87,4%*	80,4%*	91,2%*	92,3%***
	Healthcare Professional (base=no)						
	Yes	-	-	-	-	-	-
	Constant	-	-	-	-	-	-

continued on following page

Table 4. Continued

Level of trust	Variable	Relative Odds[a,b,c] (%)					
		BioNTech - Pfizer	Oxford – AstraZeneca	Moderna - National Institute of Health	Sanofi - GSK	Janssen Pharmaceutics NV	CureVac
Fully Trust	**Gender (base=male)**						
	Female	39,0%*	-	-	20,8%***	-	13,8%**
	Prefer not to say	-	-	-	-	-	-
	Age						
	16-25	-	-	-	-	-	-
	26-40	-	-	-	-	-	-
	42-55	-	-	-	-	-	-
	> 55	-	-		-	-	-
	Family net monthly income (EUR) (base = ≤ 1000)						
	1001-2000	-	-	-	-	-	-
	2001-3000	-68,3%**	-52,7%*	-57,3%*	-	-	-
	> 3000	-88,4%***	-63,3%*	-	-	-	-
	Educational qualifications (base = elementary studies)						
	Secondary studies	-	-	-	-	-	-
	Degree or Master's/ PhD degree	87,2%***	80,2%***	83,2%**	-	-	-
	Healthcare Professional (base=no)						
	Yes	-	37,9%***	-	43,3%***	-	87,8%***
	Constant	-	-	-	-	-	-

continued on following page

Table 4. Continued

Level of trust	Variable	Relative Odds[a,b,c] (%)					
		BioNTech - Pfizer	Oxford – AstraZeneca	Moderna - National Institute of Health	Sanofi - GSK	Janssen Pharmaceutics NV	CureVac
I have no opinion	**Gender (base=male)**						
	Female	-	-	-	-	44,1%*	-
	Prefer not to say	-	-	-	-	-	-
	Age						
	16-25	-	-	-	-	-	-
	26-40	-	-	-	-	-	-
	42-55	-	-	-	-	-	-
	> 55	-	-	-	-	-	-
	Family net monthly income (EUR) (base = ≤ 1000)						
	1001-2000	-	-	-	-	-	-
	2001-3000	-	-74,9%***	-67,9%**	-49,9%**	-	-
	> 3000	-45,4%**	-78,8%***	-70,9%**	-48,1%*	-57,9%**	-52,9%**
	Educational qualifications (base = elementary studies)						
	Secondary studies	-	-	-	-	-	-
	Degree or Master's/ PhD degree	-	-	-	66,2%*	96,7%*	86,9%*
	Healthcare Professional (base=no)						
	Yes	-	-	-	-55,7%**	-64,3%***	-63,8%***
	Constant	-	-	-	-	-	

Notes: [a] The base of the model is category I do not trust; [b] Relative probabilities are also called relative odds and it was calculated by Exp(B) -1, is the predicted change in odds for a unit increase in the predictor. The "exp" refers to the exponential value of B. [c] Only results with significance were showed. *$p < 0.10$ level ;** $p < 0.05$ level; *** $p < 0.01$.

brand equals the corporate brand, and in these situations, consumers may more easily perceive a company as an active relational partner. But effectively, it is important to reinforce that brand trust is distinct from closely related brand concepts such as brand attitude, brand affect, brand attachment and brand love.

As far as the pharmaceutical industry in particular (a highly competitive sector) is concerned, the branding activity came relatively late and the brands bet on strategies to increase brand awareness, in order to gain perception and recognition among customers and prescribers and consequently improve business results.

It is known that aspects such as continuous satisfaction and the high level of brand equity contribute decisively to the development of the intention to buy the product in the long term, and this will open doors for the consumer's choice to be extended, with more confidence, to other products of the organization/brand.

In this study we analyze the degree of consumer trust regarding the various brands of Covid-19 vaccines made available by different laboratories in Portugal. Trust is mainly associated with trust based on the perception that vaccines are safe and effective.

In our results we verified that the level of trust diverges significantly between vaccine brands, with BioNtech - Pfizer, Moderna - National Institute of Health and Oxford- AstraZeneca inspiring higher levels of trust among respondents. Brand trust is the most important quality that the enterprises need to improve, as part of their brand strategy. Consumers need to trust that the brand fulfills the promise and, in this case, must be safe and effective. In our results, the vaccine brands - Sanofi GSK, Janssen Pharmaceutica NV, and CureVac – need to improve the brand trust, because the respondents associated lower levels of trust or had no opinion.

Agley and Xiao (2021) highlighted that since the start of the pandemic, there has been a spread of misinformation, conspiracy theories (Sunstein & Vermeule, 2009) and unverified information about COVID-19 (Mian & Khan, 2020; Kouzy et al., 2020), which has taken the form of false/fabricated content and truthful information misrepresented (Brennen et al., 2020). In response to this context of asymmetric information, organizations like the WHO, European Union or governments have taken actions and implemented strategies to provide the public with more plentiful information. In this sense, even brands that have shown higher levels of trust cannot fail to implement strategies and transmit adequate information to consumers to ensure a higher reputation. For brands that have demonstrated a lower level of trust, they need to inspire more hope, show more effectiveness to the consumer, and should use their brand to improve society.

We also evaluated the differences between the sociodemographic characteristics of the respondents and the confidence level of vaccines against COVID-19. We verified that these variables were also found to influence the level of trust towards vaccine brands differently. Specifically, the highest levels of confidence were shown by women, people with an income level between 1001 EUR and 2000 EUR, with a high level of educational qualifications and not being health professionals. With these segmentation the pharmaceutical industry brands could tailor their strategies and create brand trust to gain brand loyalty, advocacy, and goodwill, thus allowing them to avoid complications in the future.

Limitations and Future Research

This research has limitations that could be the subject of future research. One of the limitations is the sample, we have only included Portuguese respondents and it would be interesting to have a comparison between countries to analyze if there is any cultural influence or even the time frame from the moment the sample was collected until now. Another limitation is that no scales were applied to assess other brand dimensions. Finally, it would be important to understand the perception of the effectiveness of the vaccine since most of the population has already been vaccinated and relate it to brand trust.

ACKNOWLEDGMENT

The authors are deeply grateful to ISAG – European Business School and Research Center in Business Sciences and Tourism (CICET - FCVC) for all support.

REFERENCES

Aaker, D. (1991). *Managing Brand Equity*. Free Press.

Aaker, D., & Joachimsthaler, E. (2000). *Brand Leadership*. Free Press.

Abela, A. (2003). *When Brand is a promise*. [Unpublished master's thesis. The Darden Graduate School of Business Administration, University of Virginia] doi:10.1186/s12889-020-10103-x

Agley, J., & Xiao, Y. (2021). Misinformation about COVID-19: Evidence for differential latent profiles and a strong association with trust in science. *BMC Public Health*, *21*(89), 1-12. doi:10.1186/s12889-020-10103-x

Akbarov, S. (2018). Antecedents of Customer Based Brand Equity-Research in Azerbaijan. *Journal of Business and Management Sciences*, *6*(2), 54–58. doi:10.12691/jbms-6-2-5

Akoglu, H. E., & Özbek, O. (2022). The effect of brand experiences on brand loyalty through perceived quality and brand trust: A study on sports consumers. *Asia Pacific Journal of Marketing and Logistics*, *34*(10), 2130–2148. doi:10.1108/APJML-05-2021-0333

Andre, F. E., Booy, R., Bock, H. L., Clemens, J., Datta, S. K., John, T. J., Lee, B. W., Lolekha, S., Peltola, H., Ruff, T. A., Santosham, M., & Schmitt, H. J. (2008). Vaccination greatly reduces disease, disability, death and inequity worldwide. *Bulletin of the World Health Organization, 86*(2), 140–146. doi:10.2471/BLT.07.040089 PMID:18297169

Angelmar, R., Angelmar, S., & Kane, L. (2007). Building strong condition brands. *Journal of Medical Marketing, 7*(4), 341–351. doi:10.1057/palgrave.jmm.5050101

Atulkar, S. (2020). Brand trust and brand loyalty in mall shoppers. *Marketing Intelligence & Planning, 38*(5), 559–572. doi:10.1108/MIP-02-2019-0095

Aureliano-Silva, L., Spers, E. E., Lodhi, R. N., & Pattanayak, M. (2022). Who loves to forgive? The mediator mechanism of service recovery between brand love, brand trust and purchase intention in the context of food-delivery apps. *British Food Journal, 124*(12), 4686–4700. doi:10.1108/BFJ-07-2021-0819

Baalbaki, S. (2012). *Consumer perception of brand equity measurement: A new scale*. [Doctoral Dissertation, University of North Texas]. UNT Digital Library. https://digital.library.unt.edu/ark:/67531/metadc115043/

Ballester, E. D., & Aleman, J. L. M. (2001). Brand trust in the context of consumer loyalty. *European Journal of Marketing, 35*(11), 1238–1258. doi:10.1108/EUM0000000006475

Becerra, E. P., & Badrinarayanan, V. (2013). The influence of brand trust and brand identification on brand evangelism. *Journal of Product and Brand Management, 22*(5/6), 371–383. doi:10.1108/JPBM-09-2013-0394

Brennen, J., Simon, F., Howard, P., & Nielsen, R. (2020). *Types, sources, and claims of COVID-19 misinformation*. The Reuters Institute for the Study of Journalism. https://reutersinstitute.politics.ox.ac.uk/typessources-and-claims-covid-19-isinformation

Chaudhuri, A., & Holbrook, M. B. (2001). The chain of effects from brand trust and brand affect to brand performance: The role of brand loyalty. *Journal of Marketing, 65*(2), 81–93. doi:10.1509/jmkg.65.2.81.18255

Chen, X., & Qasim, H. (2021). Does E-Brand experience matter in the consumer market? Explaining the impact of social media marketing activities on consumer-based brand equity and love. *Journal of Consumer Behaviour, 20*(5), 1065–1077. doi:10.1002/cb.1915

Chernatony, L. (2001). Succeeding with Brands on the Internet. *Journal of Brand Management, 8*(3), 186–195. doi:10.1057/palgrave.bm.2540019

Choi, N. H., Qiao, X., & Wang, L. (2020). Effects of multisensory cues, self-enhancing imagery and self-goal achievement emotion on purchase intention. *Journal of Asian Finance. Economics and Business*, *7*(1), 141–151. doi:10.13106/jafeb.2020.vol7.no1.141

Christodoulides, G. (2009, March). Branding in the post-internet era. *Marketing Theory*, *9*(1), 141–144. doi:10.1177/1470593108100071

Dam, T. (2020). Influence of Brand Trust, Perceived Value on Brand Preference and Purchase Intention. *The Journal of Asian Finance. Economics and Business*, *7*(10), 939–947. doi:10.13106/jafeb.2020.vol7.no10.939

Delgado-Ballester, E., Munuera-Alemán, J., & Yagüe-Guillén, M. (2003). Development and Validation of a Brand Trust Scale. *International Journal of Market Research*, *45*(1), 1–18. doi:10.1177/147078530304500103

DelVecchio, D., & Smith, D. (2000). Moving beyond fit: The role of brand portfolio characteristics in consumer evaluations of brand reliability. In A. Menon & A. Sharma (Eds.), *Proceedings of the 2000 Ama Winter Educators Conference: Marketing Theory & Applications* (p. 59). Amer Marketing Assn., https://www.proquest.com/scholarly-journals/moving-beyond-fit-role-brand-portfolio/docview/199493969/se-2?accountid=177838 doi:10.1108/10610420010351411

Dlacic, J., & Kezman, E. (2014). Exploring relationship between brand equity and customer loyalty on pharmaceutical market. *Economic and Business Review for Central and South - Eastern Europe*, *16*(2), 121-131.

Dwivedi, A., Johnson, L. W., Wilkie, D. C., & de Araujo Gil, L. (2019). Consumer emotional brand attachment with social media brands and social media brand equity. *European Journal of Marketing*, *53*(6), 1176–1204. doi:10.1108/EJM-09-2016-0511

Ebrahim, R. (2019). The Role of Trust in Understanding the Impact of Social Media Marketing on Brand Equity and Brand Loyalty. *Journal of Relationship Marketing*, *19*(3), 1–22. doi:10.1080/15332667.2019.1705742

Editorial. (2000). 21st century brand knowledge — towards the ADEP*T standard for brands' promise and trust. *Journal of Brand Management*, *7*(4), 220-231. doi:10.1057/bm.2000.8

Elliott, R., & Yannopoulou, N. (2007). The nature of trust in brands: A psychosocial model. *European Journal of Marketing*, *41*(9), 988–998. doi:10.1108/03090560710773309

Folse, J., Burton, S., & Netemeyer, R. (2013). Defending brands: Effects of alignment of spokes character personality traits and corporate transgressions on brand trust and attitudes. *Journal of Advertising*, *42*(4), 331–342. doi:10.1080/00913367.2013.795124

Fournier, S. (1998). Consumers and their brands: Developing relationship theory in consumer research. *The Journal of Consumer Research*, *24*(4), 343–353. doi:10.1086/209515

Fuan, L., Zhou, N., Kashyap, R., & Yang, Z. (2008). Brand Trust as a Second-Order Factor. *International Journal of Market Research*, *50*(6), 817–839. doi:10.2501/S1470785308200225

Gecti, F., & Zengin, H. (2013). The relationship between brand trust, brand affect, attitudinal loyalty and behavioral loyalty: A field study towards sports shoe consumers in Turkey. *International Journal of Marketing Studies*, *5*(2), 111–119. doi:10.5539/ijms.v5n2p111

Hannah, R., Edouard, M., Rodés-Guirao, L., Appel, C., Giattino, C., Ortiz-Ospina, E., Hasell, J., Macdonald, B., Beltekian, D., & Roser, M. (2020). *Coronavirus Pandemic (COVID-19)*. Our World in Data. https://ourworldindata.org/coronavirus

Haudi, H., Handayani, W., Musnaini, M., Suyoto, Y., Prasetio, T., Pitaloka, E., & Cahyon, Y. (2022). The effect of social media marketing on brand trust, brand equity and brand loyalty. *International Journal of Data and Network Science*, *6*(3), 961–972. doi:10.5267/j.ijdns.2022.1.015

Hess, J. (1995). Construction and Assessment of a Scale to Measure Consumer Trust. In Stern, B., & Zinkhan, G. (Eds.), Enhancing Knowledge Development in Marketing, AMA Educators' Proceedings (pp. 20-26). American Marketing Association.

Hussein, I., Chams, N., Chams, S., El Sayegh, S., Badran, R., Raad, M., Gerges-Geagea, A., Leone, A., & Jurjus, A. (2015). Vaccines Through Centuries: Major Cornerstones of Global Health. *Frontiers in Public Health*, *3*, 1–16. doi:10.3389/fpubh.2015.00269 PMID:26636066

Jacob, J., & Chestnut, R. (1978). *Brand Loyalty Measurement and Management*. John Wiley & Sons.

Jose, S. (2021). COVID vaccine and generation Z – a study of factors influencing adoption. *Young Consumers*. doi:10.1108/YC-01-2021-1276

Kapferer, J. (1991). *Strategic brand management*. Free Press.

Kavisankar, L., Balasubramani, S., Arvindhar, D. J., & Krishan, R. (2021). Scenario based vaccine status monitoring and recommendation system for Covid-19 Vaccination. *Journal of Management Information and Decision Sciences, 24*, 1–7.

Kejariwal, M., & Bhat, R. (2022). Marketing Strategies for Pharmaceutical Industry-A Review. *Journal of Pharmaceutical Negative Results, 13*(8), 3602–3606.

Keller, K. (1993). Conceptualizing, Measuring, and Managing Customer- Based Brand Equity. *Journal of Marketing, 57*(1), 1–22. doi:10.1177/002224299305700101

Koschate-Fischer, N., & Gartner, S. (2015). Brand Trust: Scale Development and Validation. *Schmalenbach Business Review, 67*(2), 171–195. doi:10.1007/BF03396873

Kwon, J.-H., Jung, S.-H., Choi, H.-J., & Kim, J. (2021). Antecedent factors that affect restaurant brand trust and brand loyalty: Focusing on US and Korean consumers. *Journal of Product and Brand Management, 30*(7), 990–1015. doi:10.1108/JPBM-02-2020-2763

Lemanski, J., & Villegas, J. (2018). Vaccine promotion: Impact of risk level on attitudes. *International Journal of Pharmaceutical and Healthcare Marketing, 12*(2), 181–197. doi:10.1108/IJPHM-04-2017-0018

Macit, C., Taner, N., Mercanoglu, G., & Mercanoglu, F. (2016). Brand Loyalty as a Strategy for the Competition with Generic Drugs: Physicians Perspective. *Journal of Developing Drugs, 5*(3). doi:10.4172/2329-6631.1000159

McCarthy, J. (2019, September 03). Big pharma sinks to the bottom of U.S. industry rankings. *Gallup News.* https://news.gallup.com/poll/266060/big-pharma-sinks-bottom-industry-rankings.aspx

Mian, A., & Khan, S. (2020). Coronavirus: The spread of misinformation. *BMC Medicine, 18*(1), 89. doi:10.118612916-020-01556-3 PMID:32188445

Montgomery, C., & Wernerfelt, B. (1992). Risk Reduction and umbrella branding. *The Journal of Business, 65*(1), 31–50. doi:10.1086/296556

Morgan, R. M., & Hunt, S. D. (1994). The commitment-trust theory of relationship marketing. *Journal of Marketing, 58*(3), 20–38. doi:10.1177/002224299405800302

Nyadzayo, M., & Khajehzadeh, S. (2016). The antecedents of customer loyalty: A moderated mediation model of customer relationship management quality and brand image. *Journal of Retailing and Consumer Services, 30*, 262–270. doi:10.1016/j.jretconser.2016.02.002

OPAS. (2020). *Folha informativa sobre COVID-19. Histórico da pandemia de COVID-19*. OPAS. https://www.paho.org/pt/covid19/historico-da-pandemia-covid-19

Pahus, L., Suehs, C. M., Halimi, L., Bourdin, A., Chanez, P., Jaffuel, D., Marciano, J., Gamez, A.-S., Vachier, I., & Molinari, N. (2020). Patient distrust in pharmaceutical companies: An explanation for women under-representation in respiratory clinical trials? *BMC Medical Ethics*, *21*(1), 72. doi:10.118612910-020-00509-y PMID:32791969

Pessemier, E. A. (1959). A New Way to Determine Buying Decisions. *Journal of Marketing*, *24*(2), 41–46. doi:10.1177/002224295902400208

Plessis, D., Sake, J. K., Halling, K., Morgan, J., Georgieva, A., & Bertelsen, N. (2017). Patient centricity and pharmaceutical companies: Is it feasible? *Therapeutic Innovation & Regulatory Science*, *51*(4), 460–467. doi:10.1177/2168479017696268 PMID:30227057

Quintanilla, C. (2021, May 05). *Consumer and brand perception in covid-19 vaccines*. CE Noticias Financieras.

Rahman, M., Masum, M., Wajed, S., & Talukder, A. (2022). A comprehensive review on COVID-19 vaccines: Development, effectiveness, adverse effects, distribution and challenges. *VirusDis*, *33*(1), 1–22. doi:10.100713337-022-00755-1 PMID:35127995

Rao, S. (2002). Pharmaceutical marketing in a new age. *Marketing Health Services*, *22*(1), 6–12. PMID:11881547

Reichheld, F. (1996). *The Loyalty Effect: The Hidden Force Behind Growth, Profits and Lasting Value*. Harvard Business School Press.

Reportlinker (2021). *COVID-19 Vaccine Market - Global Outlook and Forecast 2021-2024*. Aritzon. https://www.reportlinker.com/p06036826/?utm_source=GNW

Sabharwal, D. (2017). Determinants of Brand Reliability: A Study of the Familiarity-Assurance-Loyalty. *IJARIIE*, *3*(2), 2755–2762.

Samarah, T., Bayram, P., Aljuhmani, H., & Elrehail, H. (2022). The role of brand interactivity and involvement in driving social media consumer brand engagement and brand loyalty: The mediating effect of brand trust. *Journal of Research in Interactive Marketing*, *16*(4), 648–664. doi:10.1108/JRIM-03-2021-0072

Schuiling, I., & Moss, G. (2004). How different are branding strategies in the pharmaceutical industry and the fast-moving consumer goods sector? *Journal of Brand Management*, *11*(5), 366–380. doi:10.1057/palgrave.bm.2540182

Sharma, K., Koirala, A., Nicolopoulos, K., & Chiu, C. (2020). Coronavirus goes viral: Quantifying the COVID-19 misinformation epidemic on Twitter. *Cureus*, *12*(3). doi:10.7759/cureus.7255 PMID:32337139

Sharma, K., Koirala, A., Nicolopoulos, K., Chiu, C., Wood, N., & Britton, P. N. (2021). Vaccines for COVID-19: Where do we stand in 2021? *Paediatric Respiratory Reviews*, *39*, 22–31. doi:10.1016/j.prrv.2021.07.001 PMID:34362666

Singh, Y., Eisenberg, M., & Sood, N. (2023). Factors Associated with Public Trust in Pharmaceutical Manufacturers. *Public Health*, *6*(3), e233002. doi:10.1001/jamanetworkopen.2023.3002 PMID:36917113

Srivastava, N., Dash, S., & Mookerjee, A. (2016). Determinants of brand trust in high inherent risk products: The moderating role of education and working status. *Marketing Intelligence & Planning*, *34*(3), 394–420. doi:10.1108/MIP-01-2015-0004

Sunstein, C., & Vermeule, A. (2009). Conspiracy theories: Causes and cures. *Journal of Political Philosophy*, *17*(2), 202–227. doi:10.1111/j.1467-9760.2008.00325.x

Szilagyi, P., Thomas, K., Shah, M., Vizueta, N., Cui, Y., Vangala, S., & Kapteyn, A. (2021). The role of trust in the likelihood of receiving a COVID-19 vaccine: Results from a national survey. *Preventive Medicine*, *153*, 106727. doi:10.1016/j.ypmed.2021.106727 PMID:34280405

Wang, C., Jong, E., Faure, J., Ellington, J., Chen, C., & Chang, C. (2022). A matter of trust: A qualitative comparison of the determinants of COVID-19 vaccine hesitancy in Taiwan, the United States, the Netherlands, and Haiti. *Human Vaccines & Immunotherapeutics*, *18*(7), 2050121. doi:10.1080/21645515.2022.2050121 PMID:35349382

Chapter 3
Brand Narrative in the 21st Century

Edna Mngusughun Denga
ⓘD https://orcid.org/0000-0002-2121-242X
American University of Nigeria, Nigeria

ABSTRACT

Consumers assess the credibility of a brand by examining its brand narrative, which is crafted to distinguish it from other brands. Marketing professionals create narratives to promote their brands. Brand narratives emerge when there is a consistent and recurring set of meanings associated with a brand, portraying its place in the world. These narratives play a crucial role in reinforcing brand awareness, promotion, and positioning. Brands must effectively convey unique stories that enhance and deepen consumer relationships. As social creatures, people connect with narratives, making a robust brand narrative a powerful tool for interacting, listening to, and engaging with customers. While brand narratives are not a novel concept, social media has transformed the way they are executed. It serves as a form of content marketing, intriguing audiences without overtly promoting products or businesses.

INTRODUCTION

In an era where customers are inundated with content, a strong brand, and a thoughtful brand marketing strategy can help one brand stand out from the crowd (Sharma et al.,2022). The concept of brand marketing is not modern, before the introduction of the radio and later television, firms sought to advertise their products to smaller audiences, relying on word-of-mouth advertising from customers or newspaper advertisements to promote their offerings. In the past 25 years, advertising has

DOI: 10.4018/978-1-6684-8351-0.ch003

evolved beyond simply presenting and promoting products to encompass developing a brand narrative and communicating it through storytelling (Sharma et al.,2022). Customers are more likely to connect emotionally and personally with businesses when narrative and storytelling are employed. Studies show 55% of customers who adore a brand's story are inclined to make purchases. It makes perfect sense that countless brands are revamping their marketing tactics to concentrate on storytelling, which conveys branded messaging from the business to customers. Nowadays, marketing encompasses more than just a haphazard blend of disciplines like branding and promotions. Instead, effective marketing strategies are based on compelling narratives(Ripoll et al.,2023)

In today's digitally connected and social world, "what to say" and "how to say it" no longer matter. "What are the audience hearing and saying" is what matters. With a cell phone and a social media account, users publish content about brands across several platforms attributable to the digital era and information democratization. A meaningful brand strategy is built around a brand narrative. With a specific emphasis on the business-related shifts the brand intends to accomplish, it is founded on the information and insights gathered during the kickoff process. Brands require a solid plan for generating sales on social media when boosting revenue and attracting potential customers are top priorities for a marketing team(Sharma et al.,2022). Special deals and flash sales can undoubtedly be beneficial. But, there are many other ways to persuade potential clients to make a purchase. With the use of brand narratives, businesses may draw in audiences, win over customers, and even gradually increase customer loyalty (Ripoll et al.,2023).

Text reading skills have declined as a result of how individuals communicate and interpret pieces of information being revolutionized by technology (Burgess & Jones, 2021). In today's digital marketing environment, visual content strategy has evolved to be of significant relevance to marketers. To promote customer-based brand equity, the emphasis on brand communication has transitioned from providing decision-leading persuasion to providing a comprehensive brand experience (Chahal and Rani, 2017). Marketers have recently recognised the perks of employing brand narratives and have begun to implement them for their brands (Brechman and Purvis, 2015). Br and narratives benefit brands in a variety of ways, including informing people about how to utilize their products and offering entertaining content (Singh and Sonnenburg, 2012). This is where narratives are effective as it illustrates what something does rather than what it is (Ripoll et al.,2023). Research has proven the value of pictures and visuals with narrative components that depict customers' everyday interactions with brands. When presented with imagery information, the brain engages in episodic processing instead of making cognitive judgments, which encourages the growth of empathy (Lim & child, 2021). Consequently, Brand narrative-based visual content enhances the possibility that consumers will have favourable opinions of the brand represented in the image.

BACKGROUND

In a rapid pace evolving technological landscape where analogue and digital communication channels compete for consumer attention, new technologies, such as advancements in virtual reality and the emergence of artificial intelligence (Kim et al., 2017), offer inspiring opportunities to strengthen customer engagement. Marketing experts craft narratives to market their brands. A brand is said to have a narrative if there is a consistent and recurrent pattern of meanings that describes where it fits into the world (Sharma et al.,2022). To persuade consumers to favourably choose a specific brand, brand narratives are meticulously constructed. One of today's most popular buzzwords in marketing and communications is brand narrative. Everyone emphasizes the value of presenting a fascinating story that connects brands to a compelling narrative, but they neglect to highlight how to break through the cacophony of information to get the appropriate message to the right audience. Even though brands have more tools than ever, it is becoming increasingly difficult to reach people in this age of information overload. Since audiences are generally segregated into industrial silos, brand narratives can be particularly challenging.

Human culture and life are fundamentally centered on stories, which help people make sense of both their surroundings and themselves (Etinkaya, 2019). Storytelling has been examined by marketing academics and brand narratives in a range of settings (Sanders & van Krieken, 2018). Instead of conveying a brand's character or advantages through justifications and arguments, brand narratives leverage stories to do so. By helping consumers decipher a brand's essence, promise, and values, stories aid consumers in processing information (Kim et al., 2017) and assist brands to build their identities. Modern thinking frequently depicts brand meaning or image as narratives (Shao et al., 2015). Customers create narratives based on experiences and stories that align with their values ((Burgess & Jones, 2021)). Through their participation in the formation of brand value, these narratives add to the brand's meaning (Shao et al., 2015). Consumers' "multistories" are intricate, multifaceted, and always evolving, with a strong socio-cultural foundation intertwined with the consumer's sense of self.

Brand narrative in an internet era can affect consumer perceptions (Gilliam & Zablah 2013). Customer actions and storytelling contributions that contribute to brand value frequently outperform those of the firms (Shao et al., 2015). As a result, the dynamics of environmental inputs, firm operations, and the preexisting narratives of customers co-create brand meaning. Businesses rely heavily on their brands, yet there is currently insufficient research on how narratives fit into branding strategies. The scarce studies concentrated on the effect of narratives on audiences and how audiences employ them. Both academic research and industry practices have demonstrated the significance of brand narratives. For instance, Kennedy (2015) argued that brand narrative is paramount as a marketing strategy for the service sector. Moreover, Su et al. (2015) recommended additional research on brand narrative communication strategies on social media platforms. Brand narratives are increasingly efficiently conveyed utilizing digital technologies attributable to the information age. However, prior research has not delved into how brand narratives can be leveraged in the era of over-information as a means of enhancing brand interaction with customers in the twenty-first century.

THE CONCEPT OF BRAND NARRATIVE

A brand narrative is a succinct, well-organized story that forms the basis for a brand's communications and marketing efforts. A brand's purpose and offers are systematically plotted out into an intuitively recognizable pattern in a strategy that acknowledges (explicitly or implicitly) the interests of the consumer (Dion & Mazzalovo, 2016). The narrative is a nuanced description that aligns the need, objective, and opposition of the brand and the consumer as opposed to being a one-dimensional statement. A robust brand narrative will actively engage in conversation with a range of stakeholders and work cooperatively with partners, customers, and co-creators over time to develop its broader narrative(Burgess & Jones, 2021). Business, products, and customers are all emphasized in a brand narrative. Beyond the brand's own story, it involves every facet of the brand.

A brand narrative conveys the identity story of a brand, it describes the brand's history, mission, and operations (Delgado- Ballester,2020). The company's mission and future vision, the goals of its products or services, how it intends to serve customers, and the influence it aspires to have on the world are all significant components of a brand narrative (Signorelli, 2014). In general, a brand narrative is a technique to connect emotionally with customers and offer them compelling motives to purchase goods or services as part of a brand's brand strategy. Brand narratives contain tales that a business might utilize in its marketing initiatives. People frequently connect emotionally with stories, making them effective communication tools. They frequently feature compelling scenes, captivating characters, and thought-provoking insights that can enable people to comprehend and explain the world (Gilliam et al., 2014). They can be expressed verbally, in writing, or visually. They are a creative and expressive way of communication.

Brand narrative aids in boosting brand awareness. It is the act of storytelling a narrative integrating various digital tools, such as blog entries, photographs, and videos (Chahal and Rani, 2017). Its goal is to draw in the target audience and deepen its relationship with them to increase brand engagement. A firm can improve its relationship with its audience as the audience learns more about the brand thanks to a robust brand narrative strategy. While creating a solid brand strategy, a brand narrative is a critical element. It should include a company's mission and rationale for existing. A developed brand narrative takes into account what the key target audience needs and wants from businesses now and in the future. One integral and crucial ingredient in the ability of some of the most iconic brands to develop their enduring brand identity and brand equity is the sharing and crafting of their brand narrative from the very beginning. Think of Apple, Lego, and Coca-Cola; their brand narratives have evolved in response to shifting consumer demands, market conditions, and the pace of innovation. The most efficient and effective strategy to instil brand positioning in the market and the minds of consumers is to communicate a brand narrative at every opportunity (Signorelli, 2014).

A brand narrative is an effective instrument for communication that can significantly increase customer trust in a brand. Each communication from a brand needs to be concise, focused, consistent, and convey the personality of the brand (Rahmanian. 2021). Making more informed, strategic decisions is facilitated by ensuring that the brand narrative is in line with both internal and external business objectives. While creating a brand narrative, there are a few ground guidelines to adhere to:

- Make sure it is authentic and truthful.
- Make it informative, with supporting evidence and advantages.
- Establish an emotional connection with the target audience that will motivate them.
- Be consistent and facilitate proof to verify assertions.

Keeping these principles in mind when crafting brand narratives promotes business growth by inspiring and guiding both internal and external audiences. Brand narratives are never static. It is a communication tool that evolves as time passes. Once a brand narrative has been crafted, brands must revisit it in the future to ensure sure it is adaptable to shifting market conditions (Rahmanian. 2021). A brand and its messaging can remain relevant throughout periods of transformation by revisiting or enhancing a business's brand narrative. When a brand's values and emotional benefits are directly reflected in a brand narrative, it gives consumers a reason to choose. Moreover, brand narratives describe tangible points of differentiation and support the creation of brand experiences that alter perceptions.

How can brands tell their narratives? Excellent brand narratives tap into peoples' inherent curiosity. A captivating narrative captures consumers' interest and maintains it. In comparison to a list of product features, it is much more memorable and relatable. This innate human curiosity is harnessed by brands that utilize narrative to interact with potential customers. Particularly if the product is premium, prospective clients are more interested in learning about the business than the thing they buy (Rahmanian. 2021). They seek to understand the guiding principles of the brand they have chosen as well as the inspirations that drive its management.

Typically, the predominant objective of brand narratives is to define what and how a brand interacts with its audiences. A brand narrative needs to be believable to be effective. The objective of a brand narrative is to establish total trust in a brand from both sources both internal and external. After all, 81% of consumers concur that trust in a brand plays a role before committing to an investment. Customers are incredibly perceptive, thus, brand narratives must be genuine. Inconsistencies in made-up narratives might culminate in perplexity, dissatisfaction, and possibly a decrease in sales (Delgado- Ballester,2020). The dishonesty is noticeable if the components of a narrative don't line up. Each narrative element must flow smoothly for consumers to build trust and confidence in a brand. This may include a variety of components that contribute to a brand's overarching brand strategy, such as:

Identity: The fundamental objective of a brand or the objective of a founder is dependent upon the identities and personalities of its founders. Given that it is the cornerstone of a brand; it can be its most critical component. A team's strategy and actions can be guided by its identity and goal, which can also provide direction for what to do next. Furthermore, it assists in coordinating change initiatives with their goal.

Vision: A vision is a picture of the ideal world. Brands showcase a product or service that will enable them to accomplish their objectives while advancing their visions. Their visions widely adopt the form of a promise made to customers or a declaration of what a brand pledges to execute.

Operations: Stories that detail a brand's operations are some crucial components of a brand's narrative. This might refer to the approaches that team members design and produce products, offer services, or update operations. Their everyday operations and brand policies may also be highlighted. A brand can project credibility and draw in more customers if it is open with its audiences about how it operates and continues to evolve toward its objectives (Rahmanian. 2021).

Tone: Given that a brand narrative's fundamental focus is to create an emotional impact on its audience, the tone is one of the most significant facets of the brand narrative. The tone or mood of a narrative expresses how a brand wants its audience and customers to feel. A brand might provoke specific feelings in potential customers to support the mission it seeks to accomplish.

Marketing materials: The creation of materials, such as advertisements, that convey the brand narrative to its target audiences is the last component of a brand narrative (Yung &Khoo, 2019). This is creating tangible marketing tools that a brand may leverage to showcase to potential customers to market and sell goods and services, such as blogs, advertisements, and videos. The marketing department of a corporation should decide which marketing strategies would best promote its brand narrative. Additionally, they can utilize it to converse with their personnel about how the firm operates.

ELEMENTS OF SUCCESSFUL BRAND NARRATIVES

Businesses can establish emotional connections with their audience by developing a captivating narrative that speaks to them (Yung &Khoo, 2019). This can be accomplished by developing a brand story or by presenting client testimonials that demonstrate the positive effects of products or services on their life. Here are essential elements to shape brand narratives:

Creating A Storyline: A fascinating storyline is the initial component every brand narrative requires. The storyline creates a context in which customers can learn about the origins, core values, and distinctive features of a brand. Customers appreciate the underdog, and oftentimes a business's origin may highlight that narrative. A brand story is a narrative that conveys a company's objective, arouses feelings in the audience, and boosts consumer loyalty (Yung &Khoo, 2019). Customers are more inclined to purchase a brand's services or products if they are captivated by the brand's story. A carefully crafted brand narrative identifies a particular customer problem and presents an intriguing solution. Additionally, it effectively and inspiringly conveys a company's mission and principles. The best brand stories are Authentic, centred on the customer, consistent across channels, simple and clear with some vivid details, Structured like a story, and true to brands' personalities and voice.

Effective brand stories go beyond conveying the facts; they acknowledge and appeal to the humanity of the customer as well as their need for connection and community. The brands that can humanize themselves stand out as people are predisposed to relate to one another and their communities via storytelling. When crafting a brand story, understanding the value of excellent storytelling is essential, but creating a narrative that customers can relate to can be tricky (Yung &Khoo, 2019). Storytelling frameworks are a useful tool for organizing a narrative that will capture the interest of intended customers. As marketers construct a narrative, developing a distinctive storyline is a terrific technique to capitalize on a brand's values.

Establishing an Emotional Connection: The most powerful brand narratives elicit a favourable emotional response from the audience. To foster connections between consumers and a product or brand, emotional branding and creative brand narratives replicate consumer emotions. Marketers accomplish this by feeding their customers content that appeals to their emotions, egos, aspirations, and ambitions. Emotionally manipulative marketing has the potential to appeal to people's subconscious desires for love, power, emotional stability, and ego satisfaction (Huang et al.,2018). Customers' worth rises rapidly when they are utterly satisfied and deeply loyal to brands even as their relationship evolves at each phase.

Leverage Data to support narrative: Data from reliable sources enhances the messaging and narrative of a brand. For instance, human narratives that include statistics on wildlife numbers or climate change are frequently included in National Geographic's social media graphics. This gives the reader the chance to learn more about preserving the environment. A firm's growth over the past year or consumer interactions with the company are just two examples of how data can be utilized to create a narrative. It's interesting to discover what other people were searching for during the year by watching Google's yearly "Year in Search" video. Google's 2016 video showed how many of the same happy and terrible situations were searched for by millions of people. It received the third-highest score out of roughly 700 advertisements for technology, placing it in the top 1% of all evaluated advertisements.

Make It Resonate: Every narrative's ultimate goal is to be memorable and stick with consumers for extended periods. These components work together to assist brands in crafting compelling branded content that can strengthen relationships with customers. Once a compelling brand narrative has been established, marketers can publish that information on a variety of technology platforms to appeal to the largest or narrowest audience possible.

BENEFITS OF BRAND NARRATIVES

The assumption that brand narrative is essential to attracting and retaining customers has encouraged an increasing number of big and small firms to engage in a marketing activity called content marketing. When executed effectively, the advantages of brand narratives "nearly timeless" include:

Brand Narratives Increases Customer Engagement- Audiences are deeply and emotionally captivated by authentic brand narratives. This helps engage consumers and sustain long-term customer loyalty more than the preponderance of other marketing strategies. A straightforward value proposition or a list of product characteristics cannot compare to the depth of an emotional connection. Customers respond to communications more effectively and stay engaged longer when brands tap into their emotions. Simple brand messages are far easier for people to ignore than engaging narratives. For example, consider social media platforms. Humans are drawn to other people's stories. Many people find it nearly impossible to refrain from scrolling through an engaging life story and responding to the sub-stories that make up the overarching narrative. To what extent consumers are more engaged with brands that have mastered storytelling may be difficult to quantify. A fascinating brand narrative, however, consistently outperforms even the most personalized catchphrase, according to psychologists.

Customer retention -Positive emotional connections between brands and customers are established via narratives. Customers continue to be devoted to the brand as long as that relationship endures. Even though other businesses may launch relatively similar or superior products, emotional connections often outweigh product specifications. Compared to any other form of marketing, narratives boost consumer loyalty. Marketers can expand and incorporate additional elements into the brand story once the foundational narrative has been developed. Consider them as brand-new chapters or even as sequels for a straightforward way to visualize those extensions. The brand story must be consistent across all platforms for narratives to be successful and lead to long-term consumer retention. This holds for both the original story and its sequels. The brand team must create a relationship from one section of the narrative to the next, even if a brand changes course. This is facilitated by authenticity and consistency.

Brand Narrative Humanize Brands - Every brand has a business behind it, but those who employ great narratives in their brand messaging come off as more like an old friend than a machine that generates profits (Brechman and Purvis, 2015. By refocusing offerings on their emotional benefits and presenting a more sympathetic narrative with customers, brands may humanize their business and win over more advocates. Often, all it takes to start developing a brand is an idea. The foundation of a large percentage of businesses is the idea of identifying a problem and proposing an innovative solution to it. Brand narratives do not necessarily require a crisis. Sharing some of the more difficult times of starting a firm, however, can humanize a brand and elicit an emotional response from customers. Imagine Nike. Nike focuses on the emotional outcome such things enable—empowerment—instead of just the quality or performance of their products while trying to attract customers. The outcome? Nike routinely beats the market, ranking as the most valuable apparel brand in the world for seven years running by fostering a conversation that feels more human than transactional.

Elicit emotion- Brand Narrative has been shown to arouse emotion in research. A 2021 study found that narrative increased oxytocin levels in hospitalized patients while lowering cortisol and discomfort levels, such natural biological responses can strengthen feelings of connection when utilized in brand narrative, causing viewers to feel more connected with and attached to the brand. Brand narrative, however, can assist in engaging with the appropriate audiences in addition to merely connecting with people. Brand narratives may further fortify these relationships, helping to attract and keep the right people engaged that are required to boost sales and enhance retention, from devoted customers who are prepared to pay more for products to ideal workforce who are willing to go above and beyond for the business.

To sum up, the tradition of brand narrative dates back thousands of years, but it has not lost an of its potency. Researchers in human psychology have discovered that narratives help people relate to information more readily. A narrative forges an emotional connection, unlike a slogan for a company or the tagline of an advertisement, which they may ultimately recall. Engagement is greatly influenced by emotions. People prefer to do business with other people rather than faceless corporations because they can connect to them and build relationships. Leveraging brand ambassadors is now crucial for many brands(Brechman and Purvis, 2015). A captivating narrative is created by weaving the stories of the ambassadors and the brand together. Consumers of today are motivated by internet personal connections. Customers want to connect with brands and form relationships with them. Brand narratives are central as it fosters connection and evokes feelings in the audience. Leveraging brand narrative, brands differentiate themself from rivals and make sure they are remembered can assist with winning over customers. A strong brand narrative approach will enable brands to create an audience engagement community. It humanizes brands, enabling the development of ties that are more sincere. As people develop a personal and emotional connection with brands, these factors will contribute to fostering brand loyalty.

LEVERAGING DIGITAL PLATFORMS AND BRAND NARRATIVES TO ENHANCE SUSTAINABLE LONG-TERM GROWTH

The most potent intangible asset is a brand. Thus, managing, preserving, and measuring a brand requires an understanding of its financial value to the company. Knowing exactly how the brand affects sales allows for its improvement and strengthening to maintain the business competitive and relevant. Opportunities to increase equity are presented by new and developing digital technologies, platforms, and formats which aid in conveying brand narratives. Digital platforms can significantly increase engagement by increasing a brand's visibility and activity in the lives of its customers(Hinson et al.,2019). A consistent, pertinent, and appealing 360-degree brand narrative can further be exploited to establish and amplify brand qualities when digital media are effectively utilized (Brechman and Purvis, 2015). Customers will develop connections and perceptions as a result, which will influence their decision to adopt a particular brand. The possibility is huge, but it needs to be properly pursued.

Data capture opportunities on customer interactions and brand perception are offered by numerous digital touchpoints and interactions. This enables marketing efforts to be optimized at precisely the relevant stages throughout the customer journey to foster short-term relationships and long-term commitment. Instant feedback can be harnessed to tailor customer communications and experiences. Customers want a consistent experience across all platforms, and each encounter should be consistent with the brand's narrative, basic principles, and overall goal. The digital strategy must first be coordinated across all platforms(Hinson et al.,2019). Although it may seem obvious, just around a third of marketers have integrated digital strategies that cover social media, mobile devices, desktops, and laptops.

To connect brand experiences, digital channels are in alignment with conventional channels. Most significantly, brand narratives are utilized to communicate everything. All operations are driven by a core set of goals and serve the broader vision since the brand, marketing, and digital strategies are intimately intertwined with the overall business strategy. Combining data from many sources can yield deep insights into consumer behaviour and preferences. A storyline a brand conveys is its brand narrative. It serves as the foundation for all other brand applications, from messaging to customer service strategies(Hinson et al.,2019). It is a brand's raison d'etre (justification for existence). Since a unique brand narrative cannot be imitated, it is a significant distinction between brands and their rivals. More importantly, it is one of the most effective tools to deploy as part of a larger brand strategy intended to generate a lasting impression on the audience. A compelling brand narrative communicates the brand's value proposition, fosters audience affinities, and stands out from the competition at the same time. Any market can benefit from brand narratives, but B2B is an especially significant one because of the intense rivalry and requirement for distinctiveness.

BRAND NARRATIVE FRAMEWORKS

Brand narrative frameworks are strategic tools that help define and communicate a brand's story, values, and purpose. They provide a structured approach to developing a compelling narrative that resonates with the target audience and differentiates the brand from its competitors. Narratives are powerful. They can create meaning unforgettable in a distinctive way. Therefore, they are effective tools for businesses looking to stand out in crowded markets. One of the most effective differentiators is a captivating brand narrative. It may distinguish brands from rivals, communicate brand values, enhance the emotional impact of their messaging, and drive long-term growth (Hinson et al.,2019). 59% of brands reported that their market was "far more competitive," while 94% of brands stated that market rivalry has intensified in recent years. The traditional hurdles to market entry, such as the challenges in acquiring capital and gaining early traction, have been reduced, culminating in this heightened competition. Digital service providers like Iwoca have simplified access to business credit. A pricey office space becomes a "nice-to-have" rather than a requirement as remote work becomes more practical attributable to SaaS technologies like Slack and Asana. Even with budgetary constraints, reaching an audience has become easier.

In a considerably shorter period, businesses can be established and thrive. Existing brands are then forced to properly differentiate themselves in an attempt to stand out from the continuously burgeoning competition. Being imitated, undercut, encroached upon, and eventually crowded out is the alternative. Creating a distinctive brand is a single differentiation strategy that can never be authentically imitated (Hinson et al.,2019). And a compelling brand narrative is the cornerstone of a robust brand. The majority of stories that pique customers' interest is built around brand narrative frameworks which offer the ideal framework for crafting a brand narrative. Think of them as stories' skeleton— frameworks supporting the specifics. Brand narrative frameworks can be straightforward or complex, much like stories.

Here are six of the most effective frameworks for crafting a compelling brand narrative. Three-act Structure-One of the purest representation of a narrative is the three-act structure. It divides a narrative into three distinct acts, or segments, known as the Setup, the Confrontation, and the Resolution. Here Act One: Establish the scene; Act Two: Introduce conflict; and Act Three: Resolve the issue. The three-act structure can also be described as equilibrium, dis-equilibrium, and re-equilibrium. The integral notion is that there is a disruption in the status quo and that only a fundamental shift can a resolution be established. Character development is how this is accomplished in fiction. The main alteration for brands is their product.

Five-act structure-The German playwright Gustav Freytag popularized the five-act structure, which builds on the three-act structure's core idea but adds more depth. It involves five distinctive narrative beats; Exposition, Rising action, Climax, Falling action, and Resolution. The transition from equilibrium to dis-equilibrium and back again is at the core of this structure, but there is flexibility for additional narrative stages that add depth. Before-After-Bridge-This is a straightforward narrative structure that works effectively for brands due to its versatility in almost any format. It has three stages and can serve as the foundation of an overall marketing narrative or a single social media post. It has three phases: Before, After, and Bridge. The Before-After-Bridge framework, in contrast to the three-act and five-act forms, forgoes linear chronology in favour of a relatively sturdy hook. The After stage offers a chance to draw attention by outlining the resolution before it is reached. As a result, brands may demonstrate earlier on in their narrative their ability to alleviate customers' pain points.

Problem-Agitate-Solve-A prominent structure for marketing that fits successfully as an outline for a brand narrative is the PAS formula. Comparable to Before-After-Bridge, but with a stronger emphasis on creating emotional resonance. It entails Problem: Describe the issue that the brand's product seeks to address; Agitate: Make the issue more urgent and dangerous while stirring up emotional feelings; Solve: Present brands as the solution to the issue. When leveraged to anticipate and address the most frequent consumer concerns, the agitation in the middle beat can elicit an especially intense response. The Pixar story Framework-Simon Sinek coined the Golden Circle in his TED Talk, "How outstanding leaders inspire action." It addresses how brands can delve deeply into their value offer to establish deeper connections with their audience. The circle's three layers of self-awareness, which can be translated to stand in for various elements of a brand narrative, are depicted. It comprises the following: What: What do brands offer, sell, or do; How: The special way they carry out their work; Why: The motivations behind a brand's actions and their greater purpose.

The Golden Circle Formula Legend has it that the famed Pixar narrative structure serves as the foundation for the brand's storylines. Like other narrative frameworks, it centres on the disruption of equilibrium but extends further to analyze the repercussions more extensively. It's frequently presented as a sequence of questions that, when answered, form a comprehensive brand narrative (Lee et al., 2010). This framework is one of the easiest to utilize as the questions inherently elicit intriguing responses. There is ample possibility to introduce emotional resonance by focusing more on the consequences of the main conflict or issue. These narrative structures are all tried-and-true techniques for crafting a narrative that catches the customer's interest, develops emotional resonance, and sticks in their memories. But applying them is not as simple as filling in the blanks.

Hero's Journey: Inspired by Joseph Campbell's concept, this framework tells the brand's story by following a protagonist (the brand) on a transformative journey. It typically includes stages like a call to adventure (brand's origin), overcoming challenges (brand's growth), and achieving a resolution (brand's success). This framework taps into the universal storytelling structure that engages and captivates the audience.

Brand Archetypes: Based on Carl Jung's archetypal theory, this framework assigns a specific character archetype to the brand, representing its personality and essence. For example, the brand may embody the archetype of a hero, caregiver, or explorer. Each archetype carries certain traits and values that resonate with specific customer desires and motivations. This framework helps create a consistent and relatable brand personality.

Emotional Branding: This framework focuses on evoking specific emotions and creating an emotional connection with the audience. It identifies the primary emotions associated with the brand and crafts a narrative that triggers those emotions. The aim is to make the brand memorable, relatable, and create a deep emotional bond with customers. This framework is particularly effective for brands that want to establish an emotional attachment with their audience.

Purpose-Driven Storytelling: In this framework, the brand narrative revolves around a core purpose or mission beyond profit-making. It emphasizes the brand's commitment to a cause, whether it's environmental sustainability, social impact, or community empowerment. By highlighting the brand's purpose, this framework appeals to socially conscious consumers who align with the brand's values and aspirations.

It's important to note that these frameworks are not mutually exclusive, and brands often combine elements from multiple frameworks to create a unique and compelling narrative that aligns with their objectives and resonates with their target audience. Businesses around the globe, regardless of how large or small, arguably exist to find a solution to a problem. Establishing a stronger knowledge of the problem that they are addressing and the audience for whom they are solving must emerge foremost when brands set out to craft a brand narrative (Hinson et al.,2019).

Sentry is a perfect illustration of what a brand narrative goal looks like Their problem deals with the issue of undetected faulty code impacting application users—a problem that only affects app developers. These facts serve as the foundation of their brand narrative. Their homepage messaging specifically pinpoints the issue and offers a solution. They emphasize that their product is "developer-first" and cite the target market's popularity as proof of their suitability. Sentry's brand narrative reveals more about who they are and why they exist when delved deeper. The product's philanthropic origins as an "open-source project" utilized by the founders to "address their difficulties" are also made clear. Sentry developed a brand narrative framework that is incredibly resonant and persuasive by understanding its target market and its challenges.

Selecting a framework to guide its development comes after establishing an unambiguous knowledge of what the brand narrative must accomplish. Each well-known brand narrative framework offers a distinct method of approaching the process, but they can all result in an equally potent end. While selecting a framework to aid in developing a brand narrative, brands must test out a few and pay attention to which best captures how they intend to approach the problem at hand. Every aspect of a business should incorporate a brand narrative. It is a no-brainer to incorporate it in brand messaging, but there is more that can be done. For instance, McKinsey frequently exploits its brand narrative in content marketing initiatives. Their McKinsey Emotion Archive is a perfect illustration of a well-researched strategy for fusing narrative and content. It was made during the COVID-19 pandemic and depicts the predominant feelings experienced globally. It is based on data, incredibly perceptive, and sympathetic. In other words, it exemplifies the characteristics that McKinsey wishes to highlight in their brand narrative.

Another excellent illustration of brand narrative in marketing is SurveyMonkey, a SaaS platform for online surveys. With posts that offer odd insights from self-run surveys, they lightheartedly underscore their positioning as a tool that can obtain marketers' answers to even the most niche questions. The environmental, social, and governance (ESG) initiatives in which firms are participating are another obvious place where brand narratives are relevant. By adhering to their narrative and enacting a self-imposed "1% for the Earth" tax, they show their authenticity. The funds they generate from this tax support environmental NGOs and corroborate their brand narrative. This initiative successfully sets them apart from outdoor-wear rivals by showcasing them as a genuinely ethical company and appealing to the values of their target clientele. All brand strategies should be built around a brand narrative, especially if brands want to stand out or develop resiliency in a crowded market. Without one, the brand's principles, products, and marketing are all disjointed. Most significantly, aside from easily replicated "unique selling factors," there is nothing distinguishing brands from their rivals.

BRAND NARRATIVES IN THE 21ST CENTURY

Brands are striving to attract audiences through a sophisticated process of fusing traditional brand narrative with twenty-first-century delivery as consumer behaviour and technology evolve at an astounding rate. Consumers want to participate rather than consume, experience rather than read, and be razzle-dazzled without the glamour despite having an information overload and becoming ever-more demanding. In addition to enabling marketers a methodological approach for navigating the plethora of digital content delivery systems and deliverers, such as influencers, technology is aiding brands to deliver the experiences that consumers actively sought. With the use of data and analytics, brands can now identify target markets down to the micro-niche and offer concrete evidence of the most effective techniques for attracting them.

The tried-and-true technique adopted by marketers to capture their audience's interest and attention is brand narrative. Despite the move in the last ten years from print to online, there are more options for brand narrative in this digital age than at first glance. It is extremely vital to understand that businesses are no longer limited to traditional print and broadcast media alone since the internet offers a practically endless domain. A brand's marketing efforts are now only restricted by their marketing ingenuity when undertaken online.

Although this initially seems encouraging, there is a significant caveat when attempting to fathom the extent of reaching the internet world: Despite peoples' averaging 3 hours on their smart devices a day, our attention and activities online are continuously being pushed in many different directions, decreasing our attention spans as a result. People now establish their filters, decide what they want to pay attention to, and prioritize different things, adding to the online marketplace rivalry. How do marketers continue to capture an audience with brand narratives when the prospective customer base is constantly nearing the end of their attention spans? Word-of-mouth marketing through brand integrity is the answer, and it is an ancient marketing strategy. The likelihood of a brand's devoted consumers recommending it to their friends, relatives, and other potential customers increases significantly when it earns and upholds integrity.

In the 21st century, brand narrative has become increasingly important in shaping a brand's identity and connecting with consumers. With the rise of digital media and the constant stream of information, brands have recognized the need to tell compelling stories that resonate with their target audience. One key aspect of brand narrative in the 21st century is authenticity. Consumers today are more discerning and skeptical, and they expect brands to be genuine and transparent. Brands that can authentically communicate their values, mission, and purpose are more likely to build trust and loyalty with their customers. This requires brands to go beyond product features and benefits and instead focus on telling stories that evoke emotions and create meaningful connections.

Another important aspect is the shift from one-way communication to interactive storytelling. In the past, brands would simply broadcast their message to consumers through traditional media channels. However, the advent of social media and digital platforms has given consumers a voice and the ability to engage with brands directly. This has transformed brands' narratives into a two-way conversation, where brands actively listen to and engage with their audience. Brands that embrace this interactive approach can build stronger relationships with their customers and co-create narratives that resonate with their values.

In the 21st century, brand narratives also need to be adaptable and agile. The digital landscape is constantly evolving, and brands need to be able to respond quickly to changing trends and consumer expectations. This means being open to experimentation, embracing new technologies, and staying relevant in a fast-paced environment. Brands that can effectively adapt their narratives to different platforms and formats, while maintaining consistency in their core values, can stay connected with their audience and remain competitive. Furthermore, sustainability and social responsibility have become integral parts of brands' narratives in the 21st century. As consumers become more conscious of the impact of their purchasing decisions, they expect brands to align with their values and contribute to positive change. Brands that can demonstrate their commitment to sustainability, ethical practices, and social causes through their narratives can differentiate themselves in the market and attract like-minded consumers.

Overall, brand narrative in the 21st century is about creating authentic, interactive, adaptable, and socially responsible stories that resonate with consumers. It's about going beyond product features and benefits to build emotional connections and trust. By effectively leveraging storytelling techniques and embracing the evolving digital landscape, brands can create compelling narratives that capture the hearts and minds of their audience in today's highly competitive marketplace. With the explosive growth of social media, word-of-mouth is far more valuable today than it was ten years ago. For instance, when someone uses Facebook or Twitter to start debating about a product or brand, they broadcast it to their specific audiences, potentially influencing other people's perceptions or levels of interest in the brand. To retain positive word of mouth, brands must offer fantastic products and maintain a consistent, engaging, and reputable online and offline persona. Creating a distinctive internet marketing campaign for the launch of a new product would be a simple technique to accomplish this. A marketing campaign is more plausible to be discussed and spread among more people if it is inventive enough to draw in a new audience, particularly through humour or audio/visual appeal.

In the era before social media, word-of-mouth was arguably the most powerful and effective approach for establishing consumer trust in brands, excluding the reviews and opinions of credible people and reviewers. People would be increasingly inclined to purchase products and services if they were being positively discussed by others. By inviting customers to participate in a social media narrative strategy, social media networks provide businesses with the opportunity to harness that word-of-mouth reputation and deliver it within a coherent digital framework to a highly targeted audience of prospective customers. Brands can begin adopting the tried-and-true technique of marketing through storytelling once the attention of the online audience has been garnered. The brand narrative has evolved into a significant core component of branding since it helps people believe in a brand and its story as well as a product or service. Advertising that tells a story has always been a proven method to get people's attention, and innovative platforms like social media have rendered this feasible in a variety of inventive ways.

Instagram Stories usage is one strategy that businesses have been concentrating on as being successful. Instagram Stories are a terrific way for spreading brand information to the public due to their brief runtime of 15 seconds per post, especially for users who only use their devices occasionally. Instagram Stories may be leveraged by marketing and PR teams to highlight events, new goods, or anything else in brief bursts of time to help humanize brands(Yung &Khoo, 2019). Yet just like Snapchat, Instagram Stories only keeps postings for 24 hours. Although there are ways to archive prior posts, the vast majority of everything posted to these ephemeral platforms is only effective for the 24 hours that it is active, which reduces the effectiveness of a campaign. This justifies the need to post social content on several websites, like Twitter and YouTube. Not only do Twitter and YouTube store postings indefinitely, but it also broadens the audience reach as some users may only access one of such platforms. Marketers can boost the influence and reach of their businesses, which will raise interest in and sales of their products, by sharing an authentic story on well-known social media sites.

Brand narratives are powerful in brand marketing because it offers consumers an opportunity to discover the personality, authenticity, and values of a brand. The importance of brand narrative in this era and age is due to shifting customer behaviour. Customers demand authenticity and transparency from brands when they interact with them, which is essential to attracting prospective customers. Brands nowadays have numerous avenues than ever to reach consumers with their narrative due to the proliferation of social media and other technological advancements. Brands increasingly create films, deliver content or messages directly to a consumer's phone, or post blogs and other content on their websites for a fraction of what it previously cost.

Social media is a terrific platform for sharing real-life brand personality-enhancing narratives about businesses, products, customers, experiences, workplaces, and partnerships. Before, brands had to rely on public relations (PR), advertising, and word-of-mouth to help them build their reputations. Consistency, honesty, and transparency influence how consumers feel about brands. Social networks are the ideal platforms for delivering those attributes as they empower brands to communicate the narratives of real people who invent, develop, market, purchase, use, evaluate, and recommend products and services. As social beings, people relate to narratives. A strong brand narrative is an excellent technique to interact, listen to, and engage with customers. Although brand narratives are not a novel phenomenon, social media is altering the approach to how is been done. It is a form of content marketing, content that piques curiosity while not directly promoting any products or businesses. Social media platforms enable brands to engage followers to participate in the brand narrative in addition to sharing it with them. It is impossible to underscore the significance of incorporating data while creating narrative digital content.

Data is frequently a crucial element in generating great content and, ultimately, in conveying narratives that resonates with the target audience. It's not always necessary to employ words to convey narratives; data aids develop distinctive narratives that can be presented through interactive mediums like video, surveys, and brand apps. Marketing in the digital age can provide more positive and quantifiable outcomes by upholding brand integrity, conveying an authentic and captivating narrative, and generally staying on top of social trends to optimize reach and attention. The cornerstone of how people naturally communicate ideas and persuade each other is narrative. Narratives are also at the forefront of brand marketing when it comes to how to discuss brands engagingly. These days, digital media is leveraged to convey narratives. The emergence of social media has added complexity to the age of digital narrative. Although several of the fundamental narrative concepts hold regardless of the platform, the social media narrative has the additional challenge of having an abundance of content at the audience's fingertips. As a result, for brands to effectively convey a narrative, they must rapidly captivate their audience's attention.

These are ways brands are harnessing social media to convey their brand narratives.

Original Content. One of the primary ways brand narratives are told is through the original content that a brand releases. Over the years, there has been a dramatic increase in the quantity and variety of content. Nowadays, marketers create more than 10,000 pieces of content annually across Multiple platforms to successfully convey a narrative. This surge in content is mostly attributable to the onslaught of social media narratives.

User-Generated Content. Social media empowers brands to be narrators. Individuals can share a brand narrative with their social networks with the content they create. A business's brand narrative can be organically portrayed through user-generated content, which can also raise brand awareness(Singh and Sonnenburg, 2012). The proliferation of social media altered the notion of leveraging narrative as a marketing tactic. Marketers nowadays must consider the narratives they are crafting about themselves and those others are establishing about them. While it is humanizing to build brands to appear more like people they can interact with than abstract ideas, it also adds a brand-new element of narrative that businesses need to take into consideration. Understanding the narrative that is being communicated about brands on social media empowers brands to adopt choices about how to modify their carefully crafted and organic brand stories to portray the exact overarching narrative.

Linking to Their Website. A significant portion of a brand's story is communicated through the company website, which provides details ranging from products to the businesses' general knowledge to core values(Singh and Sonnenburg, 2012). One powerful technique to boost traffic to a website and click-through rates is social media. Technology is essential to streamlining this procedure. When artificial intelligence is employed to provide the most captivating content possible, it contributes to increased click-through rates.

Visual Narrative. The first step in engaging followers is through the content a brand publishes. There are a variety of visual accompaniments available to brands when it comes to narrative, all of which may impact consumers in different ways(Chahal and Rani, 2017). To properly communicate a narrative, the audience's attention must be attracted, especially on social media where there is a wealth of content. Understanding what creative choices pique the interest of the audience is paramount to engaging them. The process of actually creating content, including what to photograph or produce to add to a narrative, is the first step in visual narrative.

Interactions with Audience. Social media is a great platform for interacting with brand followers. A brand's personality is developed in part by how it interacts with its audience and the voice it employs. Whether they interact with audiences through a tweet or a comment, doing so helps them shape their persona(Chahal and Rani, 2017). Diverse social media platforms adopt varied approaches to interact with their audiences. Brands can interact directly with consumers on Facebook, Twitter, and Instagram by responding to comments. Customers may interact with brands live on Facebook and Instagram, which heightens the sense of conversation. Pinterest enables the exchange of ideas between people. Social media strategy involves a lot more than just content. but also how to engage with followers of a brand's posts.

YOUTUBE: OPENING DOORS FOR BRAND'S NARRATIVE

A high percentage of video marketing was accomplished before YouTube through live TV adverts and commercials as well as through specific websites. By establishing a centralized platform for posting visual content, YouTube opened up new avenues in the field of visual narrative in 2005. Overnight, YouTube surpassed all other video-sharing platforms in the entire globe. With the usages of media, visual narrative generates stories (graphics, video, photography, or other illustrations.) The presentation of concepts through visual narratives is coherent, simple to understand, and retains people captivated. YouTube revolutionized visual narrative by empowering digital marketers with a platform to create long-form visual content. YouTube transmogrified how content producers perceived brand videos in addition to boosting accessibility and lowering costs(Lee et al., 2010).

With the advent of brand channels. Brand videos took the place of traditional advertising and videos that interrupt other content. The technique for creating captivating videos that convey narratives rather than simply promote products evolved as a function of this transition. When brand videos transitioned into content, the emphasis shifted to include brand narratives. One of the most effective methods to approach content marketing nowadays is utilizing visual narrative(Chahal and Rani, 2017). Videos are the ideal narrative medium as the combination of images, storyline, and audio creates an emotional bond with the audience. A strong emotional connection is undoubtedly made by telling a compelling narrative, and this distinguishes businesses from their competitors. As visual narrative evolved, videos that focused primarily on selling products were replaced by those that conveyed narratives. The videos that share information with the audience that they desire to attract are the most captivating and appealing.

Brand Narratives' Emerging Best Practices

The components of what constitutes a good narrative have varied remarkably in the thousands of years humankind has been telling narratives (Huang et al.,2018). People entertain and connect with others through narratives, and also share knowledge about values, preferences, and aspirations. Narratives are employed by brands in the very same way, and the finest marketers are aware of how fundamental narratives are for conveying the how, what, and why of a brand's offering. The elements of a compelling narrative remain unaltered, but the tactics for conveying narratives in the digital age have transformed significantly as a response to emerging advertising technologies.

Marketers must ensure their usage of technological innovations complies with the tenets and guidelines of effective narrative and advertising. relying on standard, linear storylines, marketers nowadays can create sophisticated narrative frameworks, grabbing the interest of the appropriate user at the right time, on the ideal device, in the right place, and with the perfect blend of messages (Huang et al.,2018). Narratives are no longer confined to one trajectory and are capable of ever-increasingly original versions. An overview of the new elements of contemporary brand narrative in the digital age is described below.

The most talented storytellers in a campfire setting adjust to the reactions of their listeners and any new knowledge they may share. Digital brand narratives of today must accomplish the same, and new automation tools facilitate this. Instantaneous commercials that can utilize an array of data sources are accomplished by automation, which allows for quick data analysis and effective execution (Gilliam et al.,2017). Dynamic ads, which aid in enhancing efficiency and optimization as well as personalization, are a fundamental method of real-time advertising that may assist creativity and narrative. In other words, a dynamic ad enables the automated delivery of many variants of the same ad, allowing the same ad to communicate various things depending on the audience it is being delivered (Lim & Child, 2020). For instance, a travel operator may use real-time flight data to provide consumers with relevant vacation packages and prices based on their travel preferences, browsing history, geography, and other factors.

Advertisers can broaden their influence and target more users as access to a variety of channels is largely facilitated by advertising innovations. Advertisers have a responsibility to adapt their messaging to make the maximum use of these various platforms to take advantage of the opportunities for highly compelling and emotive narratives that originates from emerging channels and media (Huang et al.,2018). Contemporary brand narratives must be tailored to follow consumers as they switch between numerous devices for daily web browsing. Reaching the same customer across mobile, tablet, laptop, and desktop becomes increasingly challenging, especially when striving to figure out their preferences in using each device(Lim & Child, 2020). For example, when making purchases, one user might prefer utilizing an app on their mobile phone, while another user would prefer using their desktop. For effective retargeting, frequency capping, and measuring users' responses to the ad, it is important to understand their preferences, which is a hurdle. Successful sequential messaging across many platforms, a cornerstone of contemporary narrative, also requires cross-device.

Cornerstones of effective narrative have generally comprised relevance and reaction, and in the digital age, where customer expectations are higher, they are much more crucial (Gilliam et al.,2017). Data is bringing about a rebirth in relevance that might perhaps bind consumers and advertisements together. In actuality, personalization has been the primary force behind the transformation in digital advertising. Instead of shouting into the void, advertisers can now deliver narratives to consumers who they can be reasonably confident will be at least partially fascinated by their offerings. Marketers must ensure the narratives they tell are targeted to trigger the appropriate reactions since every exceptional narrative should elicit a response (Lim & Child, 2020). While marketers can leverage statistics to target the appropriate demographic and make sure their ads are seen by as many consumers as possible, to motivate the demographic to act favourable, their advertising must establish an emotional connection. Technology facilitates the continual engagement between consumers and marketers as a brand narrative evolves. In this sense, technology neither replaces nor hinders contemporary brand narratives but strengthens narratives if employed effectively.

Reporting and attribution are frequently portrayed as being the creative opposite of narrative in advertising. Yet in actuality, reporting has emerged as a vital component in the brand narrative process. Intelligent retargeting and the execution of sophisticated and flexible campaigns can both benefit from data from reliable reporting on user interactions with an advertisement. Real-time segments can be built employing user interactions logged by an ad server, which can then be integrated with creativity to build a narrative. The essential narrative framework is established through the interplay of analytics, data, and creativity(Gilliam et al.,2017).

CONCLUSION

When people hear stories, their brains come to life. Traceable back to the Homo Sapiens, humans have had a strong attraction to brand narratives. From painting on the insides of caves to the traditions of oral history, brand narratives were, and still are, a tool to transmit vital lessons, myths, and fables(Delgado- Ballester,2020). Consumers today often do not rely on major media outlets and content providers for their news and information. Instead, they rely on a combination of niche sources, content from their social media newsfeeds, and content aggregators. it is imperative to create a unified brand narrative that uses all of these channels to deliver the same message. An incredible brand narrative has the potential to continuously move people on an emotional level. Marketers are constantly looking for new ways to convey their narrative and listen to customers' stories

Consistency in brand narratives should never be underestimated. A high proportion of consumers engage with brands through many touchpoints(Delgado-Ballester,2020). Prospective buyers quickly pick up on the brand voice's lack of consistency and authenticity. If that occurs, the brand story may easily come off as fabricated. After that, customers can discontinue supporting the brand and lose trust in it. One of, if not the most effective tool available to brand managers is Brand narrative. A genuine, consistent narrative can effectively deter this from the outset. Leading organizations integrate audio, visual, and spoken narratives. Real-life stories have a powerful emotional impact on the audience. They outperform the bulk of other marketing tactics in terms of consumer engagement and long-term customer retention.

Brand narratives have grown into a necessity rather than a nice-to-have. Brands that can effectively tell their brand narrative to the globe will endure in the twenty-first century and beyond(Delgado-Ballester,2020). The following should be kept in mind when considering brand narratives:

- Take advantage of emotions. Create brand narratives that resonate with clients on an emotional level that they will remember for a long time.
- Recognize the underlying reasons behind customers' purchasing choices. Are they thinking with their heart or head?
- Don't hesitate to show vulnerability. To improve relationships, brands must share their journey with consumers.
- The finest stories come from customers, so let them tell them!

REFERENCES

Brechman, J. M., & Purvis, S. C. (2015). Narrative, transportation and advertising. *International Journal of Advertising*, *34*(2), 366–381. doi:10.1080/02650487.2014.994803

Burgess, J., & Jones, C. (2020). Exploring the forced closure of a brand community that is also a participatory culture. *European Journal of Marketing*, *54*(5), 957–978. doi:10.1108/EJM-01-2019-0075

Burgess, J., & Jones, C. (2021). Exploring lack of closure as a brand transgression. *Journal of Consumer Marketing, 38*(3), 241–250. doi:10.1108/JCM-07-2020-3937

Chahal, H., & Rani, A. (2017). How trust moderates social media engagement and brand equity. *Journal of Research in Interactive Marketing, 11*(3), 312–335. doi:10.1108/JRIM-10-2016-0104

Cho, J. Y., & Lee, E. J. (2017). Impact of interior colours in retail store atmosphere on consumers' perceived store luxury, emotions, and preference. *Clothing & Textiles Research Journal, 35*(1), 33–48. doi:10.1177/0887302X16675052

Delgado-Ballester, E. (2020). Effect of underdog (vs topdog) brand storytelling on brand identification: Exploring multiple mediation mechanisms. *Journal of Product and Brand Management*. Advance online publication. doi:10.1108/JPBM-11-2019-2639

Gilliam, D. A., Preston, T., & Hall, J. R. (2017). Frameworks for consumers' narratives in a changing marketplace: Banking and the financial crisis. *Marketing Intelligence & Planning, 35*(7), 892–906. doi:10.1108/MIP-01-2017-0005

Gilliam, D. A., Preston, T., & Hall, J. R. (2017). Frameworks for consumers' narratives in a changing marketplace: Banking and the financial crisis. *Marketing Intelligence & Planning, 35*(7), 892–906. doi:10.1108/MIP-01-2017-0005

Hinson, R., Boateng, H., Renner, A., & Kosiba, J. P. B. (2019). Antecedents and consequences of customer engagement on Facebook: An attachment theory perspective. *Journal of Research in Interactive Marketing, 13*(2), 204–226. doi:10.1108/JRIM-04-2018-0059

Huang, R., Ha, S., & Kim, S.-H. (2018). Narrative persuasion in social media: An empirical study of luxury brand advertising. *Journal of Research in Interactive Marketing, 12*(3), 274–292. doi:10.1108/JRIM-07-2017-0059

Kim, J.-E., Lloyd, S., & Cervellon, M.-C. (2016). Narrative-transportation storylines in luxury brand advertising: Motivating consumer engagement. *Journal of Business Research, 69*(1), 304–313. doi:10.1016/j.jbusres.2015.08.002

Lim, H., & Childs, M. (2020a). Visual storytelling on Instagram: Branded photo narrative and the role of telepresence. *Journal of Research in Interactive Marketing, 14*(1), 33–50. doi:10.1108/JRIM-09-2018-0115

Lim, H., & Childs, M. (2021b). Visual storytelling on Instagram: Branded photo narrative and the role of telepresence. *Journal of Research in Interactive Marketing, 14*(1), 33–50. doi:10.1108/JRIM-09-2018-0115

Mills, A. J., & Robson, K. (2020). Brand management in the era of fake news: Narrative response as a strategy to insulate brand value. *Journal of Product and Brand Management*, *29*(2), 159–167. doi:10.1108/JPBM-12-2018-2150

Pulizzi, J. (2012). The Rise of Storytelling as the New Marketing. *The Rise of Storytelling as the New Marketing*, *28*(2), 116–123. doi:10.100712109-012-9264-5

Rahmanian, E. (2021), Consumption narratives: contributions, methods, findings and agenda for future research, *Spanish Journal of Marketing - ESIC, 25*(1), 46-84. . doi:10.1108/SJME-10-2020-0179

Ripoll Gonzalez, L., & Gale, F. (2023). Sustainable city branding narratives: A critical appraisal of processes and outcomes. *Journal of Place Management and Development*, *16*(1), 20–44. doi:10.1108/JPMD-09-2021-0093

Sharma, Y., Silal, P., Kumar, J., & Singh, R. (2022). From pandemic to Prada: Examining online luxury-brand self-narrative. *Marketing Intelligence & Planning*, *40*(4), 527–541. doi:10.1108/MIP-05-2021-0153

Yung, R., & Khoo-Lattimore, C. (2019). New realities: A systematic literature review on virtual reality and augmented reality in tourism research. *Current Issues in Tourism*, *22*(17), 2056–2081. doi:10.1080/13683500.2017.1417359

ADDITIONAL READING

Bonnin, G., & Alfonso, M. R. (2019). The narrative strategies of B2B technology brands. *Journal of Business and Industrial Marketing*, *34*(7), 1448–1458. doi:10.1108/JBIM-03-2019-0112

Burgess, J., & Jones, C. (2021). Exploring lack of closure as a brand transgression. *Journal of Consumer Marketing*, *38*(3), 241–250. doi:10.1108/JCM-07-2020-3937

Çetinkaya, Ö. A. (2019). Brand storytelling and narrative advertising. In R. Yilmaz (Ed.), *Handbook of research on narrative advertising* (pp. 281–291). IGI Global. doi:10.4018/978-1-5225-9790-2.ch024

Lee, S. A., & Jeong, M. (2017). Role of brand story on narrative engagement, brand attitude, and behavioral intention. *Journal of Hospitality and Tourism Technology*, *8*(3), 465–480. doi:10.1108/JHTT-03-2016-0016

Welte, J.-B., Badot, O., & Hetzel, P. (2021). The narrative strategies of retail spaces: A semio-ethnographic approach. *European Journal of Marketing*, *55*(7), 2012–2036. doi:10.1108/EJM-03-2019-0250

KEY TERMS AND DEFINITIONS

Brand Narrative: A concise, condensed story that serves as the foundation for a company's communication and marketing efforts.

Brands: A commercial and marketing concept that aids in identifying a specific organization, product, or person.

Storytelling: The art of connecting and communicating with people in your organization, including partners, suppliers, and employees, by employing stories

Chapter 4
Neuromarketing vs. Brands

Nihan Tomris Küçün
 https://orcid.org/0000-0001-5548-6093
BILDAM Cognitive and Behavioral Research and Applications Centre, Turkey

ABSTRACT

Neuromarketing, which involves the application of neuroscience techniques to investigate the cognitive mechanisms of consumers, independent of their subjective self-reports, has gained significant traction among both commercial entities contending with a diverse target audience and scholars actively involved in associated inquiries. However, it is important to determine the potential and limitations of the techniques, to define the outputs that can be put into practice with research examples, and to create a methodological and ethical framework. In line with these priorities, in this section, neuromarketing instruments are explained and the integration with other methods is discussed. Then, it is detailed which components that effectuate consumer behavior can be monitored and to what extent they can be interpreted with neuromarketing methods. Finally, the criticisms within the framework of scientific ethics are evaluated and suggestions developed for both researchers and brands in the field in order to reach the targeted sustainable benefit.

1. INTRODUCTION: NEUROMARKETING—IS IT REALLY NEW TO CONSUMER RESEARCH?

The ever-increasing need to illuminate and even predict consumer behavior has led to an interest in new research methods. The neuromarketing approach, which can be adapted as a "complementary" to the methods used in traditional marketing research, has been met with great enthusiasm in order to understand the increasingly

DOI: 10.4018/978-1-6684-8351-0.ch004

complex consumer behaviors in parallel with the wildly increasing competition and rapidly developing communication technologies.

In numerous sources, it is commonly stated that the launch of neuromarketing is linked to the early 2000s. Specifically, the term "neuromarketing" was first introduced in 2002 by Prof. Dr. Ale Smidts, who presented a framework detailing the potential applications of neuroscience methods in the realm of consumer behavior. Following its introduction, the field rapidly gained momentum. A noteworthy development occurred when Atlanta-based advertising agency BrightHouse and Emory University collaborated on studies involving the use of fMRI to measure advertising efficacy. While this research received significant attention from both industry professionals and academics, it also elicited critical commentary from the perspectives of ethics and public health. Many non-governmental organizations and researchers have expressed their concerns that these studies will serve to robotize the consumer and lead to more uncontrolled, irresponsible and unhealthy consumption, and even demanded that the project be questioned by the US Senate (Fisher, 2010; Iloka and Onyeke, 2020). However, there are many studies that were carried out long before this discussed cooperation but were not announced within this framework. These first studies carried out in the 1960s actually form the basis of Smidts (2002) and BrightHouse initiatives, and it will not be possible to fully explain the historical development of neuromarketing without evaluating these pioneering studies (Eroğlu and Küçün, 2020).

1.1 History of Neuromarketing (A Long Way Back to 60's)

According to Zurawicki (2010), neuroscience is an interdisciplinary field that encompasses various subfields, such as molecular biology, electrophysiology, neurophysiology, anatomy, embryology and developmental biology, cellular biology, behavioral biology, neurology, cognitive neuropsychology, and cognitive sciences. In parallel, neuromarketing is a domain of research that employs neuroscience techniques to examine how consumer behavior is influenced by marketing practices. When examined within the framework of these premises, it can be said that the first examples of neuromarketing date back to the 1960s. Because is seen that the first applications of biometric measurement methods, which are still frequently used today, were made in this period.

Examples of the earliest known applications are the studies carried out by Hess and Polt (1960) and Hess (1965). Hess & Polt, (1960) conducted a study focused on pupil dilation in their first study, and as a result, it was revealed that there was a significant relationship between positive affect and pupil size. Afterward, Hess (1965) analyzed the pupil response in an emotional arousal state with the setup created with a mirror, projector, camera, light source, and screen (Picture 1) and interpreted it by associating it with the current attitudes of the participant.

Figure 1. Pioneer eye tracking applications
(Hess, E. H. (1965). Attitude and pupil size. Scientific American, 212, 46-54)

Subsequent studies have revealed that this technique, based on pupil size, has significant consistency in predicting consumers' perceptions of advertisements (Krugman, 1965; Hess, 1968; Stafford et al. 1970) and the effectiveness of advertising has started to be evaluated with cognitive responses such as interest, attention, and positive affect. In the following research carried out with eye tracking systems, fixations were started to be evaluated as a separate parameter and started to be used to measure attention towards advertisements (Pieters et al., 1999).

Immediately after, galvanic skin conductivity studies (GSR) were added to the consumer behavior research that started on the eye tracking axis. Considered one of the first studies, Aaker et al. (1986) applied GSR to determine the feelings of consumers towards marketing communication elements through "perceived warmth". In another study, LaBarbera and Tucciarone (1995) examined the determinativeness of advertisements on purchasing motivation with GSR.

The utilization of electrocardiography (ECG), a psychophysiological technique, has made a substantial contribution towards broadening the methodological approaches and extending the domains of inquiry in the realm of research oriented towards identifying emotions. Frost & Stauffer (1987) conducted one of the studies focusing on the relationship between vascular activity and arousal and using the method. Although it is not possible to accept the related research as direct marketing-oriented, it was possible to examine the physiological responses to communication elements in terms of social class, gender, and personality, and important input was provided for further studies.

Electromyography (EMG), another psychophysiological measurement method, is among the methods used for emotion identification in the early period. In the study designed by Cacioppo and Petty in 1989 with a focus of social psychophysiology, it was aimed to determine the patterns of facial muscle activity against certain conditions. In the research conducted by Hazlett and Hazlett (1999), emotional responses to television advertisements were analyzed.

The historical development of the subject has a significant turning point just before the introduction of neuromarketing as a term, and this belongs to Prof. Dr. Jerry Zaltman. In 1998, Zaltman and Kossyln, both scholars at Harvard University, submitted a patent application titled "Neuroimaging as a Marketing Tool," which facilitated the evaluation of consumers' cognitive responses to marketing communication components via EEG. Despite the gradual progress of Zaltman's endeavors in the field, which picked up pace only when ethical guidelines were established, his patent application and research have established him as a key contributor to the development of neuromarketing (Chandwaskar, 2019).

As a result, the development of neuromarketing, which is a multidisciplinary approach, has taken place at the end of a cumulative process, just like in other disciplines. The irresistible curiosity about human nature has caused researchers in different fields to adapt neuroscience methods to their studies in a way that has never been done before, and one more step has been taken to take a closer look at the consumer mind.

2. NEUROMARKETING METHODS AND INSTRUMENTS

Psychophysiological measures, which involve performing physical manipulations and observing corresponding physiological reactions, are employed in research to ascertain the link between the mental and physical processes of lifeforms. Once compared to data obtained from conscious responses triggered by emotional stimulation, psychophysiological techniques are assumed to be more reliable and relatively objective because they measure autonomous responses. The various methodologies employed in neuromarketing research are classified based on the data parameters, such as the region of gathering, the transmission method, and the type of processing. "Neurometric, biometric, and psychometric measurements" (Stipp, 2015), which are explained in more depth below, are the most frequently used measurement type grouping method in the literature.

2.1 Biometrical Measurements (Eye-Tracking, Galvanic Skin Response, Electrocardiography, Electromyography, Thermal Imaging, Complementary Methods)

As detailed above, eye-tracking systems are used in the pioneer studies carried out in neuromarketing. Eye trackers can determine the area of view by tracking the pupils of individuals with the help of infrared rays. When the infrared rays produced by the device come into the eye, it is refracted in the cornea and reflected back to the eye tracking system, thus creating reference intervals for tracking. These reflection angles, called Purkinje reflections, are significant for the device to confidently detect the eye. It is crucial that the repeated calibration process of eye tracking systems for each participant is carried out with this principle (Rosa, 2015).

Eye trackers use hardware to monitor factors such as where the eye is looking, changes in pupil size, and quick eye movements called saccades. This is achieved by utilizing an infrared or near-infrared radiation source and detector. The data collected is then analyzed by software that interprets the information. The sampling frequency of the hardware determines the resolution of the system. There are over ten variables that can be measured, but fixation, blink, pupil size, saccade, and scan path are the most commonly used in neuromarketing research (Wedel and Pieters, 2017).

Fixation refers to the brief period when the eye is focused on a specific location, and the duration and number of these fixations can be recorded. The duration of fixation can be used to determine the length of time someone focuses on one thing or the combined time spent focusing on multiple items within their field of vision. It's important to consider the context and other data when analyzing why someone may be more focused on a specific area, as it could be due to a psychological feature that is particularly prominent or not well understood (Djamasbi, 2014).

Blinking is another type of eye movement, and research has shown that an increase in blinking frequency is associated with behaviors like withdrawal and avoidance (Maffei and Angrilli, 2019).

When visual attention arises eyes undergo structural changes as well as organized eye movements. One of these changes is the size of the pupil, which adjusts to let more or less light into the eye to improve vision (Iloka and Anukwe, 2020). Pupil dilation can be caused by various factors like changes in brightness, emotional response, and task difficulty, and it can also be used to predict what stimuli will capture someone's automatic attention, such as contrast, density, brightness, or movement (Binder et al., 2020).

Saccade data refers to the rapid movements of the eye as it transitions from one point of focus to another. According to Hopp and Fuchs (2004), the order of these focuses can be determined, and a long saccade might indicate that attention has shifted to a new area. When there are short-distance saccades between focuses, it suggests that attention is more continuous in a particular area. Combining fixation and saccade data results in a scan path, which can be visualized as a heat map that shows how intensely the participant was looking at different stimuli.

In sum, eye movements can provide important insights into a person's cognitive processes. Eye-tracking devices are advantageous for neuromarketing research because they are easy to transport and use, and they don't require physical contact with the participant.

The other instrument that collects psychophysiological responses is galvanic skin response (GSR), in other words; electrodermal activity (EDA). The analysis of skin conductance (GSR) is based on the principle of measuring the electrical activity that occurs on the surface of the skin. Sweat glands become active during changes in an emotional state, resulting in a shift in the balance of positive and negative ions on the skin surface (Wang et al., 2018). By tracking this change with GSR sensors, it is possible to gain information about the process experienced by the individual.

GSR results are the autonomic response of the somatic nervous system and are mainly associated with arousal. Although this change in skin conductivity is generally associated with stress (Tonacci et al., 2020) in the literature, excitement, which actually describes relatively positive arousal, is also associated with excitement (Cuesta et al., 2018) may be experienced. For this reason, it is essential to use it in an integrated way with other devices in order to determine which of the positive/negative ends of the effect is close.

An electrocardiogram (ECG) captures the heart's electrical activity across various phases and perspectives, which are contingent upon the situation and configuration (Sarkar and Etemad, 2020). Cardiovascular responses are mainly used in neuromarketing studies in two ways. The first is the heart rate (HR), and the second is the peripheral blood flow (Tirandazi et al., 2022). While heart rate is monitored with an electrocardiogram, blood flow is usually performed with pulse-oximetry devices that monitor blood flow (oxygen density) from the fingertip in this type of research (Ambach and Gamer, 2018).

Thorson and Lang (1992) note that an increase in heart rate is linked to feelings of excitement and interest, while a decrease is associated with concentration and relaxation. The method employed in this approach focuses on evaluating the effect along the "positive-negative" and "arousal-withdrawal" axes. Accordingly, a number of studies in the literature utilize ECGs as the sole modality for recognizing emotions. ECGs are referred to as widely used biosensors for recognizing emotions by Rattanyu et al. (2011) on account of their ease of use, high precision, capability to gather data from diverse body parts, and cost-effectiveness.

Kose et al. (2021) describe electromyography (EMG) as a technique that involves sensors to capture and interpret the electrical activity due to muscle contraction. EMG involves the placement of three electrodes connected to a signal collector on the face, followed by measuring the signals generated by the stimuli.

The muscles in which the electrodes are placed are the corrugator supercili, zygomaticus major, and orbicularis occuli muscle groups (Larsen et al., 2003). Research on emotion identification using EMG associates the zygomaticus major with positive emotions, while the corrugator supercili is associated with negative emotions (Kehri et al., 2019). As a method that enables us to identify emotions and determine their intensity, EMG is extensively used in emotion recognition research (Sato et al., 2013).

The last biometric measurement method to be addressed in this section is thermal imaging. In order to gain accurate insights into human emotions, researchers have recently explored the use of thermal imaging for automated emotion identification (Rooj et al., 2023).

Thermal imaging technology captures thermal radiation emitted by an object and produces an image in which each pixel represents the temperature distribution of the scene. When applied to a person's face, a thermal image reveals fluctuations in localized skin temperature resulting from changes in blood flow associated with emotional states (Lee et al., 2022). This unique "thermal signature" is an involuntary physiological response and cannot be easily manipulated, thus making it a reliable indicator of a person's true emotional state (Rooj et al., 2023).

Although thermal imaging enables experiments to be conducted in natural settings without direct contact with the participants, the high cost of the instrument and the need for additional image processing efforts limits its use in neuromarketing research (Moses and Clark, 2020). As a result, the method is not yet widely adopted in this field as initially anticipated.

2.2 Neurometrical Measurements (Electroencephalography, Functional Magnetic Resonance, Functional Near-Infrared Spectroscopy)

Neurometric measurement methods allow direct monitoring of cognitive activity in specific brain regions through biosignals. Among these methods, Positron Emission Tomography (PET) and Magnetoencephalography (MEG) are two imaging techniques that fall under this category. However, due to certain technical limitations and the advantages of alternative methods, their use in neuromarketing research tends to decrease. As a result, this section focuses on the more widely used methods in this field.

Electroencephalography (EEG) involves measuring the weak electrical potential on the surface of the scalp that is generated by changes in the cerebral cortex of the brain. These electrical signals correspond to instantaneous changes in electrical rhythms during cognitive processes and are categorized according to their type and size, such as delta, theta, alpha, beta, and gamma waves. By analyzing these waves, EEG enables researchers to identify the specific brain regions responsible for signal generation and to simultaneously measure the micro-electricity levels produced by cognitive activity (Khruana et al., 2021). As a result, EEG can be used to aid in emotion recognition by detecting specific wave types.

Electroencephalography (EEG) has a long history of application in marketing research, dating back to the early 1970s. Pioneering studies by Krugman (1977) and Hansen (1981) used EEG to investigate consumer behavior in the context of perception and recall. Alwitt (1985) subsequently used EEG to examine how consumers' initial exposure to advertising content influences their purchasing decisions. EEG's popularity as an imaging method in neuromarketing research surged in the 1990s, following a series of studies by Rothschild et al. (1986), Rothschild and Hyun (1990), and Swartz (1998). As a result, EEG has become one of the most commonly used methods in this field.

EEG is a popular method in neuromarketing research due to several reasons. First, it is a non-invasive technique that does not require intervention (Aldayel et al., 2020). Second, it has a temporal resolution of less than a millisecond, allowing for precise measurements of brain activity (Zamani and Naieni, 2020). Third, EEG is more cost-effective than other neuroimaging methods, making it an attractive option for researchers with limited budgets (Aldayel et al., 2020). Finally, EEG is relatively easy to use. However, the method has some limitations, including its inability to collect data from deeper brain regions beyond the cortex and its high sensitivity to environmental factors (Urigüen & Zapirain, 2015).

Despite the spatial resolution limitations of EEG, functional magnetic resonance (fMRI) possesses a sufficiently high resolution to enable the acquisition of data from all regions of the brain. The transportation of oxygen to the body's tissues is facilitated by hemoglobin found in red blood cells. In essence, fMRI works by monitoring changes in the consumption of oxygenated blood in the tissue of interest, whereby an increase in oxygen consumption and subsequent blood flow in a specific brain region indicates activation in response to a given stimulus (Amaro and Barker, 2006). The level of activation can be monitored by fMRI, as it is directly correlated to the level of oxygen consumption. For this reason, fMRI is a highly promising measurement technique for neuromarketing research, owing to its capability to detect detailed and specific metabolic activity (Alsharif et al., 2021).

Nevertheless, fMRI usage is often constrained by the high cost and limited accessibility of the technology. Additionally, some participants may experience claustrophobia in the fMRI scanner, and integrating additional devices for conducting diverse experiments is challenging due to the presence of a strong magnetic field. (Fisher et al., 2010).

The advantages and disadvantages of these two neurometric measurement methods, which are most frequently used in neuromarketing studies, lead researchers to look for different alternatives, especially for emotion recognition studies. In this context, it is seen that more user-friendly methods with lower research costs are increasingly finding their place in the field (Krampe et al. 2018). One of these relatively new methods is functional near-infrared spectroscopy (fNIRS).

Functional near-infrared spectroscopy (fNIRS) is a non-invasive tool for neuroimaging that determines hemoglobin concentration in the outermost layer of the brain, known as the cortex. The density of oxygenated hemoglobin (oxyHb) indicates cognitive processes occurring in the detected area (Grossmann and Friederici, 2012). As a result, the hemodynamic response observed by fNIRS enables the analysis of an individual's cognitive responses to the experienced process.

fNIRS operates by emitting rays at two different wavelengths and monitoring the values of oxyhemoglobin (Hbo2) and deoxygenated hemoglobin (HbR) (Villringer et al., 1993). The technique leverages the optical window, in which skin, tissue, and bone are transparent to NIR light (700-900 nm spectral range), to detect hemoglobin (Hb) and oxygen-free hemoglobin (deoxy-Hb). The differences in the absorption spectra of deoxy-Hb and oxy-Hb enable the monitoring of the attenuation of light at different wavelengths, enabling the measurement of relative changes in hemoglobin concentration (Kirilina et al., 2012). Although optodes transmit these rays that can penetrate the scalp and skull, they have certain spatial resolution limitations. Nevertheless, many researchers consider fNIRS a valuable approach for assessing hemodynamic changes accompanying brain activation (Villringer et al., 1993).

The aforementioned discussion highlights both benefits and challenges of neuroscience methods which are adopted by marketing scholars to study consumer behavior. Notably, each method measures different cognitive states and involves distinct procedures for data collection, artifact removal, and analysis. Therefore, researchers often employ an integrated approach that combines multiple methods to enhance the accuracy and dependability of the findings. To achieve this, it is crucial to design the experiment appropriately, select suitable participants for the sample, and implement proper data collection procedures for the techniques.

3. NEUROMARKETING AND EXPERIMENTAL DESIGN

The standard approach employed in neuromarketing studies is commonly referred to as event-based or stimulus-based (Hakim and Levy, 2019). This methodology closely resembles the traditional controlled-experimental design preferred by most researchers (Lee et al., 2017).

Neuromarketing's experimental approach considers the brain to be a reactive system that responds to sensory inputs with neural activity, resulting in a cognitive or behavioral response. In this approach, participants are exposed to a carefully crafted experimental stimulus, and their brain activity is measured alongside a behavioral response, such as a decision-making process. Additional physiological and psychological variables may be measured as control responses. This approach is prevalent in cognitive neuroscience and is the primary methodology employed in neuromarketing research (Lee et al., 2017).

Naturally, the equipment employed has a significant impact on shaping the different stages of an experiment. A crucial factor to consider is whether the study will take place in a controlled laboratory environment or in the real world. When conducting laboratory-based research, wired devices can be preferred or computer screens can be utilized to present stimuli. However, for studies conducted in the real world, wireless devices are preferable, and the devices must be calibrated to suit the environmental conditions. The range of the equipment should be regulated, and any potential disruptive stimuli in the environment should be minimized as much as possible.

It is essential to ensure that the stimuli possess adequate manipulation power in both scenarios, as mentioned previously. In other words, similar to traditional marketing research methods, the stimuli utilized in neuromarketing studies must be appropriately positioned in terms of power, intensity, validity, and reliability. While existing affective stimuli databases can be utilized, it is also possible to conduct pre-tests specific to the study to determine whether the selected stimuli are suitable for the sample.

It is important to use an experiment presentation program integrated with the devices to convert the selected stimuli into an experimental set. At this stage, it is seen that software tools such as ePrime (Isa and Mansor, 2020), SensLab (Moya et al., 2020), and Paradigm (Ozkara and Bagozzi, 2021) are frequently used in neuromarketing studies. The use of these software is extremely important in order to determine what kind of psychophysiological response the participant gave in which second of the experiment. Because these customized softwares add time stamps called "triggers" to the moments when the stimuli are displayed, making it possible to monitor these changes during the analysis of the data. In order to make such a marking, the experiment presentation program must be able to communicate with the devices.

During the presentation of the stimuli to the participants, several techniques are applied in order to make the brain, which is constantly active and interacting with the internal and external factors, as neutral as possible. The most frequently used of these presentation interval techniques is to show a blank screen for a certain period of time among the stimuli. In this way, visual stabilization is provided, brain signals are neutralized and the response to the next stimulus is prevented from being affected by the previous ones.

One of the most important elements in experimental design is, of course, determining the size of the sample and selecting participants with representative ability. At this point, the experimental designs are primarily decisive for the sample. The patterns chosen are critical for the analysis of the data and the statistical methods to be used, and ultimately for the determination of the sample size. After identifying participants who are capable of representing the sample and obtaining their consent for the experimental procedure, the data collection phase can commence.

To minimize the influence of confounding variables, Neuromarketing studies frequently employ strict participant selection criteria. Specifically, experiments are typically conducted with individuals who are right-handed, possess normal or corrected-to-normal vision, are not taking any medications that may affect the central nervous system, and have no prior history of neuropathology (Calvert et al., 2019). Such measures are implemented to enhance the internal validity of the study and ensure the reliability of the findings.

Finally, as briefly mentioned in the devices section, it should be taken into account that all neuromarketing methods have their own data collection steps. Similarly, the unit of measurement used by all of them also differs. All devices have customized calibration processes in line with their own working principles. Similarly, the areas where the data is stored differ depending on the adopted devices and their models. In some techniques, it is possible to store data directly on the researcher's computer, while in others, storage is carried out via the cloud.

Another important point regarding data collection and analysis is the integration of multiple devices. Many researchers state that the use of more than one integrated measurement method allows an increase in the accuracy of the findings and makes it possible to obtain more comprehensive results by balancing the advantages/disadvantages of each technique (Shukla, 2019). Likewise, it is plausible to amalgamate neuromarketing methodologies with conventional research techniques, namely surveys, interviews, or focus group sessions. Notably, the pivotal consideration at this juncture pertains to the capacity of the researcher to opt for the most appropriate method(s) that align with the targeted variables, while avoiding bias and attaining congruity across the derived outcomes (Royo- Vela and Varga, 2022).

4. NEUROMARKETING APPROACH FOR COGNITIVE FUNCTIONS (EMOTION RECOGNITION, ATTENTION, AROUSAL, LEARNING, MEMORY, AND RECALL)

Cognitive functions are the central area of interest in the field of neuromarketing, as it offers the potential to gain insight into the consumer psyche. The extent of these functions can vary greatly depending on the capabilities of the devices employed, making them a critical consideration. As such, this section aims to explore the connections between commonly utilized devices and fundamental cognitive functions.

One of the primary purposes of neuromarketing studies is to determine the emotional state of consumers against marketing communication elements. In this context, it is seen that the most powerful methods are neurometric measurement methods (Gill and Singh, 2020). Of course, there are important differences between the emotion identification methods of the mentioned instruments. For example, the main emotion identification methods that can be determined at valence and arousal bases for EEG; are hemispheric asymmetries (Ding et al., 2021), event-related potentials (Mansor et al., 2021), evoked potentials (Vecchiato et al., 2011), QEEG (quantitative analysis of the frequency of the electroencephalography), and deep neural networks (Song et al., 2018). On the other hand, since fMRI has an improved spatial resolution that can reach not only the cortex but also the internal structures of the brain compared to EEG, it is possible to make more specific emotion recognition (Campanella et al., 2013). Despite this success of neurometric measurement methods, it should not be overlooked that instruments measuring at the biometric level also provide important data on emotion recognition. For instance, ECG (Jing et al., 2009), EMG (Jerritta et al., 2014), GSR signals (Nakasone et al., 2005), and fixation scores obtained by eye tracking (Maughan et al., 2007) also provide important clues.

Concerning the critical role of attention in shaping consumer behavior, the foremost modality that comes to mind is eye tracking, given its acknowledged ability to serve as a proxy for visual attention (Shagass et al., 1976). An eye tracker offers an important variety of data in order to examine the participant's attention to the stimulus they are faced with in the physical environment or through a digital screen. Parameters such as eye movements towards all stimuli from the first point of view, gaze orders, fixation duration, saccades, and revisit scores make it possible to have information about the attention stages at the conscious level and before. When all these parameters are evaluated in terms of stimuli and within the intervals specified in the literature, getting a clear view of triggered attention can be reached (Wedel, 2013). However, eye tracking is not the only method used to detect attention in neuromarketing. EEG (Pazharliev et al., 2015), ECG (Alsharif et al., 2022) and fNIRS (Meyerding and Risius, 2018) can also provide important findings about attention and related cognitive load.

Psychological arousal refers to a state of heightened physiological and psychological activation, often associated with increased levels of excitement, alertness, and readiness for action. Thus arousal is basically related to the approach/avoidance system. It can be triggered by a wide range of stimuli, including stress, anxiety, fear, excitement, and sexual desire.

Psychologically, it can manifest as a feeling of being on edge, jittery, or energized. In terms of physiology, arousal is characterized by an increase in heart rate, blood pressure, respiration rate, and muscle tension. The listed psychophysiological responses make ECG (Wang et al., 2018) and EMG (Xu et al., 2019), especially GSR (Rimm and Litvak, 1969) suitable for the detection and intensity of arousal.

The overwhelming majority of marketing communication tactics are formulated to generate, strengthen, or modify consumer attitudes. In the course of this undertaking, the phases of learning, and recall assume crucial importance for the efficacy and durability of the communication endeavor. How consumers respond to these efforts is one of the most important focal points of neuromarketing. Memory and recall, one of these complex cognitive processes, has been frequently investigated with neurometric methods such as fMRI (Hsu and Cheng, 2018), EEG (Camarrone and Van Hulle, 2019). In addition, since the first step of this cognitive process is attention, there are also important studies conducted with eye tracking systems (Zhang and Yuan, 2018).

5. PRACTICAL APPLICATIONS

The primary motivation of neuromarketing is to make the intrinsic dynamics that shape consumer behavior more understandable. Consumers' responses, which they are sometimes unaware of, sometimes forced to suppress due to social norms, and sometimes completely impulsive, may completely fail the expectations of a carefully planned marketing program. For this reason, in addition to all approaches that have the potential to get one step closer to the consumer mind, neuromarketing applications also have an important potential with the advantage of obtaining information simultaneously (Hsu, 2017).

Neuromarketing has a broad application within the realm of marketing activities. One of the areas with the most extensive research is marketing communication (Bočková et al., 2021). Findings such as the activation of trust-related regions in the consumer's brain when celebrities or physically attractive individuals are used in advertisements (Hubert and Kenning, 2008), the discovery of subconscious marketing techniques, and the elucidation of their legitimate use (Brierley et al., 2020), or the identification of advertising elements that facilitate recall (Balconi et al., 2014) have propelled the field forward and enriched the practical findings acquired. These findings enable companies to adapt and choose their advertisements in a way that incorporates elements facilitating improved brand recall and enhanced consumer attention retention.

Another important topic in which the approach of neuromarketing provides significant contributions is the evaluation of products and their associated features from the consumer's perspective. In this context, models that enable the monitoring of consumer perception towards innovative product designs (Deng and Wang, 2019), studies that reveal cognitive responses to irrelevant/relevant product varieties in brand extension activities, or research that enables the tracking of user experience in the digital/physical domain can be grouped under this heading (Briesemeister and Trebbe, 2022).

Neuromarketing also offers important tips for digital and physical marketplaces. For example, in the study conducted by Küçin and Güler (2021), using an eye tracker, it was revealed that consumers' experiences with the brand are more dominant than sales promotion tools and social impact in the visual attention orientation and purchasing process. In the study carried out by Singh (2020), it was investigated how consumers perceive the shelf designs of online retailers by using eye tracking, mouse tracking, and emotion measurement.

Neuromarketing can make a valuable contribution to marketing practices by focusing on the dynamics of the consumer-brand relationship. Evidence from a study conducted by Pozharliev et al. (2015) indicates that consumers exhibit heightened attention toward luxury brands when they are in the presence of others, as observed through electroencephalogram (EEG) measurements. Similarly, the research conducted by Garczarek-Bąk and Disterheft (2018) employed a comprehensive approach utilizing electromyography (EMG), galvanic skin response (GSR), eye tracking, and EEG. Their findings revealed that the type of brand (i.e., national versus private label) influences consumers' purchasing decisions. Furthermore, the results demonstrated that the frontal asymmetry index, assessed through EEG, can be utilized as a predictive measure for determining consumers' likelihood of making a purchase. Another interesting study was developed for brand loyalty and the underlying psychophysiological responses. Through the utilization of functional magnetic resonance imaging (fMRI), a study examined the selection of retail brands by consumers. Notably, when consumers made purchases from brands to which they exhibited loyalty, activation in the ventromedial prefrontal cortex was observed (Hubert & Kenning, 2008). This specific brain region is known to be associated with the reward system, implying its involvement in processing the pleasurable aspects of consumer behavior linked to brand loyalty.

The aforementioned aspects and studies represent only a fraction of the diverse array of domains in which neuromarketing can be applied. The extensive applicability of neuromarketing stems from its capacity to explore the cognitive processes of individuals with a heightened level of precision. The methodologies encompassed within neuromarketing hold significant potential for advancing our understanding of human cognition in various contexts.

5.1 Responsibilities of Brands and Ethical Issues

According to Luna-Nevarez (2021), Neuromarketing has been assessed as a valuable methodology for firms to augment their marketing efforts since its inception. Indeed, the fact that neuromarketing research is not only applied to existing products and services but also can be conducted on products and services that have not yet been put on the market provides an important chance to reduce financial risk. Additionally, it has made important contributions to the understanding of consumers' implicit motivations with the new methods it has brought to marketing research and has created an important framework for the re-evaluation of marketing communication strategies.

Notwithstanding the considerable contributions made by pioneering neuromarketing research conducted by prominent brands, it has faced extensive criticism from the public, non-governmental organizations, and some researchers. In this period, when neuromarketing does not yet have a framework of ethical rules like other applied sciences, corporations have faced significant reproach for their employment of neuromarketing practices, primarily for commercial advantage, without providing adequate safeguards to subjects participating in their research (Alexander et al., 2019). The utilization of highly sensitive data techniques on human participants has elicited significant ethical concerns due to the potential for revealing extensive information about consumers' neural processes to companies. Thus various consumer advocacy groups, including Commercial Alert and the Advertising Research Foundation (ARF), have articulated concerns and urged the government to establish standards and more stringent regulations for research firms undertaking neuromarketing studies (Madan, 2010).

Neuromarketing is associated with two major ethical concerns, namely the potential for manipulative use of a "buy button" in the brain to influence consumer choice, and the resulting unfair advantage for marketers who employ it over those who do not (Isa et al., 2019). In actuality, the aim of neuromarketing is to aid companies in developing superior products and advertisements that appeal to consumers, rather than manipulating their thought processes. The manipulation potential of neuromarketing is significant, which highlights the need for companies to focus on creating a favorable impression of their product and generating consumer interest, rather than resorting to deceptive tactics. Ultimately, companies should endeavor to cultivate a positive mood in consumers that enhances their perception and enjoyment of their product offerings. (Savelli, 2022).

Another ethical concern is about the potential to pose a significant risk to small businesses that cannot adapt such research methods to their production and marketing processes (Elouadifi and Essakallı, 2022). However, The aforementioned limitation is not exclusive to the field of neuromarketing, but rather related to the financial resources that enterprises can allocate toward all forms of marketing research. For this reason, many businesses have to outsource this type of research. However, this practice also requires sharing the ethical responsibility of neuromarketing research among stakeholders.

At this juncture, two variants of responsibility can be delineated that have the potential to yield a resolution. The first proposal is to make sure that all studies carried out by consultancy companies, advertising agencies, and independent researchers conducting research and commercial collaborations in this field are carried out in line with the established ethical codes. In this context, inclusive initiatives such as NMSBA (The Neuromarketing Science & Business Association) are considered to be important platforms for both academia and sector representatives. However, it is clear that it will not be enough to simply declare adherence to these ethical codes and, as in all clinical studies, the importance of sustainable monitoring of these collaborations in terms of international standards and compliance levels with them.

The second one pertains to the practicality and accessibility of scientific research conducted by academics in the domain of practitioners. It must be noted that this proposition does not seek to constrain scientific research solely for commercial motives. Rather, our suggestion is to disseminate the pragmatic discoveries derived within the ambit of scientific research ethics, in order to elicit a contribution to the sector.

6. CONCLUSION

The post-modern consumer is someone who desires, recreates, and shares the experience in their interaction with brands. For this reason, today's consumers are now considered as individuals who are more sensitive, more judgmental, far from loyalty, influencing and affecting, shaping and maintaining communication. All these factors necessitate brands to have more information on the individual and society levels, that is, on the psychological and sociological axis. In other words, brands now have to do much more than just produce products or services and deliver them under promised conditions in order to survive. Since many phenomena that make up traditional marketing theories have been diversified and renewed. The acceptance of a dual world consisting mainly of the physical and digital environment has become a reality that cannot be ignored thanks to today's technology.

Just about 10 years ago, while barriers such as access to the internet, attitudes towards online shopping, and the impact of demographic factors were discussed, online consumers suddenly became a direct target for brands, with factors such as the pandemic, the global market approach, the increasing interest in online platforms, the rapid development of information and communication technologies. In this new era shaped by information technologies, brands have no time to lose. Because the digital world is an opportunity independent of scale and also a field of struggle for all brands. In parallel with all these, consumer demand has reached a greater determinant on the market than it has ever been. Moreover, this demand is no longer just about services and products.

Consumers create a perception with all the tangible and intangible dimensions that the brand makes them feel, promises and provides from the first moment they come face to face with the brand. Moreover, thanks to advanced communication technologies, they have become able to access information in a shorter time and easily share their opinions with others. Additionally, a large part of this information flow takes place outside the brand's intervention area.

Consumers' expectations are evolving towards offering unique value propositions tailored to them. In addition, brands need to be able to appeal to the masses and compete at the global level. These expectations can make strategic marketing communication much more complex in the digital world where there are no borders. Of course, it is not a fair approach to ignore the important tools that the developing technology offers to brands. Brands can now know what is consumed more at what time of the day, which product is demanded at the individual level, under what conditions, and much more. Moreover, they all have the opportunity of uninterrupted communication with their target audience. Indeed, all these improvements have the potential to provide important inputs for the brands in terms of both developing new strategies and evaluating the effectiveness of existing applications.

The desire for deepening experience, diversified products and services, and the rapid development of communication channels have also positively affected consumers' adaptation to innovations. The adaptation of people, who wake up to new technologies every day, to a new application or innovation is now much faster. Therefore, there is no time to waste for brands. In this period, which is called the information era, brands have to reconsider their unique value propositions, address them both at the level of the individual and the society, perform communication at an "optimal" level, and closely monitor and direct their audience with technology support in order to survive.

A new brand often has only one chance to convey the message it has developed for all these purposes. Therefore, this shot must hit the target so that the consumer can recognize and prefer it when they see the brand again in this crowd. Well-known brands are seen as relatively luckier than new ones, with components such as brand reputation, prestige, and value they already have. However, they also have important goals in front of them such as adapting their operations to changing conditions, keeping the consumer portfolio, reaching new audiences, and being sustainable.

In addition to all these challenges, the chance for brands to contact consumers and express themselves is gradually decreasing. Because individuals who are tired of one-sided communication strategies may find communication efforts managed by brands insecure, unconvincing or insincere. Or they may simply directly block or ignore such a communication effort. In order to overcome these obstacles, brands try to enrich their experiences by being close to their target audiences at every step with digital tools that are diversifying day by day. But here, too, there is an important psychophysiological threshold barrier. Thanks to the filtering ability, which is the perfect protection mechanism of the human brain, millions of stimuli encountered are passed through a cognitive filter, and only messages that are worth crossing that perception threshold remain. Although this elimination is the first step of rational thinking, the brain does not always produce the same output from the same input, as it also includes many prejudices. This is exactly the point that refers to the area called the "black box" in the marketing literature, that is, the brain where the decision-making process takes place.

The human brain has the ability to think, evaluate and make decisions shaped by the interaction of many internal and external dynamics. This complex process makes it possible to get different answers from the same person even under the same conditions. Moreover, the reasoning process of an individual alone and the decision-making dynamics of a group are quite different from each other. But all these factors are not absolute barriers to understanding the cognitive activities of the human mind. Because there are psychometric, biometric and neurometric measurement methods developed for monitoring many cognitive activities in this field that have been studied for a long time.

"Neuromarketing" (aka consumer neuroscience), which can be summarized as a field in which neuroscience methods are used to shed light on consumer behavior, is an approach developed to understand precisely these complex and uncertain processes. These methods, which enable the monitoring of the brain and related biometric activations in the face of stimuli, promise an important potential for behavioral studies in terms of providing results independent of self-report. Because when consumers are asked their opinions about a brand, they may not be able to give the correct answer for many different reasons. Many factors such as the careless responder effect, social norms, self-evaluations, and irrational decision-making tendencies may cause consumers to be inadequate or unwilling to explain their own behavior.

Despite these factors, neuromarketing makes it possible to monitor answers that consumers are often unaware of at the conscious level. Because the vast majority of neuromarketing methods are methods that can make simultaneous measurements and report changes at the millisecond level. Moreover, since it focuses directly on psychophysiological responses, it is possible to generalize to populations. All these advantages provide brands with important input to test new "phygital" marketing strategies or to make sense of consumer feedback.

Despite all these promising strengths, it is not possible to accept neuromarketing as a miraculous key to understanding and predicting consumer behavior. Because each of the methods used has its difficulties and limitations, sample sizes create scaling problems and studies both require a multidisciplinary approach and cause high costs. Moreover, neuromarketing is not a candidate to replace traditional marketing research. On the contrary, most neuromarketing research also adopts mixed methods in which other research methods such as questionnaires or interviews are used together. Forwhy human behavior is an output that is too complex to be explained by the interpretation of collected signals alone.

For the reasons mentioned, although neuromarketing has received a rapidly increasing interest in the academic field, especially in the last 20 years, the demand for its application has not reached the expected level yet. This is because these researches require brands to follow a different path from traditional consumer research and acquire different expertise. The fact that the marketing teams, which have developed and diversified in parallel with the speed and needs of digitalization in the recent period may not rapidly adopt the neuromarketing approach. However, as the perception threshold rises, the importance of diversifying consumer research and conducting this process based on human nature for critical goals such as reaching consumers who have become blind and unresponsive to brand communication efforts, designing and presenting the desired experience, and evaluating its effectiveness becomes clear.

REFERENCES

Aaker, D. A., Stayman, D. M., & Hagerty, M. R. (1986). Warmth in advertising: Measurement, impact, and sequence effects. *The Journal of Consumer Research*, *12*(4), 365–381. doi:10.1086/208524

Aditya, D., & Sarno, R. (2018). Neuromarketing: State of the arts. *Advanced Science Letters*, *24*(12), 9307–9310. doi:10.1166/asl.2018.12261

Aldayel, M., Ykhlef, M., & Al-Nafjan, A. (2020). Deep learning for EEG-based preference classification in neuromarketing. *Applied Sciences (Basel, Switzerland)*, *10*(4), 1525. doi:10.3390/app10041525

Alexander, J., Shenoy, V., & Yadav, A. (2019). Ethical challenges in neuromarketing: A research agenda. *Indian Journal of Marketing*, *49*(3), 36–49. doi:10.17010/ijom/2019/v49/i3/142145

Alsharif, A. H., Salleh, N. Z., & Khraiwish, A. (2022). Biomedical Technology in Studying Consumers' Subconscious Behavior. *International Journal of Online & Biomedical Engineering*, *18*(8).

Alsharif, A. H., Salleh, N. Z. M., & Baharun, R. (2021). Neuromarketing: The popularity of the brain-imaging and physiological tools. *Neuroscience Research Notes*, *3*(5), 13–22. doi:10.31117/neuroscirn.v3i5.80

Amaro, E. Jr, & Barker, G. J. (2006). Study design in fMRI: Basic principles. *Brain and Cognition*, *60*(3), 220–232. doi:10.1016/j.bandc.2005.11.009 PMID:16427175

Ambach, W., & Gamer, M. (2018). Physiological measures in the detection of deception and concealed information. In *Detecting concealed information and deception* (pp. 3–33). Academic Press. doi:10.1016/B978-0-12-812729-2.00001-X

Balconi, M., Stumpo, B., & Leanza, F. (2014). Advertising, brand and neuromarketing or how consumer brain works. *Neuropsychological Trends*, *16*(16), 15–21. doi:10.7358/neur-2014-016-balc

Binder, A., Naderer, B., & Matthes, J. (2020). A "forbidden fruit effect": An eye-tracking study on children's visual attention to food marketing. *International Journal of Environmental Research and Public Health*, *17*(6), 1859. doi:10.3390/ijerph17061859 PMID:32183015

Bočková, K., Škrabánková, J., & Hanák, M. (2021). Theory and practice of neuromarketing: Analyzing human behavior in relation to markets. *Emerging Science Journal*, *5*(1), 44–56. doi:10.28991/esj-2021-01256

Brierley, G., Ozuem, W., & Lancaster, G. (2020). Subconscious marketing communication techniques and legal implications. *Journal of Decision Systems*, *29*(2), 69–78. doi:10.1080/12460125.2020.1752047

Briesemeister, B. B., & Trebbe, J. (2022). Welcome to the Real World: Neuromarketing for the Stationary Point of Sale to Quantify the Customer Experience. *Neuromarketing in Business: Identifying Implicit Purchase Drivers and Leveraging them for Sales*, 91-108.

Cacioppo, J. T., & Petty, R. E. (1983). *Social psychophysiology*. The Guilford Press.

Calvert, G. A., Pathak, A., Ching, L. E. A., Trufil, G., & Fulcher, E. P. (2019). Providing excellent customer service is therapeutic: Insights from an implicit association neuromarketing study. *Behavioral Sciences (Basel, Switzerland)*, *9*(10), 109. doi:10.3390/bs9100109 PMID:31615003

Camarrone, F., & Van Hulle, M. M. (2019). Measuring brand association strength with EEG: A single-trial N400 ERP study. *PLoS One*, *14*(6), e0217125. doi:10.1371/journal.pone.0217125 PMID:31181083

Campanella, S., Bourguignon, M., Peigneux, P., Metens, T., Nouali, M., Goldman, S., Verbanck, P., & De Tiège, X. (2013). BOLD response to deviant face detection informed by P300 event-related potential parameters: A simultaneous ERP–fMRI study. *NeuroImage*, *71*, 92–103. doi:10.1016/j.neuroimage.2012.12.077 PMID:23313569

Chandwaskar, P. (2019). A Review on: Neuromarketing as an emerging field in consumer research., International Journal of Management. *Technology And Engineering*, *8*(11), 2281–2287.

Cuesta-Cambra, U., Niño-González, J. I., & ve Rodríguez-Terceño, J. (2017). The Cognitive Processing of an Educational App with EEG and'Eye Tracking'. Comunicar. *Media Education Research Journal, 25*(2).

Deng, L., & Wang, G. (2019). Application of EEG and interactive evolutionary design method in cultural and creative product design. *Computational Intelligence and Neuroscience*, *2019*, 2019. doi:10.1155/2019/1860921 PMID:30733799

Ding, Y., Robinson, N., Zhang, S., Zeng, Q., & Guan, C. (2021). Tsception: Capturing temporal dynamics and spatial asymmetry from EEG for emotion recognition. arXiv preprint arXiv:2104.02935.

Djamasbi, S. (2014). Eye tracking and web experience. *AIS Transactions on Human-Computer Interaction*, *6*(2), 37–54. doi:10.17705/1thci.00060

Elouadifi, S., & Essakallı, M. (2022). Conceptual model of the factors impacting the adoption of Neuromarketing Technologies. *International Journal of Accounting, Finance, Auditing, Management and Economics, 3*(4-2), 1-23.

Fisher, C. E., Chin, L., & Klitzman, R. (2010). Defining neuromarketing: Practices and professional challenges. *Harvard Review of Psychiatry*, *18*(4), 230–237. doi:10.3109/10673229.2010.496623 PMID:20597593

Frost, R., & Stauffer, J. (1987). The effects of social class, gender, and personality on physiological responses to filmed violence. *Journal of Communication, 37*(2), 29–45. doi:10.1111/j.1460-2466.1987.tb00981.x

Garczarek-Bąk, U., & Disterheft, A. (2018). EEG frontal asymmetry predicts product purchase differently for national brands and private labels. *Journal of Neuroscience, Psychology, and Economics, 11*(3), 182–195. doi:10.1037/npe0000094

Gill, R., & Singh, J. (2020, December). A review of Neuromarketing techniques and emotion analysis classifiers for visual-emotion mining. In *2020 9th International Conference System Modeling and Advancement in Research Trends (SMART)* (pp. 103-108). IEEE. 10.1109/SMART50582.2020.9337074

Grossmann, T., & Friederici, A. D. (2012). When during development do our brains get tuned to the human voice? *Social Neuroscience, 7*(4), 369–372. doi:10.1080/1 7470919.2011.628758 PMID:22017313

Hakim, A., & Levy, D. J. (2019). A gateway to consumers' minds: Achievements, caveats, and prospects of electroencephalography-based prediction in neuromarketing. *Wiley Interdisciplinary Reviews: Cognitive Science, 10*(2), e1485. doi:10.1002/ wcs.1485 PMID:30496636

Hazlett, R. L., & Hazlett, S. Y. (1999). Emotional response to television commercials: Facial EMG vs. self-report. *Journal of Advertising Research, 39*(2), 7–7.

Hess, E. H. (1965). Attitude and pupil size. *Scientific American, 212*(4), 46–54. do i:10.1038cientificamerican0465-46 PMID:14261525

Hess, E. H. (1968). Pupillometrics. In *F. M. Bass, C. W. King, & E. A. Pessemier Applications of the sciences in marketing management*. John Wiley & Sons.

Hess, E. H., & Polt, G. M. (1960). Pupil size as related to interest value of visual stimuli. *Science, 132*(3423), 349–350. doi:10.1126cience.132.3423.349 PMID:14401489

Hopp, J. J., & Fuchs, A. F. (2004). The characteristics and neuronal substrate of saccadic eye movement plasticity. *Progress in Neurobiology, 72*(1), 27–53. doi:10.1016/j.pneurobio.2003.12.002 PMID:15019175

Hsu, M. (2017). Neuromarketing: Inside the mind of the consumer. *California Management Review, 59*(4), 5–22. doi:10.1177/0008125617720208

Hubert, M., & Kenning, P. (2008). A current overview of consumer neuroscience. *Journal of Consumer Behaviour: An International Research Review, 7*(4-5), 272–292. doi:10.1002/cb.251

Iloka, B. C., & Anukwe, G. I. (2020). Review of eye-tracking: A neuromarketing technique. *Neuroscience Research Notes*, *3*(4), 29–34. doi:10.31117/neuroscirn. v3i4.61

Iloka, B. C., & Onyeke, K. J. (2020). Neuromarketing: A historical review. *Neuroscience Research Notes*, *3*(3), 27–35. doi:10.31117/neuroscirn.v3i3.54

Isa, S. M., & Mansor, A. A. (2020). Rejuvenating the marketing mix through neuromarketing to cultivate the green consumer. *International Journal of Information Management*, *5*, 66–75.

Isa, S. M., & Mansor, A. A., & Razali, K. (2019). Ethics in neuromarketing and its implications on business to stay vigilant. *KnE Social Sciences*, 687-711.

Jerritta, S., Murugappan, M., Wan, K., & Yaacob, S. (2014). Emotion recognition from facial EMG signals using higher order statistics and principal component analysis. *Zhongguo Gongcheng Xuekan*, *37*(3), 385–394. doi:10.1080/02533839 .2013.799946

Jing, C., Liu, G., & Hao, M. (2009, July). The research on emotion recognition from ECG signal. In *2009 international conference on information technology and computer science* (*Vol. 1*, pp. 497-500). IEEE.

Kehri, V., Ingle, R., Patil, S., & Awale, R. N. (2019). Analysis of facial EMG signal for emotion recognition using wavelet packet transform and SVM. In *Machine intelligence and signal analysis* (pp. 247–257). Springer Singapore. doi:10.1007/978-981-13-0923-6_21

Kirilina, E., Jelzow, A., Heine, A., Niessing, M., Wabnitz, H., Brühl, R., Ittermann, B., Jacobs, A. M., & Tachtsidis, I. (2012). The physiological origin of task-evoked systemic artefacts in functional near infrared spectroscopy. *NeuroImage*, *61*(1), 70–81. doi:10.1016/j.neuroimage.2012.02.074 PMID:22426347

Kose, M. R., Ahirwal, M. K., & Kumar, A. (2021). A new approach for emotions recognition through EOG and EMG signals. *Signal, Image and Video Processing*, *15*(8), 1863–1871. doi:10.100711760-021-01942-1

Krampe, C., Gier, N. R., & Kenning, P. (2018). The application of mobile fNIRS in marketing research—Detecting the "first-choice-brand" effect. *Frontiers in Human Neuroscience*, *12*, 433. doi:10.3389/fnhum.2018.00433 PMID:30443210

Krugman, H. E. (1965). The impact of television advertising: Learning without involvement. *Public Opinion Quarterly*, *29*(3), 349–356. doi:10.1086/267335

Küçün, N. T., & Güler, E. G. (2021). Examination of Consumer Purchase Decisions via Neuromarketing Methods: A Social Psychology Approach. *Prizren Social Science Journal*, 5(2), 14–29. doi:10.32936/pssj.v5i2.245

LaBarbera, P. A., & Tucciarone, J. D. (1995). GSR reconsidered: A behavior-based approach to evaluating and improving the sales potency of advertising. *Journal of Advertising Research*, 35(5), 33–54.

Lee, J. M., An, Y. E., Bak, E., & Pan, S. (2022). Improvement of Negative Emotion Recognition in Visible Images Enhanced by Thermal Imaging. *Sustainability*, 14(22), 15200. doi:10.3390u142215200

Lee, N., Brandes, L., Chamberlain, L., & Senior, C. (2017). This is your brain on neuromarketing: Reflections on a decade of research. *Journal of Marketing Management*, 33(11-12), 878–892. doi:10.1080/0267257X.2017.1327249

Luna-Nevarez, C. (2021). Neuromarketing, ethics, and regulation: An exploratory analysis of consumer opinions and sentiment on blogs and social media. *Journal of Consumer Policy*, 44(4), 559–583. doi:10.100710603-021-09496-y

Maffei, A., & Angrilli, A. (2019). Spontaneous blink rate as an index of attention and emotion during film clips viewing. *Physiology & Behavior*, 204, 256–263. doi:10.1016/j.physbeh.2019.02.037 PMID:30822434

Mansor, A. A., Isa, S. M., & Noor, S. S. M. (2021). P300 and decision-making in neuromarketing. *Neuroscience Research Notes*, 4(3), 21–26. doi:10.31117/neuroscirn.v4i3.83

Maughan, L., Gutnikov, S., & Stevens, R. (2007). Like more, look more. Look more, like more: The evidence from eye-tracking. *Journal of Brand Management*, 14(4), 335–342. doi:10.1057/palgrave.bm.2550074

Meyerding, S. G., & Risius, A. (2018). Reading minds: Mobile functional near-infrared spectroscopy as a new neuroimaging method for economic and marketing research—A feasibility study. *Journal of Neuroscience, Psychology, and Economics*, 11(4), 197–212. doi:10.1037/npe0000090

Moses, E., & Clark, K. R. (2020). The Neuromarketing Revolution: Bringing Science and Technology to Marketing Insight. In Anthropological Approaches to Understanding Consumption Patterns and Consumer Behavior (pp. 449-464). IGI Global.

Moya, I., García-Madariaga, J., & Blasco, M. F. (2020). What can Neuromarketing tell us about food packaging? *Foods*, *9*(12), 1856. doi:10.3390/foods9121856 PMID:33322684

Nakasone, A., Prendinger, H., & Ishizuka, M. (2005, September). Emotion recognition from electromyography and skin conductance. In *Proc. of the 5th international workshop on biosignal interpretation* (pp. 219-222). Citeseer.

Ozkara, B. Y., & Bagozzi, R. (2021). The use of event related potentials brain methods in the study of conscious and unconscious consumer decision making processes. *Journal of Retailing and Consumer Services*, *58*, 102202. doi:10.1016/j.jretconser.2020.102202

Pieters, R., Rosbergen, E., & Wedel, M. (1999). Visual attention to repeated print advertising: A test of scanpath theory. *JMR, Journal of Marketing Research*, *36*(4), 424–438. doi:10.1177/002224379903600403

Pozharliev, R., Verbeke, W. J., Van Strien, J. W., & Bagozzi, R. P. (2015). Merely being with you increases my attention to luxury products: Using EEG to understand consumers' emotional experience with luxury branded products. *JMR, Journal of Marketing Research*, *52*(4), 546–558. doi:10.1509/jmr.13.0560

Rattanyu, K., & Mizukawa, M. (2011). Emotion recognition based on ecg signals for service robots in the intelligent space during daily life. *J. Adv. Comput. Intell. Intell. Inform.*, *15*(5), 582–591. doi:10.20965/jaciii.2011.p0582

Rimm, D. C., & Litvak, S. B. (1969). Self-verbalization and emotional arousal. *Journal of Abnormal Psychology*, *74*(2), 181–187. doi:10.1037/h0027116 PMID:5783231

Rooj, S., Routray, A., & Mandal, M. K. (2023). Feature based analysis of thermal images for emotion recognition. *Engineering Applications of Artificial Intelligence*, *120*, 105809. doi:10.1016/j.engappai.2022.105809

Rosa, P. (2015). What do your eyes say? Bridging eye movements to consumer behavior. *International Journal of Psychological Research*, *8*(2), 90–103. doi:10.21500/20112084.1513

Royo-Vela, M., & Varga, Á. (2022). Unveiling Neuromarketing and Its Research Methodology. *Encyclopedia*, *2*(2), 729–751. doi:10.3390/encyclopedia2020051

Sarkar, P., & Etemad, A. (2020, May). Self-supervised learning for ecg-based emotion recognition. In *ICASSP 2020-2020 IEEE International Conference on Acoustics, Speech and Signal Processing (ICASSP)* (pp. 3217-3221). IEEE. 10.1109/ICASSP40776.2020.9053985

Sato, W., Fujimura, T., Kochiyama, T., & Suzuki, N. (2013). Relationships among facial mimicry, emotional experience, and emotion recognition. *PLoS One, 8*(3), e57889. doi:10.1371/journal.pone.0057889 PMID:23536774

Savelli, E. (2022). Neuromarketing: ethical dilemma and consumers' perception. In *21th International Marketing Trends Conference* (pp. 1-7). AE Mark.

Shagass, C., Roemer, R. A., & Amadeo, M. (1976). Eye-tracking performance and engagement of attention. *Archives of General Psychiatry, 33*(1), 121–125. doi:10.1001/archpsyc.1976.01770010077015 PMID:1247358

Shukla, S. (2019). Neuromarketing: A change in marketing tools and techniques. *International Journal of Business Forecasting and Marketing Intelligence, 5*(3), 267–284. doi:10.1504/IJBFMI.2019.104044

Singh, S. (2020). Impact of neuromarketing applications on consumers. *Journal of Business and Management, 26*(2), 33–52.

Song, T., Zheng, W., Song, P., & Cui, Z. (2018). EEG emotion recognition using dynamical graph convolutional neural networks. *IEEE Transactions on Affective Computing, 11*(3), 532–541. doi:10.1109/TAFFC.2018.2817622

Stafford, J. E., Birdwell, A. E., & Van Tassel, C. E. (1970). Integrated advertising: White backlash. *Journal of Advertising Research, 10*, 15–20.

Stipp, H. (2015). The Evolution Of Neuromarketing Research: From Novelty To Mainstream. *Journal of Advertising Research, 55*(2), 120–122. doi:10.2501/JAR-55-2-120-122

Thorson, E., & Lang, A. (1992). .The Effects Of Television Videographics And Lecture Familiarity On Adult Cardiac Orienting Responses And Memory. *Communication Research*, 346-369.

Tirandazi, P., Bamakan, S. M. H., & Toghroljerdi, A. (2022). A review of studies on internet of everything as an enabler of neuromarketing methods and techniques. *The Journal of Supercomputing*, 1–42.

Tonacci, A., Dellabate, A., Dieni, A., Bachi, L., Sansone, F., Conte, R., & Billeci, L. (2020). Can Machine Learning Predict Stress Reduction Based on Wearable Sensors' Data Following Relaxation at Workplace? A Pilot Study. *Processes (Basel, Switzerland), 8*(4), 448. doi:10.3390/pr8040448

Urigüen, J. A., & Garcia-Zapirain, B. (2015). EEG artifact removal—state-of-the-art and guidelines. Journal of neural engineering, 12(3), .

Vecchiato, G., Astolfi, L., Fallani, F. D. V., Toppi, J., Aloise, F., Cincotti, F., & Babiloni, F. (2011). Understanding cerebral activations in neuromarketing: A neuroelectrical perspective. In *International Conference on Bio-Inspired Systems and Signal Processing, BIOSIGNALS 2011* (pp. 91-97). Research Gate.

Villringer, A., Planck, J., Hock, C., Schleinkofer, L., & Dirnagl, U. (1993). Near infrared spectroscopy (NIRS): A new tool to study hemodynamic changes during activation of brain function in human adults. *Neuroscience Letters*, *154*(1), 101–104. doi:10.1016/0304-3940(93)90181-J PMID:8361619

Wang, C. A., Baird, T., Huang, J., Coutinho, J. D., Brien, D. C., & Munoz, D. P. (2018). Arousal effects on pupil size, heart rate, and skin conductance in an emotional face task. *Frontiers in Neurology*, *9*, 1029. doi:10.3389/fneur.2018.01029 PMID:30559707

Wedel, M. (2013). *Attention research in marketing: A review of eye tracking studies*. Robert H. Smith School Research Paper No. RHS, 2460289.

Wedel, M., & Pieters, R. (2017). A review of eye-tracking research in marketing. *Review of marketing research,* 123-147.

Xu, S., Ni, Q., & Du, Q. (2019). The effectiveness of virtual reality in safety training: Measurement of emotional arousal with electromyography. In *ISARC. Proceedings of the International Symposium on Automation and Robotics in Construction* (Vol. 36, pp. 20-25). IAARC Publications.

ve Kossylyn, Z. (1998). *Neuroimaging as a Marketing tool*. US6099319A. Google. https://patents.google.com/patent/US6099319A/

Zamani, J., & Naieni, A. B. (2020). *Best feature extraction and classification algorithms for EEG signals in neuromarketing*. Frontiers in Biome.

Zhang, X., & Yuan, S. M. (2018). An eye tracking analysis for video advertising: Relationship between advertisement elements and effectiveness. *IEEE Access: Practical Innovations, Open Solutions*, *6*, 10699–10707. doi:10.1109/ACCESS.2018.2802206

Zurawicki, L. (2010). Neuromarketing: Exploring the Brain of the Consumer. Springer, and London, UK.

Chapter 5

Motivational Factors That Influence the Intention to Watch a Spectator Sports Product:
The Case of the National Women's Soccer League

Sebastiano Mereu

ⅈD https://orcid.org/0000-0003-2607-1782

Sports Business Research Academy, Switzerland

ABSTRACT

This empirical research examines how motivational factors for sport consumption affect the intention to watch the National Women's Soccer League (NWSL) in the USA. The motivation scale for sport consumption (MSSC) was adopted to collect quantitative data through an online questionnaire from a convenience sample of 302 spectators in the USA who follow the NWSL. The hypothesized relationships were tested via structural equation modeling (SEM). The results indicate that aesthetics, social interaction, escape, and physical skill of the performing athletes have a significant and positive influence on consumption intention or consumption frequency for watching NWSL matches. This study contributes to the body of knowledge for the business of women's sports with an empirical examination on motives for watching the NWSL, a popular women's football league, and explores possible marketing communications tactics necessary to promote the sports brand and encourage people to consume the sports product offered by the NWSL.

DOI: 10.4018/978-1-6684-8351-0.ch005

INTRODUCTION

The history of women's football, also known as women's soccer, can be traced back to the 1880s (Williams, 2011; Scottish Government, 2019). The first golden age lasted until the 1920s, by which certain matches counted audiences as large as 53,000, as was the case on Boxing Day 1920, when the popular *Dick, Kerr Ladies F.C.* played at Goodison Park in Liverpool, England (Alexander, 2005; Skillen et al., 2022). In 1921, however, the English Football Association banned women from playing football on grounds with spectators, a decision that was adopted by other countries as well (Williams, 2003; Dator, 2019). Nevertheless, women's football started gaining new popularity in the 1970s due to new gender equality laws (e.g. Title IX in the USA) resulting in promotional efforts fostering gender equality in sports in different countries (Williams, 2011; Mumcu et al., 2016). Further important milestones were reached in the 1990s. The first Women's World Cup sanctioned by the Fédération Internationale De Football Association (FIFA), an international governing body of association football, was held in China in 1991 and the second was held in Sweden in 1995 (Williams, 2003). Additionally, women's football debuted as an Olympic discipline in Atlanta, USA, in 1996 (Olympics, 2019), presenting the sport to a wider audience.

These large-scale promotional platforms led to a considerable increase in global viewership in the decades to come. For example, 1.12 billion people watched coverage of the 2019 FIFA Women's World Cup staged in France (FIFA, 2019). Moreover, the 2022 UEFA European Women's Football Championship held in England became the most watched Women's Euro in history with more than 280 million viewers across Europe (EBU, 2022; UEFA, 2022a). The popularity of the 2022 tournament and the English women's team winning the trophy may have had a positive impact on the popularity of the English Women's Super League (WSL), England's top-tier of women's football. Various clubs reported that sales of season-tickets increased as much as 254% from the previous season in the final week of the 2022 Women's Euro (Mians & Majid, 2022). Similarly, the sport's increasing popularity led to more lucrative sponsorship deals. For example, Barclays, a British multinational financial institution, signed a £30 million deal to sponsor the English Football Association Women's Championship from 2022 to 2025 (Sky Sports, 2021).

In order to support the current momentum, continued professionalization of the sport and categorical marketing efforts are needed to exploit the growing interest in women's football and increase sponsorship, fandom, and credibility (Leslie-Walker & Mulvenna, 2022; Rosen, 2022). Various federations and leagues across the globe have professionalized women's football, especially in Europe and the USA (Adachi et al., 2022). Although two professional women's football leagues in the USA had to be discontinued due to financial instability and lack of fan support in 2003 and 2012 respectively (Mumcu et al., 2016), the National Women's Soccer League (NWSL), the third attempt and current professional league in the USA, has seen substantial viewership growth and interest from investors since its inauguration in 2013, possibly due to a more elaborate marketing and media coverage strategy (Reuters, 2021; Schad, 2022). This is also underlined by the presence of high-profile owners of NWSL franchises, such as actor Natalie Portman co-owning Los Angeles-based Angel City FC (Herbst, 2022), basketball player James Harden owning a minority stake in Houston Dash (DuBose, 2020), and former Bed Bath & Beyond CEO Steven Temares being a majority owner of NJ/NY Gotham FC (Gotham FC, 2022), to name a few. These kind of investments in the NWSL add status and prestige to the league's profile.

Nonetheless, according to Haley Rosen, a former professional football player and now CEO of Just Women's Sports, a media company, women's sports have a marketing problem (Rosen, 2022), which may also apply to the NWSL. Although women's sports are gaining popularity and keep breaking records, it still has to compete for sports fans' attention with a wide range of other spectator sports offerings (Economist, 2019; UEFA, 2022b). Furthermore, women's sports receive a much smaller share of media coverage compared to men's sports (Cooky et al., 2021). In order to build upon the above-mentioned momentum and increase viewership of women's football, including the season-long NWSL competition, it becomes necessary to examine the salient motives for their viewers, as well as what influence those motives have on consumption intentions (see Trail & James, 2001; Won & Kitamura, 2006). Based upon respective findings, explicit promotional tactics should be conceptualized and implemented to strengthen the appeal for potential viewers and spectators to follow the sports brand, e.g. the NWSL, across various media channels and ultimately reinforce the intention to consume the respective sports product, i.e. the season-long NWSL competition, and increase frequency, either in the stadium or through broadcast.

This study applies the above-mentioned objectives to the NWSL and their fans and spectators in the USA. It further provides the necessary foundation for recommendations on how the organization can foster consumption intentions and frequency through integrated marketing communications activities. The guiding research question for this study is therefore defined as follows: What are the motives for fans and spectators of the NWSL in the USA that influence the consumption intention and frequency for watching the offered sports product? The question will be answered by reviewing extant literature on motives for sport consumption and synthesizing appropriate literature with a statistical analysis of primary data collected for this study from fans and spectators of the NWSL in the USA.

THEORETICAL BACKGROUND

Measuring Motives for Sport Consumption

A variety of scales that measure the motives for consuming an entertainment media product, such as a women's football competition, have been proposed with views from different perspectives. Gantz (1981) suggested to investigate the motives for watching televised sports through a 'uses and gratifications' approach and found that the motives were grouped into four dimensions: to thrill in victory, to let loose, to learn, and to pass time. However, he relativized his findings and noted that the offered list may be incomplete due to limitations of the study. Wann (1995) developed the Sport Fan Motivation Scale (SFMS), which includes eight factors: self-esteem, aesthetics, escape, group affiliation, family, entertainment, eustress, and economic (gambling). Despite the scale's wide adoption in research, concerns regarding its content validity were raised by Trail and James (2001). They raised concern that the scale would offer an incomplete elaboration on the development of its items, as well as inaccurate labelling and wording of certain motives and items. Trail and James (2001) went on to develop the Motivation Scale for Sport Consumption (MSSC), which comprises nine factors: achievement, aesthetics, escape, social interaction, family, drama, acquisition of knowledge, physical attraction, and physical skill. A comparison with the SFMS shows similarities regarding the proposed factors. Wann and James (2019) raised the point that although the MSSC is supported with evidence of statistical validity, a main concern with the scale is, similar to the SFMS, the possibly misleading wording of the items that may offer a description of a consumer's behavior instead of information about the motivation for the respective consumption. It needs to be considered that Wann and James (2019) referred to the first version of the MSSC developed. An updated version of the MSSC was proposed by Trail (2012) with adapted items after tests with new data sets, as well as with the exclusion of the factor 'family' and inclusion of the factors 'enjoyment of aggression' and 'novelty'. This study applies the updated version of the MSSC, as its questionnaire items seem appropriate for reaching the research objectives discussed above.

The Influence of Motives on Consumption Intention and Frequency

The MSSC was developed to measure the motivations of sport spectator consumption behavior (Trail & James, 2001). This offers sports organizations a better understanding of the underlying stimuli for spectators to consume the sports product, which further enables organizations to emphasize marketing communications efforts that strengthen spectators' relevant motives (Wann & James, 2019). The MSSC can also be used to evaluate causal relationships between motives and the intention to consume a given spectator sports product (Won & Kitamura, 2006; Macey et al., 2022), as well as between motives and the frequency of the respective consumption (Hamari & Sjöblom, 2017). As mentioned above, the updated version of the MSSC as presented by Trail (2012) consists of ten factors, which can individually influence the consumption intention and frequency for watching a sports product such as the NWSL. The ten motivational factors are defined in the following paragraphs and respective hypotheses are presented accordingly.

Trail (2012) defines vicarious achievement as "the need for social prestige, self-esteem and sense of empowerment that an individual can receive from their association with a successful team" (p. 4). This motivation implies a social component based upon the feeling of belonging to a community consisting of other supporters and the team (Hamari & Sjöblom, 2017). Invested fans may even see themselves as the '12th player' of the team they support and, with that, an essential part of the team (Haridakis, 2010). It can therefore be argued that spectators of a NWSL match may feel a certain degree of vicarious achievement, because of the real or imagined relationships with other spectators and their team. Hence, the following hypothesis is suggested:

H1: Vicarious achievement positively influences (a) the consumption intention and (b) the frequency of watching the NWSL.

Aesthetics of a sport can motivate people to watch and enjoy a given sports product, because it highlights "the artistic beauty and grace of the sport" (Hsieh et al., 2011, p. 141). Nevertheless, visual stimuli, such as the subjective beauty captured in a media product or the pleasure of watching the respective media product, affect how aesthetics are perceived by consumers and can lead to a desired behavior (Im et al., 2010; Xiao, 2020). This suggests that the perceived aesthetics of a women's football match can be influenced by the overall media production of the NWSL. Thus, spectators may experience aesthetic characteristics of the sport not only through the protagonists of the show, i.e. the performing athletes, but also, more subliminally, through the company producing the broadcast and delivering it to the audience. This leads to hypothesize the following:

H2: Aesthetics positively influence (a) the consumption intention and (b) the frequency of watching the NWSL.

Hamari and Sjöblom (2017) define escapism in a media consumption context as "the degree to which media enables an escape from day-to-day routines, and provides a distraction from everyday activities" (p. 216). Won and Kitamura (2006) found that escapism can positively influence the intention to consume football in the future. Consumers with different levels of emotional attachment to a sport or team, i.e. occasional spectators or invested fans, can find motivation in escaping from everyday life by consuming a specific sports product (Trail et al., 2003). Therefore, escapism may be a relevant motivation for all spectators of the NWSL. The following hypothesis is therefore suggested:

H3: Escapism influences (a) the consumption intention and (b) the frequency of watching the NWSL.

In the context of this study, social interaction refers to the consumption of spectator sports to gratify the need of interacting and socializing with like-minded others in order to obtain the feeling of belonging to a group (Trail, 2012). Social interaction can influence consumption intention for watching a sports product (Kim et al., 2021), as well as its frequency (Won & Kitamura, 2006). Leslie-Walker and Mulvenna (2022) highlight that social interaction during a football match fosters positive feelings about the experience. As with escapism, interaction with others is a relevant motivator for spectators with different degrees of investment in the sport (Trail et al., 2003). Spectators of the NWSL can interact in person in the stadium or in a public place, or they can interact and socialize via digital devices, for example on social media. Hence:

H4: Social interaction influences (a) the consumption intention and (b) the frequency of watching the NWSL.

Drama can refer to "the enjoyment of uncertainty and dramatic turns of events in media content such as sports" (Hamari & Sjöblom, 2017, p. 216). The term is occasionally used interchangeably with the term eustress (Wann & James, 2019). The outcome of a football match is uncertain because of its unscripted nature and the unpredictable events during the match. These events can be affected by chosen tactics, performance, or behavior of the players, coaches, and referees. Thus, the product may offer various dramatic surprises to its spectators and viewers. Kim et al. (2008) confirmed a significant relationship between drama and sports media consumption. Consequently, the following hypothesis can be defined:

H5: Drama influences (a) the consumption intention and (b) the frequency of watching the NWSL.

Acquisition of knowledge refers to "the need to learn about the team or players through interaction and media consumption" (Trail, 2012, p. 4). Viewers and fans may be motivated to watch NWSL matches, because they want to increase their knowledge about the sport, the league, the game's strategy, or technical aspects of the sport. The motivation to acquire knowledge about a sport can affect the consumption intention for a sports product (Hsieh et al., 2011), and it can impact the frequency to consume it (Hamari & Sjöblom, 2017). Therefore:

H6: Acquisition of knowledge influences (a) the consumption intention and (b) the frequency of watching the NWSL.

The MSSC seeks to further evaluate if spectators consume the offered sports product because they find performing athletes to be physically attractive or radiate a certain sex appeal (Trail, 2012). Mutz and Meier (2016) found that physical attractiveness of female football players has a significant influence on public interest. An attractive or specific appearance can also help athletes distinguish themselves from other athletes, as it functions as a personal brand attribute and can strengthen their recognizability (Arai et al., 2014). Moreover, physical attractiveness can intensify fan loyalty (Mahmoudian et al., 2021). Hence, physical attractiveness of NWSL athletes could establish a distinct appearance that motivates spectators to regularly tune in or attend games in the stadium. This leads to the next hypothesis:

H7: Physical attractiveness influences (a) the consumption intention and (b) the frequency of watching the NWSL.

The motivational factor 'physical skill of participating athletes' refers to the intention for spectators to watch the sports product in order to enjoy a skillful and athletic performance (Hsieh et al., 2011). Clarke et al. (2022) found that physical skill was the strongest motivation for highly identified fans for watching the English women's national football team play. Similarly, the physical skill of players in the J.League, the professional Japanese football league, was found to have a significant influence on the intention to attend future games (Won & Kitamura, 2006). Furthermore, Allison (2018) explains that the Portland Thorns, a NWSL franchise, emphasize their fan culture with "an appreciation for skilled soccer [that] coexists with desires to support diverse women's rights and opportunities" (p. 994). Hence:

H8: Physical skill influences (a) the consumption intention and (b) the frequency of watching the NWSL.

Enjoyment of aggression can be described as the motivation for spectators to watch a sports product in order to enjoy rough play during the game, a macho atmosphere, aggressive behavior of the players, or hostility and intimidation (Trail, 2012). This motivational factor is related to the relief arising from watching aggressive behaviors that are part of the football match on the pitch (Wang et al., 2011). This is further manifested through the ubiquitous physicality in team sports such as women's football, especially at a professional level. However, extant research shows that women's sports exhibit less aggression compared to the same sports played by men (Muhammad, 2019). Still, enjoyment of aggression was found to influence consumption intentions of mediated sports products (Hamari & Sjöblom, 2017). Thus:

H9: Enjoyment of aggression influences (a) the consumption intention and (b) the frequency of watching the NWSL.

Novelty is the last element in the adapted MSSC for this study and addresses the gratification of having a new team or player join the league, as well as having the opportunity to watch them play (Trail, 2012). It is in the nature of the NWSL to expand by introducing more teams to make the competition and, therefore, the offered product more attractive (Kassouf, 2022). Furthermore, new football players can join a NWSL team from within the league or from abroad adding novelty to a team and the championship. This kind of novelty can affect the intention to consume sports (dos Santos et al., 2021). The last hypothesis is therefore defined as follows:

H10: Novelty influences (a) the consumption intention and (b) the frequency of watching the NWSL.

It is crucial for marketing practitioners to understand the functionality of the motivational factors described above and how they influence consumption intention and frequency for watching the NWSL. This lays the foundation for an accurate conceptualization and delivery of effective promotional efforts. The hypothesized model is illustrated in Figure 1.

METHOD AND RESULTS

Quantitative data was collected through a self-administered online questionnaire with closed questions adapted from the MSSC as proposed by Trail (2012). The questionnaire was made available in June 2022 to people who follow the official NWSL channels on various social media platforms. All users following the accounts

Figure 1. Hypothesized model. ACH: vicarious achievement, AES: aesthetics, DRA: drama, ESC: escape, KNO: acquisition of knowledge, SKI: physical skills, SOC: social interaction, ATT: physical attractiveness, AGG: Enjoyment of Aggression, NOV: Novelty, INT: Consumption intention, FRE: consumption frequency.

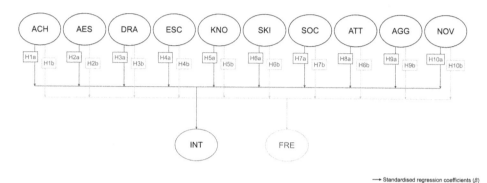

were welcome to respond to the survey; no remuneration was offered for completing the questionnaire.

Sample of the Study

A convenience sample of 302 people responded to the questionnaire. All responses were accepted as they were all complete and no pattern response violations were detected. Of the 302 respondents 69.5% identified as female, 23.2% as male, and 7.3% as non-binary. The largest age group of the sample consists of people between the ages of 25 and 34 years (37.4%), followed by people between 35 and 44 years (20.2%), 18 and 24 years (19.9%), and 45 and 54 years of age (13.9%). The rest of the sample encompasses less than 10% in aggregate. Most of the respondents live in the USA (88.4%) with the rest of the sample watching the NWSL from a wide range of countries. The sample reports a balanced distribution across NWSL team affiliations with only 8.3% of the sample watching the NWSL without supporting a specific team. Accordingly, the sample of this study represents the perspectives of a rather female and Millennial audience in the USA that supports a wide array of teams. Table 1 offers an overview of the demographic characteristics of the sample.

Measurement Tool

The items from the MSSC were adapted to the context of the NWSL, while staying as close as possible to the original wording. The same applies to the consumption

Table 1. Demographic characteristics of the sample (N=302)

	N	%
Gender		
Female	210	69.5
Male	70	23.2
Non-binary	22	7.3
Age		
0-17	5	1.7
18-24	60	19.9
25-34	113	37.4
35-44	61	20.2
45-54	42	13.9
55-64	14	4.6
65+	7	2.3
Country		
USA	267	88.4
Canada	9	3.0
UK	5	1.7
Germany	3	1.0
Rest of the world	18	5.9
Team affiliation		
Angel City FC	52	17.2
NJ/NY Gotham FC	38	12.6
Portland Thorns FC	36	11.9
Washington Spirit	31	10.3
OL Reign	29	9.6
No specific team	25	8.3
San Diego Wave FC	19	6.3
Chicago Red Stars	17	5.6
Houston Dash	14	4.6
Kansas City Current	13	4.3
North Carolina Courage	11	3.6
Racing Louisville	10	3.3
Orlando Pride	7	2.3

intention scale, which was adopted from Macey et al. (2020). A seven-point Likert scale was utilized to measure the individual items ranging from 'disagree very strongly' (1) to 'agree very strongly' (7). An exception is the dependent variable of consumption frequency (FRE), which was measured with five options, including 'never', 'once a year', 'once a month', 'once a week', and 'daily'. The consumption frequency scale was applied following the example of Hamari and Sjöblom (2017). Table 2 provides an overview of the utilized questionnaire items.

Validity and Reliability

Cronbach's Alpha (α) values of the applied scales measured above the suggested 0.7 cut-off value, which suggests a good internal consistency. Likewise, composite reliability (CR) and average variance extracted (AVE) values measured above the suggested thresholds of 0.7 and 0.5 respectively. An exploratory factor analysis found that all items recorded factor loadings above the recommended threshold of 0.5. Table 3 offers the respective overview.

Discriminant validity was supported with the square root of each factor's AVE value being greater than the respective inter-construct correlations, as shown in Table 4. Furthermore, the model fit was assessed with IBM SPSS Amos 27 and computed the measures CMIN/DF=1.555, RMSEA=.043, CFI=.953, NFI=.881, TLI=.941, and GFI=.878, suggesting good model fit.

Results

The collected data was analyzed through structural equation modeling (SEM) in SPSS Amos 27 in order to assess causal relationships between the dependent and independent variables. The computed standardized regression weights (β) indicate that aesthetics (H2a, .213, $p < .01$), social interaction (H4a, .205, $p < .01$), and physical skill of the athletes (H8a, .178, $p < .05$) have a statistically significant and positive influence on the intention to watch the NWSL. Furthermore, aesthetics (H2b, .180, $p < .05$), escape (H3b, .145, $p < .05$), and social interaction (H4b, .141, $p < .05$) have a statistically significant and positive influence on the frequency for watching the NWSL. All other standardized regression weights show no statistically significant association between the independent variables and the dependent variables. With reference to Cohen's statistical power analysis, the coefficient of determination for consumption intention ($R^2 = .256$) explains a large effect size on the variable, and the coefficient of determination for consumption frequency ($R^2 = .124$) describes a medium effect size on the variable for the given sample size of this study (Cohen, 1992). Table 5 outlines the results.

Table 2. Adapted motivation scale for sport consumption (MSSC)

Item	Questionnaire item
Factor 1: Vicarious Achievement	
ACH1	I feel a personal sense of achievement when my favorite women's soccer team(s) do/does well.
ACH2	I feel like I have won when my favorite team(s) win(s).
ACH3	I feel proud when the team(s) I support play(s) well.
Factor 2: Aesthetics	
AES1	I enjoy the artistic value of women's soccer.
AES2	I like the beauty and grace of women's soccer.
AES3	I consider women's soccer to be a form of art.
Factor 3: Escape	
ESC1	Women's soccer provides me with an opportunity to escape the reality of my daily life for a while.
ESC2	I can get away from the tension in my life through women's soccer.
ESC3	Women's soccer provides me with a distraction from my daily life for a while.
Factor 4: Social Interaction	
SOC1	I like to socialize with others regarding women's soccer.
SOC2	I like having the opportunity to interact with others through women's soccer.
SOC3	I enjoy talking to other people through women's soccer.
Factor 5: Drama	
DRA1	I prefer close games rather than one-sided games.
DRA2	I like games where the outcome is uncertain.
DRA3	A tight game between two teams is more enjoyable than a blowout.
Factor 6: Acquisition of Knowledge	
KNO1	By watching women's soccer, I can increase my knowledge about the sport.
KNO2	By watching women's soccer, I can increase my understanding of the game's strategy.
KNO3	By watching women's soccer, I can learn about the technical aspects of the sport.
Factor 7: Physical Attractiveness	
ATT1	I enjoy watching female soccer players who are physically attractive.
ATT2	The main reason I watch women's soccer is because I find the players physically attractive.
ATT3	An individual female soccer player's sex appeal is a big reason why I watch women's soccer.
Factor 8: Physical Skill	
SKI1	I enjoy the skill of female soccer players.
SKI2	I enjoy the performance of female soccer players.
SKI3	I enjoy the athleticism of female soccer players.
Factor 9: Enjoyment of Aggression	
AGG1	I enjoy rough play in women's soccer.
AGG2	I enjoy aggressive behavior of the players.
AGG3	I enjoy when there is hostility and intimidation that are part of the game.

continued on following page

Table 2. Continued

Item	Questionnaire item
Factor 10: Novelty	
NOV1	I enjoy the novelty of a new team or player.
NOV2	I like having the opportunity to watch a new team or player.
NOV3	The opportunity to watch games of a new team or player is fun.
Factor 11a: Consumption Intention	
INT1	I predict that I will keep watching women's soccer in the future at least as much as I have done lately.
INT2	I intend to watch women's soccer at least as often within the next month as I have previously done.
INT3	I plan to watch women's soccer during the next month.
Factor 11b: Consumption Frequency	
FRE	How often do you watch women's soccer?

Table 3. Factor loadings, validity, and reliability

Item	Factor loading	α	CR	AVE	M	SD
Factor 1: Vicarious Achievement		.820	.857	.666		
ACH1	.822				5.42	1.492
ACH2	.862				5.86	1.287
ACH3	.762				6.47	0.913
Factor 2: Aesthetics		.835	.857	.667		
AES1	.829				6.15	1.126
AES2	.829				5.99	1.272
AES3	.776				5.48	1.569
Factor 3: Escape		.952	.937	.831		
ESC1	.908				5.89	1.467
ESC2	.913				5.70	1.512
ESC3	.914				5.91	1.386
Factor 4: Social Interaction		.902	.892	.733		
SOC1	.856				5.89	1.325
SOC2	.855				5.91	1.339
SOC3	.858				5.95	1.326

continued on following page

Table 3. Continued

Item	Factor loading	α	CR	AVE	M	SD
Factor 5: Drama		.816	.877	.704		
DRA1	.860				5.59	1.177
DRA2	.784				5.67	1.251
DRA3	.870				5.79	1.319
Factor 6: Acquisition of Knowledge		.903	.907	.765		
KNO1	.854				6.33	1.017
KNO2	.898				6.31	0.939
KNO3	.871				6.23	1.018
Factor 7: Physical Attractiveness		.713	.863	.681		
ATT1	.689				4.21	1.957
ATT2	.906				1.74	1.266
ATT3	.864				1.49	1.087
Factor 8: Physical Skill		.886	.880	.710		
SKI1	.849				6.79	0.526
SKI2	.866				6.82	0.474
SKI3	.812				6.80	0.555
Factor 9: Enjoyment of Aggression		.851	.889	.728		
AGG1	.843				4.12	1.527
AGG2	.889				4.07	1.579
AGG3	.826				3.57	1.771
Factor 10: Novelty		.910	.900	.750		
NOV1	.823				5.44	1.212
NOV2	.899				5.72	1.185
NOV3	.875				5.77	1.147
Factor 11a: Consumption Intention		.795	.830	0633		
INT1	.737				6.70	0.682
INT2	.834				6.73	0.650
INT3	.813				6.88	0.512
Factor 11b: Consumption Frequency		n/a	n/a	n/a		
FRE	.541				4.09	0.572

Table 4. Correlation matrix

	ACH	AES	DRA	ESC	KNO	SKI	SOC	ATT	AGG	NOV	INT	FRE
ACH	1											
AES	.328	1										
DRA	.023	.175	1									
ESC	.291	.384	.223	1								
KNO	.130	.333	.042	.216	1							
SKI	.269	.374	.027	.176	.535	1						
SOC	.434	.300	.024	.288	.261	.349	1					
ATT	.008	.068	.070	.090	-.033	-.056	-.023	1				
AGG	.219	.127	.258	.221	.051	.074	.270	.194	1			
NOV	.388	.295	.308	.252	.224	.256	.332	-.067	.259	1		
INT	.265	.316	.080	.209	.134	.243	.333	-.052	.069	.266	1	
FRE	.135	.255	.057	.244	.128	.119	.215	.038	.095	.162	.377	1

Table 5. Results. *p < .05; **p < .01. IV: independent variable, DV: dependent variable

Hypotheses no.	IV	(a) DV: Consumption Intention ($R^2 = .256$)		(b) DV: Consumption Frequency ($R^2 = .124$)	
		β	p	β	p
H1	Vicarious Achievement	.004	.957	-.063	.386
H2	Aesthetics	**.213****	.005	**.180***	.014
H3	Escape	.059	.367	**.145***	.026
H4	Social Interaction	**.205****	.005	**.141***	.049
H5	Drama	.036	.598	-.032	.641
H6	Acquisition of Knowledge	-.114	.122	-.005	.945
H7	Physical Attractiveness	-.076	.205	.049	.413
H8	Physical Skill	**.178***	.020	-.017	.818
H9	Enjoyment of Aggression	-.011	.865	.009	.891
H10	Novelty	.123	.082	.083	.238

DISCUSSION

Women's football has been gaining popularity since the turn of the century and has the potential to establish itself as a socially and commercially viable alternative to other professional spectator sports played by women or men in the near future (UEFA, 2022b). Rising numbers of fans and spectators across various women's football competitions highlight the momentum that the sport has been enjoying, especially since the 2010s (FIFA, 2019; Reuters, 2021; UEFA, 2022a). However, women's football is said to have a major marketing problem, which includes the inequality in how the sport is resourced, marketed, and, especially, in how it is covered by the media as compared to men's football (Rosen, 2022). Thus, it is essential to solve that problem by allocating more human and financial resources to promotional efforts that foster the image and appeal for women's football products, such as the NWSL, hence, enriching the brand and making it more visible and competitive across different communication channels.

This empirical research demonstrates that the motivational factors including aesthetics (H2a, b), escapism (H3b), social interaction (H4a, b), and physical skill of the footballers (H8a) have a positive and statistically significant influence on fans and spectators of the NWSL in the USA to consume the offered sports product. These findings are supported by extant research undertaken in different sports. Hsieh et al. (2011) found that aesthetic (H2a) motives had a significant and positive effect on sports consumption. This finds further support in research by Hamari and Sjöblom (2017), who established a significant and positive effect on consumption frequency through aesthetic (H2b) and escape (H3b) motives. Social interaction (H4a, b) was found to have a significant and positive influence on consuming a sports product (Kim et al., 2021) and its respective consumption frequency (Won & Kitamura, 2006). Lastly, Clarke et al. (2022) uncovered a significant and positive effect of physical skill of the footballers (H8a) on the consumption for women's sports. Marketing professionals responsible for promoting the NWSL product should consider emphasizing integrated marketing communications tactics that highlight these four factors. The next section elaborates on recommended marketing communications activities to be implemented by marketing practitioners.

Practical Recommendations

Football is often referred to as 'the beautiful game', which implies a certain aesthetic beauty to the sport. Trail (2012) defines artistic value, beauty, and grace of a sport as the main aesthetic characteristics that motivate spectators to consume that sport. However, valuable skills inherent to play and win a game of football constitute an essential part of the aesthetics offered by the game (Ryall, 2015). This underlines the association between the aesthetics of football and the physical skill of the players, giving credence to the interpretation that physical skills contribute to the aesthetics of football. In support of that statement, Davis (2015) notes that the aesthetic meaning of the goal, a climactic moment during the football match, results from the dramatic struggle leading up to the goal. It can further be reasoned that the immersion in the drama of the competition creates the aesthetic experience for fans and spectators (Borge, 2015), which leads back to the characteristics proposed by Trail (2012).

Therefore, aesthetics and physical skills may need to be considered in reference with each other when conceptualizing and creating promotional tactics and content. The brand experience perspective suggests to create an overall sensory experience through an integrated marketing communications mix enhanced by promotional tactics; these tactics shall add value to a brand or product like the NWSL by emphasizing aesthetic characteristics or excitement, thereby differentiating itself from other brands' offerings (Schmitt, 1999). This means that marketers may want to consider including aesthetics specific to the NWSL in communication and respective content, such as imagery of protagonists (i.e. teams and people in the NWSL), aesthetics of locations (e.g. stadiums, arenas, cities, etc.), or cultural heritage of the team and its hometown. Additionally, communication and content that highlights the physical skill of NWSL protagonists, directly or indirectly, could heighten the effectiveness of the messages.

Escapism is found to have a positive and statistically significant influence on the frequency for watching the NWSL. A possible interpretation is that people who follow a season-long football competition like the NWSL may create a ritualized watching experience around it (Aubrey et al., 2012). This can strengthen the commitment and, therefore, the regularity of the occurrence. Escaping the reality of daily life and regularly distracting oneself with unscripted entertainment such as the NWSL can become a habitual pastime through which viewers may seek recreation or excitement (Rubin, 1981; Wann & James, 2019). Schmitt (1999) suggests that company and brands implement promotional tactics that emphasize how such an escape could enrich the lives of consumers "by targeting their [active] experiences, showing them alternative ways of doing things, alternative lifestyles and interactions" (p. 68). This could include engaging with fans and spectators to discuss NWSL topics before, during, or after a matchday, showing them how the NWSL can positively affect their lives, or accentuating the gratification that viewers can experience from escaping daily life for at least 90 minutes on a regular basis.

The statistically significant and positive influence that social interaction has on consumption intention and frequency for watching the NWSL, highlights that socializing and having the opportunity to interact and talk with others through the happenings around the NWSL is an essential motivation for its fans and spectators. Wann and James (2019) explain that sport fandom usually takes place within a social setting, be it in the comfort of one's home, a bar, or the respective sports venue. Such socialization and interaction with like-minded others around sports also applies to social media channels (Sanderson, 2011). Social media is one of the more effective communication channels for connecting people with each other and with the brand and is considered an essential marketing vehicle (Sutera, 2013; Batra & Keller, 2016). Relational marketing tactics should expand beyond addressing an individual's self-interest and foster an inclusive brand experience. This creates the need for individuals to be perceived positively by like-minded others while belonging to a social system, therefore building and maintaining strong relations with the brand and other fans (Schmitt, 1999). Given the potentially wide reach of social media channels, marketers for the NWSL should aim to engage their followers with communication requesting specific interactions such as, for example, contributing to a relevant topic with a statement or photo, participating in a quiz about the team, or joining an online Q&A with a player or staff member. Another opportunity could be to engage spectators via second-screening (Cunningham & Eastin, 2017).

Figure 2 offers a visualization of the final conceptual model emphasizing the statistically significant causal relationships discussed above. Nevertheless, although the results of this empirical research highlight the importance to focus on the elements with statistical significance, it can be argued that motivational factors that were not found to be statistically significant in the case of this study, may still need to be considered to a certain degree in practical marketing communication efforts. Batra and Keller (2016) suggest to implement integrated marketing communication efforts along a defined consumer journey by applying an adequate mix of various communication channels in order to achieve specific communication objectives. Furthermore, Pine and Gilmore (2019) describe the need for companies and brands to offer a holistic brand experience to current and potential customers including a mix of brand aesthetics, entertainment, information, and escapism.

Figure 2. Conceptual model with results. ACH: vicarious achievement, AES: aesthetics, DRA: drama, ESC: escape, KNO: acquisition of knowledge, SKI: physical skills, SOC: social interaction, ATT: physical attractiveness, AGG: enjoyment of aggression, NOV: novelty, INT: consumption intention, FRE: consumption frequency.

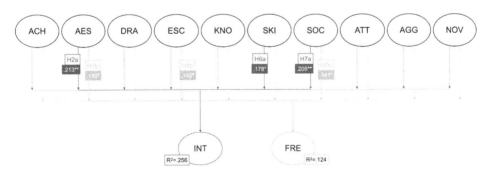

CONCLUSION

Women's football is enjoying great momentum as a spectator sport. International championships have sparked interest in the sport and fueled the growth of national competitions, such as the NWSL in the USA. Nevertheless, women's sports in general are said to have a marketing problem that needs to be solved. This study assesses how motivations for sport consumption influence the intention to watch the NWSL in the USA by applying the MSSC on a sample of 302 respondents that reflects a mainly female and Millennial view. Results computed through SEM found that aesthetics of women's football, escape from daily life, social interaction with like-minded others, and physical skill of the athletes influence consumption intentions and respective frequency for watching the league (see Figure 2). Explicit integrated marketing communications efforts that emphasize the above-mentioned motivations should be considered for implementation in order to improve the NWSL's marketing efforts.

Limitations of this study include the rather small sample size and its respondents being recruited soley through social media. Nevertheless, this study fills a gap in the body of knowledge for the business of women's football with regard to motivation for sport consumption and offers students and practitioners the chance to reflect on promotional tactics to strengthen consumption intention for women's football. Future research could investigate the same research question while addressing a wider demographic audience. Similarly, an analysis comparing the consumption intention of the audience in the home market and audiences in foreign markets would be beneficial for the NWSL to better organize its marketing communication efforts for the different audiences.

There are no competing interests to declare with regard to this study.

REFERENCES

Adachi, N., Yamashita, R., & Matsuoka, H. (2022). How does spectator marketing in women's leagues differ from that in men's leagues? *International Journal of Sport Management and Marketing*, *22*(1–2), 1–18. doi:10.1504/IJSMM.2022.121259

Alexander, S. (2005). Trail-blazers who pioneered women's football. *BBC News.* http://news.bbc.co.uk/sport2/hi/football/women/4603149.stm

Allison, R. (2018). Women's soccer in the United States: Introduction. *Sport in Society*, *21*(7), 993–995. doi:10.1080/17430437.2018.1401361

Arai, A., Ko, Y. J., & Ross, S. (2014). Branding athletes: Exploration and conceptualization of athlete brand image. *Sport Management Review*, *17*(2), 97–106. doi:10.1016/j.smr.2013.04.003

Aubrey, J. S., Olson, L., Fine, M., Hauser, T., Rhea, D., Kaylor, B., & Yang, A. (2012). Investigating personality and viewing-motivation correlates of reality television exposure. *Communication Quarterly*, *60*(1), 80–102. doi:10.1080/0146 3373.2012.641830

Batra, R., & Keller, K. L. (2016). Integrating marketing communications: New findings, new lessons, and new ideas. *Journal of Marketing*, *80*(6), 122–145. doi:10.1509/jm.15.0419

Borge, S. (2015). An agon aesthetics of football. *Sport, Ethics and Philosophy*, *9*(2), 97–123. doi:10.1080/17511321.2015.1061045

Clarke, E., Geurin, A. N., & Burch, L. M. (2022). Team identification, motives, and behaviour: A comparative analysis of fans of men's and women's sport. *Managing Sport and Leisure*, 1–24. doi:10.1080/23750472.2022.2049455

Cohen, J. (1992). Quantitative methods in psychology: A power primer. *Psychological Bulletin*, *112*(1), 155–159. doi:10.1037/0033-2909.112.1.155 PMID:19565683

Cooky, C., Council, L. D., Mears, M. A., & Messner, M. A. (2021). One and done: The long eclipse of women's televised sports, 1989–2019. *Communication & Sport*, *9*(3), 347–371. doi:10.1177/21674795211003524

Cunningham, N. R., & Eastin, M. S. (2017). Second screen and sports: A structural investigation into team identification and efficacy. *Communication & Sport*, *5*(3), 288–310. doi:10.1177/2167479515610152

Dator, J. (2019). *A short history of the banning of women's soccer*. SB Nation. https://www.sbnation.com/soccer/2019/7/6/18658729/banning-womens-soccer-world-cup-effects

Davis, P. (2015). Football is football and is interesting, very interesting. *Sport, Ethics and Philosophy*, *9*(2), 140–152. doi:10.1080/17511321.2015.1020855

dos Santos, R. L., Petroll, M. D. L. M., Boeing, R., & Scussel, F. (2021). Let's play a new game: The drivers of eSports consumption. *Research. Social Development*, *10*(5), e40710515188. Advance online publication. doi:10.33448/rsd-v10i5.15188

DuBose, B. (2020). *As part owner, James Harden celebrates NWSL title by Houston Dash*. https://rocketswire.usatoday.com/2020/07/26/as-part-owner-james-harden-celebrates-nwsl-title-by-houston-dash/

EBU. (2022). *EBU members on a high after record UEFA Women's EURO TV viewing figures.* https://www.ebu.ch/news/2022/08/ebu-members-on-a-high-after-record-uefa-womens-euro-tv-viewing-figures

The Economist. (2019). Competition between sports for fans' money and attention is increasingly fierce. *The Economist.* https://www.economist.com/international/2019/10/05/competition-between-sports-for-fans-money-and-attention-is-increasingly-fierce

FIFA. (2019). *FIFA Women's World Cup 2019 watched by more than 1 billion.* FIFA. https://www.fifa.com/tournaments/womens/womensworldcup/france2019/news/fifa-women-s-world-cup-2019tm-watched-by-more-than-1-billion

Gantz, W. (1981). An exploration of viewing motives and behaviors associated with television sports. *Journal of Broadcasting & Electronic Media*, 25(3), 263–275. doi:10.1080/08838158109386450

Gotham, F. C. (2022). *Steven Temares.* Gotham FC. https://www.gothamfc.com/steven-temares

Hamari, J., & Sjöblom, M. (2017). What is eSports and why do people watch it? *Internet Research*, 27(2), 211–232. doi:10.1108/IntR-04-2016-0085

Haridakis, P. M. (2010). Rival sports fans and intergroup communication. In H. Giles, S. Reid, & J. Harwood (Eds.), *The dynamics of intergroup communication* (pp. 249–262). Peter Lang.

Herbst, J. (2022). *How Natalie Portman and her Angel City FC cofounders are changing the game for women's soccer.* FastCompany. https://www.fastcompany.com/90739855/how-natalie-portman-and-her-angel-city-fc-cofounders-are-changing-the-game-for-womens-soccer

Hsieh, L. W., Wang, C. H., & Yoder, T. W. (2011). Factors associated with professional baseball consumption: A cross-cultural comparison study. *International Journal of Business and Information*, 6(2), 135–159.

Im, H., Lennon, S. J., & Stoel, L. (2010). The perceptual fluency effect on pleasurable online shopping experience. *Journal of Research in Interactive Marketing*, 4(4), 280–295. doi:10.1108/17505931011092808

Kassouf, J. (2022). *As expansion race heats up, NWSL faces tough questions about its future with Utah expected to join in 2024.* ESPN. https://www.espn.com/soccer/united-states-nwsl/story/4692534/as-expansion-race-heats-upnwsl-faces-tough-questions-about-its-future-with-utah-expected-to-join-in-2024s

Kim, S., Greenwell, T. C., Andrew, D. P., Lee, J., & Mahony, D. F. (2008). An analysis of spectator motives in an individual combat sport: A study of mixed martial arts fans. *Sport Marketing Quarterly*, *17*(2), 109–119. https://oaks.kent.edu/flapubs/17

Kim, S., Morgan, A., & Assaker, G. (2021). Examining the relationship between sport spectator motivation, involvement, and loyalty: A structural model in the context of Australian Rules football. *Sport in Society*, *24*(6), 1006–1032. doi:10.1080/17430437.2020.1720658

Leslie-Walker, A., & Mulvenna, C. (2022). The Football Association's Women's Super League and female soccer fans: Fan engagement and the importance of supporter clubs. *Soccer and Society*, *23*(3), 314–327. doi:10.1080/14660970.2022.2037218

Macey, J., Tyrväinen, V., Pirkkalainen, H., & Hamari, J. (2022). Does eSports spectating influence game consumption? *Behaviour & Information Technology*, *41*(1), 181–197. doi:10.1080/0144929X.2020.1797876

Mahmoudian, A., Sadeghi Boroujerdi, S., Mohammadi, S., Delshab, V., & Pyun, D. Y. (2021). Testing the impact of athlete brand image attributes on fan loyalty. *Journal of Business and Industrial Marketing*, *36*(2), 244–255. doi:10.1108/JBIM-10-2019-0464

Mians, J., & Majid, U. (2022). WSL clubs see ticket demand surge after Lionesses' Euro 2022 win. *The Guardian*. https://www.theguardian.com/football/2022/aug/03/wsl-clubs-see-ticket-demand-surge-after-lionesses-euro-22-win

Muhammad, H. (2019). Gender differences and aggression: A comparative study of college and university sport players. *Humanities and Social Sciences*, *26*(2), 1–16.

Mumcu, C., Lough, N., & Barnes, J. C. (2016). Examination of women's sports fans' attitudes and consumption intentions. *Journal of Applied Sport Management*, *8*(4), 25–43. doi:10.18666/JASM-2016-V8-I4-7221

Mutz, M., & Meier, H. E. (2016). Successful, sexy, popular: Athletic performance and physical attractiveness as determinants of public interest in male and female soccer players. *International Review for the Sociology of Sport*, *51*(5), 567–580. doi:10.1177/1012690214545900

Olympics. (2019). *Best of team USA women's football at the Olympics: Top moments.* [Video]. Youtube. https://www.youtube.com/watch?v=X2ByJNAsct4

Pine, B. J., & Gilmore, J. H. (2019). *The experience economy: Competing for customer time, attention, and money.* Harvard Business Review Press.

Reuters. (2021). *Record viewership for 2021 NWSL finale.* Reuters. https://www.reuters.com/lifestyle/sports/record-viewership-2021-nwsl-finale-2021-11-23/

Rosen, H. (2022). *The problem with women's sports | Haley Rosen.* TEDxBoston. https://www.youtube.com/watch?v=vG6P9gfgO6g

Rubin, A. (1981). The interaction of television uses and gratifications. *Journal of Broadcasting, 27,* 37–51. doi:10.1080/08838158309386471

Ryall, E. (2015). Good games and penalty shoot-outs. *Sport, Ethics and Philosophy, 9*(2), 205–213. doi:10.1080/17511321.2015.1020854

Sanderson, J. (2011). *It's a whole new ballgame: How social media is changing sports.* Hampton Press.

Schad, T. (2022). 'Where the heck are the women?' Why women's sports could see financial boon in future TV deals. *USA Today.* https://eu.usatoday.com/story/sports/2022/07/12/womens-sports-tv-financial-boon-coming/7810802001/

Schmitt, B. (1999). *Experiential marketing: How to get customers to sense, feel, think, act, relate to your company and brands.* Free Press.

Scottish Government. (2019). *Unveiling a plaque at the Hibs Supporters' Club to commemorate the first women's international football match in 1881.* Scootish Government. https://twitter.com/scotgovhealth/status/1201846754603347968

Skillen, F., Byrne, H., Carrier, J., & James, G. (2022). 'The game of football is quite unsuitable for females and ought not to be encouraged': A comparative analysis of the 1921 English Football Association ban on women's football in Britain and Ireland. *Sport in History, 42*(1), 49–75. doi:10.1080/17460263.2021.2025415

Sky Sports. (2021). WSL: Barclays extends FA and Premier League partnership and will sponsor FA Women's Championship. *Sky Sports.* https://www.skysports.com/football/news/28508/12496102/wsl-barclays-extends-fa-and-premier-league-partnership-and-will-sponsor-fa-womens-championship

Sutera, D. (2013). *Sports fans 2.0: How fans are using social media to get closer to the game.* Scarecrow Press.

Trail, G. (2012). *Manual for the Motivation Scale for Sport Consumption (MSSC).* Sports Research Consultants. https://sportconsumerresearchconsultants.yolasite.com/resources/MSSC%20Manual%20-%202012.pdf

Trail, G., & James, J. D. (2001). The Motivation Scale for Sport Consumption: Assessment of the scale's psychometric properties. *Journal of Sport Behavior*, *24*(1), 108–128.

Trail, G. T., Robinson, M., Dick, R., & Gillentine, A. (2003). Motives and points of attachment: Fans versus spectators in intercollegiate athletics. *Sport Marketing Quarterly*, *12*, 217–227.

UEFA. (2022a). *UEFA Women's EURO 2022 becomes most watched Women's EURO in history*. UEFA. https://www.uefa.com/insideuefa/news/0277-15b76971bb48-092500679b6d-1000--uefa-women-s-euro-2022-becomes-most-watched-women-s-euro-in-his/

UEFA. (2022b). *The business case for women's football*. UEFA. https://editorial.uefa.com/resources/0278-15e121074702-c9be7dcd0a29-1000/business_case_for_women_s_football-_external_report_1_.pdf

Wang, R. T., Zhang, J. J., & Tsuji, Y. (2011). Examining fan motives and loyalty for the Chinese Professional Baseball League of Taiwan. *Sport Management Review*, *14*(4), 347–360. doi:10.1016/j.smr.2010.12.001

Wann, D. L. (1995). Preliminary validation of the sport fan motivation scale. *Journal of Sport and Social Issues*, *19*(4), 377–396. doi:10.1177/019372395019004004

Wann, D. L., & James, J. D. (2019). *Sport fans: The psychology and social impact of fandom* (2nd ed.). Routledge.

Williams, J. (2003). *A game for rough girls? A history of women's football in Britain*. Routledge.

Williams, J. (2011). *Women's Football, Europe and professionalization 1971-2011*. International Centre for Sports History and Culture.

Won, J. U., & Kitamura, K. (2006). Motivational factors affecting sports consumption behavior of K-league and J-league spectators. *International Journal of Sport and Health Science*, *4*, 233–251. doi:10.5432/ijshs.4.233

Xiao, M. (2020). Factors influencing eSports viewership: An approach based on the theory of reasoned action. *Communication & Sport*, *8*(1), 92–122. doi:10.1177/2167479518819482

KEY TERMS AND DEFINITIONS

Media Product: A product that consists of media content such as text, images, audio or video files and is intended to satisfy the need for entertainment and information.

Motivation Scale for Sport Consumption (MSSC): A scientific scale that measures the motives for watching spectator sports, including vicarious achievement, aesthetics, drama, escape, acquisition of knowledge, physical skills, social interaction, physical attractiveness, enjoyment of aggression, and novelty.

National Women's Soccer League (NWSL): The professional women's football/soccer league at the top of the league system in the USA, established in 2012.

Spectator Sports Fans: Enthusiastic consumers that watch or follow a sport with interest and identification with a league, team, or athlete.

Spectator Sports: Sports that people watch or follow for entertainment purposes without getting involved in the action.

Uses and Gratifications: An approach in media studies that views the recipient of an entertainment media product as an active subject, who selects an available media product with the intention to satisfy his or her media needs or wants.

Women's Football (or Women's Soccer): The team sport of association football played by women at the professional level.

Chapter 6
The Use of Digital Technologies for Traceability:
An Analysis of Consumer and Firm Perceptions

Francesco Pacchera
https://orcid.org/0000-0002-5809-392X
Tuscia Univeristy, Italy

Chiara Cagnetti
Tuscia University, Italy

Mariagrazia Provenzano
Tuscia University, Italy

Tommaso Gallo
Tuscia University, Italy

Cecilia Silvestri
https://orcid.org/0000-0003-2528-601X
Tuscia University, Italy

ABSTRACT

Digital transformation (DT) affects companies' competitiveness mainly in terms of innovation, efficiency, and cost reduction and affects global value chains in specialization, geographic scope, governance, and upgrading. In food, digital tools can improve competitive advantage by supporting companies in ensuring food quality and safety. However, many companies still struggle to respond adequately to DT challenges by adopting new technology concepts as a trend and not a real company imperative, misallocating internal resources and capabilities around technology, and expecting good results. There are no studies in the literature that consider both the adoption of digital technologies and consumer perception in the olive oil sector at the same time. This study has two purposes. The first is to analyse the use of digital technologies by companies in the olive oil sector, and the second is to understand consumer perceptions of the use of digital technologies in traceability.

DOI: 10.4018/978-1-6684-8351-0.ch006

1. INTRODUCTION

The Mediterranean area is the leading producer of olive oil, where Italy and Spain account for almost all world exports (60% Spain and 20% Italy) (Ismea, 2021). Italian production covers on average 15% of world production, and even on the import side, the largest customer in Italy, followed by the United States (US). World demand for olive oil grew slowly - averaging 1% annually - but steadily until 2012. From then on, world consumption also stabilized below the 3 million tons threshold until 2018, when it returned steadily above that threshold. For Italy, production for the 2020/21 marketing year stood at 255,000 tons, a 30% reduction from the previous year (Ismea, 2021). Due to the COVID-19 pandemic, average prices in 2020 fell sharply compared to 2019. However, there is a positive sign for exports to the US, Germany, and France. At the national level, olive oil represents a key product on the market supply-side and demand-side. The oil supply chain consists of several actors and different production phases. In the agricultural phase, olive companies are involved in the production of olives. In the industrial phase, oil processing and extraction companies are involved. Finally, the canning, packaging, and sales companies close the production chain. The Italian supply chain is characterized by a highly developed agricultural sector with high potential found in the suitable territory and the presence of certified products and traced supply chains. The main weaknesses of the olive sector are the small size of the companies and the lack of innovation. The processing phase (mills) sees more focus on investment in research and development. The Italian companies is also characterized by a strong propensity to export, justified by the large size of the operators holding large market shares (MIPAF, 2016). The Italian olive supply chain is therefore poorly organized the activities that make up the agricultural and primary processing phase of the supply chain are fragmented. Large and multinational companies dominate the secondary processing companies and the sales phase (Carlucci et al., 2014). Olive oil represents a key product to which the consumer contributes and increasingly pushes companies to produce quality products (Ismea, 2021). Quality is a strategic tool to compete in the oil market. The consumer is greatly influenced by the range of products on the market, which often offers very wide expectations. Considering extra virgin olive oil (EVOO oil), consumers are greatly influenced by the characteristics of the product and the information they have access to. Examples of this are the information on compositional characteristics (on the label or communicated by the producer), the presence/absence of compounds depending on nutritional requirements, specificity of processing, and raw material characteristics. All this should be communicated correctly to the consumer, and digital technologies are an efficient and effective method of transparent communication.

The consumer represents one of the main protagonists in the olive oil supply chain because the continuous growth of EVOO oil consumption and consumer preferences pushes companies to make more and more quality products (Ismea, 2021) through digital technologies (Carlucci et al., 2015). Indeed, in this context, new technologies can play an important role in ensuring food quality and safety by addressing the main issues related to this topic: food fraud, food safety and recall, regulatory compliance, social issues, and consumer information (Burke, 2019). However, few companies still use digital technologies for this purpose. In the literature, there are studies on the use of digital technologies for traceability in olive oil production (Conti, 2022; Guido et al., 2020; Ktari et al., 2022; Violino et al., 2020) other studies analyse consumer perceptions of the adoption of digital technologies by olive companies (Aparicio-Ruiz et al., 2022; Marozzo et al., 2022; Violino et al., 2019) but there are no studies that consider these two aspects together and analyse the potential developments. To bridge this gap the study has two purposes. The first is to analyse the actual use of digital technologies by companies in the agri-food sector, with a focus on the olive oil sector. The second is to understand consumer perceptions of the use of digital technologies in traceability. For this reason, the research questions are as follows:

RQ1: What digital technologies do companies for the traceability of EVOO oil?
RQ2: What is the perception of consumers regarding the use of technologies for the traceability of EVOO oil?

The chapter is organized as follows. Section 2 defines a review of the literature on the traceability of products. Section 3 introduces the methodology used to collect and analyse the data, and section 4 presents the findings. Section 5 introduces the discussions, and finally, Section 6 includes the conclusions, implications, and limits.

2. REVIEW OF THE LITERATURE

The agri-food sector is one of the most important worldwide but is considered the most vulnerable one due to the perishability of food, often subject to spoilage and contamination. Current social situations, such as the dissemination of COVID-19, have increased consumer awareness, who are increasingly aware and informed about the characteristics, quality, and safety of food products (Cao et al., 2023; Gupta et al., 2023). Food safety is a very important issue, especially in recent years due to global population growth and other aspects such as increasing demand for food and climate change. One aspect related to the demand for food is the loss resulting from the reduction in quantity and consequent quality produced (Cao et al., 2023; Conti, 2022;

Corallo et al., 2021; Ktari et al., 2022; Latino et al., 2022; Liberatore et al., 2018; Marozzo et al., 2022; Menozzi, 2014; Tharatipyakul & Pongnumkul, 2021). These negative factors are caused by the actions and decisions of different stakeholders belonging to the agri-food chain. The main causes of food loss are found within the agri-food supply chain, namely inadequate storage facilities, crop inefficiency, mismanagement, and logistical problems. Specific actions, such as the adoption of food policies and technological investments by companies, can be used to overcome the problems of food loss (Gupta et al., 2023). In recent years, companies have initiated a process of digital transformation (DT), which involves significant changes in their operations (Giua et al., 2022). DT is starting to develop in many sectors and supply chains, including agri-food, and involves the use of modern digital technologies, which influence the competitiveness of companies mainly in terms of innovation, efficiency, and cost reduction and affect global value chains in terms of specialization, geographical extension, governance, and upgrading (Leão & da Silva, 2021). Digital technologies contribute to improving competitive advantage by supporting companies in ensuring food quality and safety, addressing major food-related issues such as food fraud, food safety and recalls, regulatory compliance, social issues, and consumer information (Burke, 2019; Martini & Menozzi, 2021; Parra-López et al., 2021). Food safety is a major concern of consumers (Caro et al., 2018), who also focus on the origin of products (Ben-Ayed et al., 2013; Carzedda et al., 2021; Latino et al., 2022; Liberatore et al., 2018) as well as the quality of goods (Conti, 2022; Corallo et al., 2021; Marozzo et al., 2022; Polenzani et al., 2020; Tharatipyakul & Pongnumkul, 2021) and services (Carzedda et al., 2021; Power, 2019). To solve the problem of food safety and the origin of agri-food products, companies introduce traceability systems to release useful information to consumers. According to some authors, traceability represents the ability to access information, in whole or in part, about an object under examination, during its life cycle, through recorded process identification (Guido et al., 2020; Schwägele, 2005). Traceability makes it possible to trace agri-food products throughout the production chain, making information about agri-food products transparent and meeting the information needs of consumers (D. Biswas et al., 2023; Carzedda et al., 2021; Gupta et al., 2023). Information transparency succeeds in meeting the needs of companies and their business processes, improving the production efficiency of the company and the market, but most importantly it aims to communicate product quality to consumers (Corallo et al., 2021). Information sharing is timely and accurate and covers the entire agrifood supply chain and allows it to operate at the local level, i.e., at the level of the individual company or supply chain, through relationships involving different stakeholders (Conti, 2022; Latino et al., 2022). The sharing of information is timely and accurate and concerns the entire agri-food supply chain and allows it to operate at a local level, i.e. at the level of the individual companies or the level of the supply chain, through relationships involving different stakeholders (Latino et al.,

2022). Communication of information increases consumers' awareness of using information that is correct and responsive to their needs (Corallo et al., 2021). Through traceability, consumers can follow the product, as mentioned above, throughout the supply chain, using proper documentation and recording useful information (Guido et al., 2020; Lozano-Castellón et al., 2022). Traceability can be voluntary or mandatory. Voluntary traceability makes transparent a series of information that can guarantee consumers the safety and quality characteristics of products, increasing the competitiveness of companies on the market. Consumers, who are increasingly attentive to product information, perceive voluntary traceability as increasing their trust in the company. Compulsory traceability, defined by EC Regulation 178/2002, requires agri-food operators to keep information on goods bought and sold and their quantity, as well as on all those involved in the transitions. EU Regulation 1169/2021 is also important, as it concerns the provision of information on agri-food products to consumers. The regulation allows consumers to be protected concerning food products by indicating the place of production, the production batch number, the indication of origin, and the shelf life (Ben-Ayed et al., 2013). Voluntary and non-voluntary information can be found on the labels of agrifood products, which are considered the first information tool used by consumers at the time of purchase (Martini & Menozzi, 2021). At present, the traceability of agri-food products takes place both with the use of simple labels and with modern digital technologies, which make it possible to monitor products and places of production, increasing consumer satisfaction regarding quality, origin, sustainability, and authenticity (Ben-Ayed et al., 2013; Lozano-Castellón et al., 2022). The most widely used technologies for the traceability of agri-food products are Radio Frequency Identification (RFID) (A. Biswas & Roy, 2015; Conti, 2022; Guido et al., 2020; Gupta et al., 2023; Ktari et al., 2022; Tharatipyakul & Pongnumkul, 2021; Violino et al., 2019, 2020), Near Field Communication (NFC) (A. Biswas & Roy, 2015; Conti, 2022; Tharatipyakul & Pongnumkul, 2021; Violino et al., 2019, 2020), QR Code (Cao et al., 2023; Conti, 2022; Guido et al., 2020; Ktari et al., 2022; Latino et al., 2022; Tharatipyakul & Pongnumkul, 2021; Violino et al., 2019), and lot (Conti, 2022; Guido et al., 2020). Digital Technologies are tools that can reassure the consumer because they offer additional information beyond that on the label, where the latter no longer reassures the consumer concerning the quality and safety of the product because the consumer is increasingly demanding (Guido et al., 2020). The technologies are all low-cost and accessible via smartphones and allow companies to release useful information to consumers, although not all technologies have direct access to databases. Some digital technologies only display information from the company's website, without direct access to tracking databases, as is the case with the QR Code. Among the agri-food products that are tracked is olive oil, which is present in several types. Olive product information has precise terms to be used on labels, defined by the European Union. Standards regulate the physical, chemical, and organoleptic characteristics of the product, which depend on where it is marketed (Conti, 2022). Some countries lack specific laws on oil production, but general regulations on product traceability exist and are used by companies (Guido et al., 2020). The study analyses traceability systems for EVOO oil considered the most valuable and highest priced. Companies with traceability systems for EVOO oil can increase consumer confidence by increasing control systems and certifications (Polenzani et al., 2020). Although, to date, it is still difficult to predict how and in what way digital technologies will succeed in transforming the agri-food sector, they are the key to improving food traceability systems (Monfared, 2016). However, many companies still struggle to respond adequately to the challenges of DT, adopting new technology concepts as a trend and not a real business imperative, misallocating internal resources and capabilities around the technology, and expecting good results. Furthermore, studies on the impact of DT on corporate competitiveness are, for the time being, still at an early stage of development (Leão & da Silva, 2021), as are the relevant impact assessment criteria (Lisienkova et al., 2022). For better comprehension, Table 1 below summarizes the topics discussed in the text.

Table 1. Evidences from literature review

Authors	Digital Technologies				Consumers			
	Lot	NFC	QR Code	RFID	Food safety	Origin of products	Food quality	Awareness
(Conti, 2022)	X	x	x	x	x		x	
(Tharatipyakul & Pongnumkul, 2021)		x	x	X	x		x	x
(Violino et al., 2019)		x	x	X				x
(Violino et al., 2020)		x		x				
(D. Biswas et al., 2023)		x		x				
(Guido et al., 2020)	x		x	x				
(Latino et al., 2022)			x		x	x		x
(Cao et al., 2023)			x		x			
(Ktari et al., 2022)			x	x	x			
(Gupta et al., 2023)				x				
(Liberatore et al., 2018)					x	x		
(Marozzo et al., 2022)					x		x	x
(Corallo et al., 2021)					x		x	x
(Menozzi, 2014)					x			x
(Ben-Ayed et al., 2013)						x		
(Carzedda et al., 2021)						x		
(Polenzani et al., 2020)							x	x

Source: our elaboration

3. MATERIAL AND METHODS

To meet the proposed aims, the study used two different methodologies for data collection. For the first purpose, a documentary analysis was used to extract secondary data from websites, official documents, and financial statements. For the second aim, a questionnaire (Bowen, 2009) was used to collect primary data. The primary data and secondary data were then triangulated for further interpretation of the results (Flowerdew & Martin, 2005). The research design with the steps taken is explained in the following Figure 1.

Figure 1. Design of research
Source. *Authors' elaboration*

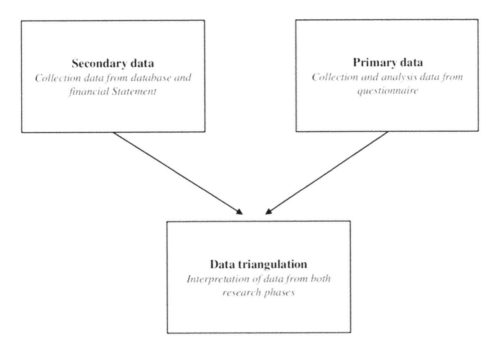

3.1. Dataset Analysis

The companies selected from the sample are derived from the AIDA platform (https://aida.bvdinfo.com/), considering ATECO code 10.41, "production of oils and fats." The selected companies have a turnover of more than 10 million euros as of 12/31/2021. The sample consists of 33 oil-producing companies; three do not produce extra virgin olive oil. Therefore, the final sample consists of 30 companies.

Companies with the highest turnover include "Lucchese olii e vini S.p.A." (298 mln €), "Carapelli Firenze S.p.A." (247 mln €), and "Casa Olearia Italiana S.p.A." (222 mln €). Of the companies in the sample, we looked for information useful for analysis. The objective was to identify what information was contained on product labels, such as storage, use, type of extraction, certifications, the words "Made in Italy" and "Unfiltered." The information was obtained by analysing the website and in more detail, analysing the labels of individual EVOO oil products. In addition to this information, we researched information related to traceability, identifying what technologies were currently used by companies.

3.2. Questionnaire

The questionnaire investigates consumer perceptions of the traceability of EVOO oil and the use of digital technologies. The questionnaire derives from a literature review, considering the factors used in other surveys and creating questions specific to this analysis. The questionnaire is anonymous to protect data and information about consumer participants. The questionnaire is in Italian language and analyses the following two sections:

- Consumer's analysis: containing information about consumers' perception concerning traceability and use of digital tools.
- Consumer profile: containing information on socio-demographic features.

Data were collected from December 2022 to March 2022 through Google Forms and social media (Brito et al., 2021; Majeed et al., 2022; Sarfraz et al., 2021). Social media allow a lot of data to be collected in a short period and without cost (Theodoridis & Zacharatos, 2022). The difficulty of clearly identifying the customer population led to the adoption of a non-probabilistic sampling scheme, specifically accidental sampling, as widely used in market research (Bracalente, B., Cossignani, M., & Mulas, A., 2009; Theodoridis & Zacharatos, 2022). Specifically, the procedure used to collect the questionnaire is the snowballing and convenience method (Theodoridis & Zacharatos, 2022). For this reason, data were collected from consumers from all regions of Italy. The questions in the questionnaire are in most cases answered using the Likert scale, which measures the perceptions of sustainable consumers by assigning respondents a score ranging from 'strongly disagree' (value 1) to 'strongly agree' (value 6) (Likert, 1932). A total of 464 questionnaires were answered, but not all answers were used for the analysis. The results were filtered based on the objective of the survey. The sample analysis involves a descriptive analysis of the respondents, including age, gender, income, and educational qualification. The data sample collected by administering the questionnaire was 464 people, and the statistical software used to carry out the analysis is "STATA 12 Data Analysis and Statistical Software" (www.stata.com).

4. RESULTS

This section presents the results of the survey conducted on the questionnaire and dataset containing the companies.

4.1. Companies

There are 30 oil companies in the sample, and among them, 15 (38.5%) make organic products, 14 (35.90%) "Protected designation of origin (PDO)/ Protected geographical indications (PGI) products", and 10 (25.6%) ensure product "Traceability" as shown in Table 2. As can be seen from the results, few companies realize product traceability, an important element that could be useful for consumers when buying the product. Presumably, a consumer who is highly attentive to product characteristics might be very interested in the traceability systems used by the company. "Traceability" could be an additional element that assures the quality of the product and, as a result, could result in greater consumer confidence in the product they are purchasing. Investing in traceability can be a key and strategic element in improving business results, selling more products, and increasing consumer trust and awareness of the products made by that specific company.

Table 2. Dimensions of EVOO oil

Dimensions	*f*	%
Bio	15	38.50%
PDO/PGI	14	35.90%
Traceability	10	25.60%
Total	39	100.00%

Source: author's elaboration

Regarding traceability, 8 out of 10 companies use the "Lot", 5 use the "QR Code", and five use "label info" (Table 3). A "lot", also as evidenced by the results, is the most widely used traceability tool by companies. This tool, which is the most common and the most widely used, is an important guarantee for the traceability of a product and greater safety for the consumer. Nowadays, many businesses are gearing

Table 3. Traceability tools

Tools	f	%
Lot	8	44.4%
QRCode	5	27.8%
Label information	5	27.8%
Total	18	100.0%

Source: Author's elaboration

up to be up to date to meet consumer demands inherent in traceability. More and more consumers, perhaps also facilitated using technological and digital tools such as smartphones, also tend to inform themselves using these devices (smartphones, tablets, etc.). The "QR Code", for example, can be an important traceability tool aimed at better assurance to consumers, through which they can access information inherent in product traceability. With the "QR Code", one can acquire specific information quickly without it having to be on the product packaging. By doing so, the consumer can access it easily and without having to look for it on the packaging. Therefore, the "QR Code", but in general technologies that facilitate the use of digital devices to acquire information, is essential for a consumer who wants to be increasingly up-to-date and informed about the products he or she decides to purchase.

For traceability, companies used use the three tools in combination. The "Lot", which turns out to be the main tool, is combined with "QR Code" and label info.

The third stage of the analysis considers the type of information on the label. The table 4 shows that most companies (23 out of 30) include the "Made in Italy" label; 18 have information on extraction, while 11 reports the mode of "Preservation". Consumers may be very interested in the origin and thus provenance of a product,

Table 4. Type of information

Type of Information	f	%
Made in Italy	23	30.30%
Extraction	18	23.70%
Preservation	11	14.50%
Certifications	9	11.80%
Unfiltered oil	8	10.50%
Usage	7	9.20%
Total	76	100.00%

Source: author's elaboration

especially if it is "Made in Italy". As is well known, "Made in Italy" is very effective in the world as it is often associated with quality products. A product made in Italy represents a certainty for the consumer, who is certain that he is buying a product that will meet his needs and, probably, exceed his expectations. Nowadays, in an increasingly competitive market in which competition, partly due to globalization has increased in many market sectors, getting recognized and making a quality product is essential to enable a company to grow and survive within the market. Therefore, if the consumer notices that a product is "Made in Italy", there may be a greater likelihood of purchasing the product.

In addition, it is also important to understand how to preserve a product to be able to keep it longer (this especially applies to food products such as oil). The consumer, at the time of purchase wants to be informed to know how he or she will be able to store that product to maintain its quality or, as in the case of oil, its flavor, taste, smell, and perhaps even its colour Having information on preservation could be critical in getting the consumer to buy that product rather than that of a competitor.

Again, the presence of information allows combinations with others of it. For example, on the label, there is information combined with "Made in Italy", "Extraction", mode of "Preservation" and the presence of "Certifications".

4.2. Consumers

The first part of the result includes the descriptive statistics of 464 consumers. The analysis considers only a sample of 457 consumers, i.e., those who habitually consume EVOO oil. The descriptive analysis allows for obtaining relevant information about the socio-demographic profiles of respondents (M. Nekmahmud and M. Fekete-Farkas (2020)). Regarding "Gender", 58% (n=263) were women, and 42% (n=194) were men. The age of participants is 16% (n=72) for those aged 18-25 years, 26% (n=121) for those aged 26-33, 12% (n=54) for the age 34-41, 10% (n=47) for the age 42-49, 20% (n=92) for the age 50-57 and finally, 16% (n=71) of the sample was over 58 years. Regarding the "Level of education", 1% (n=6) of participants had middle school licenses, 20% (n=90) had a higher diploma, 17% (n=76) of participants had a bachelor's degree, the 29% (n=133) of participants had master's degree and, in finally, 33% (n=152) of participants had a post-degree (Master, Ph.D.). Regarding the "Geographical area of consumer residence", 9% (n=42) live in the North Italy region, 79% (n=361) of consumers live in the regions of South Italy, 11% (n=50) of consumers live in the regions of middle Italy, and in finally, only 1% of consumers lives in the island. Considering the "Responsibility for family purchasing", 77% (n=351) purchase products and 23% (n=106) don't purchase products. Finally, the "Household size" of the respondents is 11% (n=49) for one-person households, 22% (n=199) for two-person households, 24% (n=112) for three-person households, 33%

(n=150) for four-person households, and finally, 10% (n=46) for households of more than four persons. The following Table 5 summarizes the results.

Table 5. Descriptive statistics of the sample

Dimension	Items	f	%
Gender	Woman	263	58%
	Man	194	42%
Total		457	100%
Age	18-25years	72	16%
	26-33 years	121	26%
	34-41 years	54	12%
	42-49 years	47	10%
	50-57 years	92	20%
	Over 58 years	71	16%
Total		457	100%
Geographical area of residence	North	42	9%
	South	361	79%
	Middle	50	11%
	Island	4	1%
Total		457	100%
Responsible for family purchasing	Yes	351	77%
	No	106	23%
Total		457	100%
Qualification	Middle school license	6	1%
	Higher Diploma	90	20%
	Bachelor's degree	76	17%
	master's degree	133	29%
	Post-degree (Master, Ph.D.)	152	33%
Total		457	100%
Household	1	49	11%
	2	100	22%
	3	112	24%
	4	150	33%
	>4	46	10%
Total		457	100%

Source: author's elaboration

Considering the sample of respondents (n=457), consumers consider it important to know the traceability of the EVOO oil they intend to buy. Respondents gave the importance of EVOO oil traceability a score of 5.42 (on a Likert scale of 1 to 6). To have product traceability, respondents are willing to spend more especially if traceability is achieved using new technologies. Therefore, the respondents give a score of 4.77 (on a Likert scale of 1 to 6) for buying EVOO oil traced with new digital technologies at a higher price.

Among the digital technologies considered important for the traceability of EVOO oil is the "QR Code" (30%), followed respectively by "Web Site" (18%), "Mobile App" (16%), and "Bar Code" (16%). The two technologies considered unimportant by consumers are "RFID" (12%) and "NFC" (11%). The result is shown in Figure 2.

Figure 2. Traceability technologies
Source: Author's elaboration

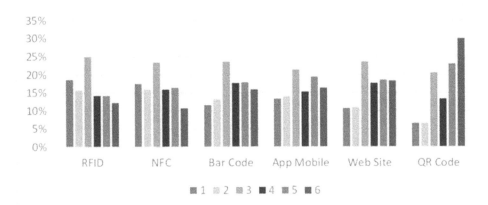

Regarding the questions in the questionnaire, consumers were asked to express their preferences regarding the information on the label. Labels are the first source of information for any food product, including EVOO oil. EVOO oil labels contain mandatory information that allows products and places of production to be traced, increasing consumer satisfaction regarding quality, origin, sustainability, and authenticity. (Lozano-Castellón, J., López-Yerena (2022); Ben-Ayed, R., Kamoun-Grati, N., & Rebai, A. (2013). Based on the results of the questionnaire, expressed as an average value, the "Country of origin of the olives" has a value of 5.3, followed by the "Country of processing" of the product with an average value of 5.16, and the "Certifying body of the controls", with an average value of 5.02. These three pieces of information are considered the most important by consumers, followed by information such as the "Extraction method" and "Presence of voluntary controls", both with an average value of 4.77, information on the "Polyphenol content", with an average value of 4.65, and finally, the "Olive variety" with an average value of 4.62 (Table 6).

Table 6. Label information

Label information	Average value
Country of origin of olives	5.29
Country of product processing	5.16
Certifying the body of the controls	5.02
Presence of voluntary controls	4.77
Extraction method	4.77
Polyphenol content	4.65
Olives variety	4.62

Source: Author's elaboration

Considering that some information on the label is mandatory by law, through the questionnaire consumers were asked to identify what information might be relevant to include on EVOO oil labels. According to consumers, it might be important to include a "QR code containing all EVOO oil traceability information" with an average value of 5.00. For consumers, it might also be important to include "Information on the sensory characters of the oil(degree of aromatic intensity, fruity, spicy, bitter) with a mean value of 4.52, "Information on how extra virgin olive oil (EVOO) is harvested and produced" equal to 4.46, and a "QR code linking to the producer's website" equal to 4.31. Finally, consumers do not consider it important to include "Information about the types of recipes/food to be paired with the extra virgin olive oil purchased", with a mean value of 3.40. The following Table 7 show the results.

Table 7. Addition of information

Addition of information	Average value
QR code containing all extra virgin olive oil traceability information	5.00
QR code linking to the producer's website	4.31
Information about the types of recipes/food to be paired with the extra virgin olive oil purchased	3.40
Information on how extra virgin olive oil (EVOO) is harvested and produced	4.46
Information on the sensory characters of the oil (degree of aromatic intensity, fruity, spicy, bitter)	4.52

Source: Author's elaboration

5. DISCUSSION

This study uses a twofold inquiry to answer the research questions. On the one hand, it analyzes companies in the olive supply chain, identifying the main information on the label and the digital technologies used for the traceability of EVOO oil. The other element of the survey is consumers, who were given a questionnaire to identify information regarding their perceptions of EVOO oil traceability and the information currently on the label. The label and in particular the brand are fundamental aspects that influence consumer perception. A brand is able to provide transparent and reliable information on the origin, production and distribution of its products, this increases credibility and consumer trust (Mellens et al., 1996). Traceability can positively influence the value of a brand (Yin et al., 2017). The ability to know and verify all information about a product provides transparency and increases consumer trust in the brand (Garaus & Treiblmaier, 2021). Further information that can be conveyed through the traceability of a product concerns the aspect of sustainability and quality (Burnier et al., 2021). This provides the product brand with a guarantee and veracity with respect to these aspects. Traceability can also be a distinctive element for the brand, which can make the product more competitive in the market (Xue et al., 2007). In addition, traceability strengthens the bond between brand and consumer, knowing the origins of the product gives the consumer a sense of belonging to the brand (Van Rijswijk & Frewer, 2008). Regarding the RQ1 (*What digital technologies do companies for the traceability of EVOO oil?*), the results for olive farms highlight the main information reported on the label and the digital tools and technologies used for EVOO oil traceability. The main information reported on the label concerns the type of extraction and the words "Made in Italy." Regarding digital technologies and traceability tools, olive farms mainly use the batch to show information to consumers. Compared to the RQ2 (*What is the perception of consumer regarding the use of technologies for the traceability of EVOO oil?*), the results highlight the importance of buying EVOO oil, which needs to be traced through specific technologies, mainly using a QR Code. Consumers also have the propensity to spend a higher price to buy EVOO oil that uses methodologies to be traced.

Combining the results of the companies' analysis with those of consumers, interesting insights emerge. First, consumers express a strong interest in oil traceability, paying particular attention to the information on the label. Indeed, the presence of information influences purchases intention (Leão & da Silva, 2021). Tools can improve companies' competitive advantages in ensuring food quality and safety (Burke, 2019). Investments geared toward greater food safety also result in greater security for those who purchase products. Consumers can feel reassured that if a company makes investments aimed at ensuring product quality and safety, as a result, those investments are an important factor that can greatly influence consumer purchases. The traceability of a product plays a key role in both the authenticity of the product and the willingness of consumers to pay more for a product with traceable information (Marozzo et al., 2022). This means that consumers today increasingly demand to be more informed than in the past when purchasing a product. The information that a product can provide, such as traceability, can be a key factor in a company's success in getting more and more consumers to buy that product. Traceability, therefore, can be identified as synonymous with greater assurance for the consumer and, at the same time, as a key element in increasing sales. Consumers consider it important and more reliable if EVOO oil uses digital tools and technologies for traceability. The consumer's preferred digital technology is the QR code, which provides relevant information about the product, directly accessing a virtual label that can show information about composition, sustainability, quality, and use (Latino et al., 2022). The QR code is an important digital technology for consumer perception because it is easy to access and provides transparency, safety, and reliability to consumers (Violino et al., 2019). The QR allows consumers to access specific information and is usually placed on the product label. The information can influence the propensity to purchase EVOO oil, but it also allows the consumer to express information regarding his or her perception of EVOO oil (Guido et al., 2020). According to studies and from the analysis of olive oil companies, the issue of traceability is still not particularly popular. Only 10 out of 30 olive oil companies provide consumers with information about the traceability of EVOO oil. To improve this, companies need to raise awareness regarding the issue of traceability, considering the considerable importance consumers attach to it, with the potential to increase revenues. On the digital side, it also emerges that companies are behind consumers, who attach particular importance to digital technologies to ensure the security of traceability systems. Only 5 out of 10 companies (dealing with traceability) use the QR Code system, which is preferred by consumers. Therefore, if companies want to try to increase their competitive advantage against more direct competitors and acquire new customers, they should invest/intervene in this aspect to meet what is an explicit demand of customers according to the results obtained from the questionnaire.

The analysis of label information shows the relationships between consumers and the companies in the sample. "Made in Italy" information was important to 65 percent of respondents and presented in 23 labels, followed by the presence of "Certifications" (requested by 42% of respondents and presented in 9 out of 30 labels). "Made in Italy" information was found to be important for 65% of respondents and featured in 23 labels, followed by the presence of "Certifications" (requested by 42% of respondents and featured in 9 out of 30 labels). Among the information on the label, the extraction method is present in 18 out of 30 labels. However, the average value of this information is very low. However, the average value of this information, as shown in Table 5 above, in terms of its importance to the consumer is 4.77. However, the average value of this information in terms of importance by consumers is 4.77. Compared to other studies, consumers do not seem to perceive this information as particularly important (Menozzi, 2014).

There are three main aspects of the gap between consumers and companies:

- Label information
- QR code
- Certification

Consumers attach high importance to these three aspects, unlike companies for whom the level of importance varies from low to medium.

This shows that companies need to increase the role of digital technologies in their operations by trying to use new methods to provide more information to consumers.

QR, through an easy-to-learn interactive approach, offers more information to help consumers understand product features, also increasing consumer trust in a specific product (Rotsios et al., 2022). Consumers are also willing to pay a higher price for products with QR codes (Violino et al., 2019). Based on the results obtained from the survey, consumers prefer to buy EVOO oil, at a higher price, mainly within supermarkets, as shown in the study by (Carlucci et al., 2014), which highlights the growth of the market share of in-store sales. Consumers today pay close attention to the information they can get about a product by using the QR code placed on the packaging. The growing focus on information has prompted companies to equip themselves with useful tools to try to meet the needs and wants of consumers. The QR code is a useful innovative element in trying to get more information that is not on the product label or packaging. The use of technology and devices allows consumers to be more informed about products and the aspects that then lead them to choose to buy that product. Traceability, for example, as seen above, is a critically important element in enabling consumers to have greater assurance in terms of product quality and health. Therefore, QR codes and other useful tools are emerging to provide certainty in terms of quality and professionalism to consumers. The use of innovative technologies and useful tools to give more information to the consumer could also enable a relationship of trust with companies that provide cutting-edge tools and methodologies that can meet the needs of consumers. In addition to the QR code, companies need to provide information using traditional methods such as labels. Labels indicate quality (Chrysochou et al., 2022), raising consumer awareness of product characteristics and environmental impact (Erraach et al., 2021). The final Figure 3 summarizes the significant findings of this research.

Figure 3. Relevance of aspects for consumer and company
Source: author's elaboration

Consumers / Companies	Label information	Lot	QR Code	Extraction	Made in Italy	Used	Certification
Label information	▲ ⊚						
Lot	⊚	⊚					
QR Code			▲ ⊚				
Extraction				⊚ ⊚			
Made in Italy					⊚ ⊚		
Used						▢ ▢	
Certification							▢ ⊚

Legend

⊚	High
▢	Medium
▲	Low

6. CONCLUSION

The objective of this research was to analyse the entire national olive-oil supply chain to understand the level of application of digital technologies by major companies in the sector, and to understand consumer perceptions regarding using digital technologies in traceability through consumer research. The analysis highlights the need for greater alignment between consumer demands in terms of label information and traceability and capacity on the part of companies to meet those demands. At the research level, it would be appropriate to further investigate the digital technologies used to share product information by focusing on consumer perception and how their use can increase awareness of product purchases. From a managerial point of view, the results, therefore, highlight the need to invest more in digital technologies, especially the QR code, to increase the trustworthiness of the products offered and reach more consumers with transparent information. Consumer trust is conditioned by the information made available by the company where the use of digital technologies can overcome the information asymmetry. At the policy level, policies can be implemented that incentivize the use of digital technologies by companies to make information more transparent and educate consumers to read and understand the information on labels. The research has some limitations. First and foremost is the sample of companies analysed. Future research must be oriented on a larger sample that allows a greater depth of the topic and completeness of data. Finally, the study involves the use of digital technologies to foster greater consumer awareness at the time of purchase. The paper highlights the importance of the use of digital technologies by olive oil companies. Their application allows companies to improve consumer awareness. Thus, consumers will buy more products from a company that uses digital technologies rather than another one that does not use them.

REFERENCES

Aparicio-Ruiz, R., Tena, N., & García-González, D. L. (2022). An International Survey on Olive Oils Quality and Traceability: Opinions from the Involved Actors. *Foods*, *11*(7), 1045. doi:10.3390/foods11071045 PMID:35407132

Ben-Ayed, R., Kamoun-Grati, N., & Rebai, A. (2013). An overview of the authentication of olive tree and oil. *Comprehensive Reviews in Food Science and Food Safety*, *12*(2), 218–227. doi:10.1111/1541-4337.12003

Biswas, A., & Roy, M. (2015). Green products: An exploratory study on the consumer behaviour in emerging economies of the East. *Journal of Cleaner Production*, *87*(1), 463–468. doi:10.1016/j.jclepro.2014.09.075

Biswas, D., Jalali, H., Ansaripoor, A. H., & de Giovanni, P. (2023). Traceability vs. sustainability in supply chains: The implications of blockchain. *European Journal of Operational Research*, *305*(1), 128–147. doi:10.1016/j.ejor.2022.05.034

Bowen, G. A. (2009). Document analysis as a qualitative research method. *Qualitative Research Journal*, *9*(2), 27–40. doi:10.3316/QRJ0902027

Brito, K. D. S., Filho, R. L. C. S., & Adeodato, P. J. L. (2021). A Systematic Review of Predicting Elections Based on Social Media Data: Research Challenges and Future Directions. In IEEE Transactions on Computational Social Systems (Vol. 8, Issue 4, pp. 819–843). Institute of Electrical and Electronics Engineers Inc. doi:10.1109/TCSS.2021.3063660

Burke, T. (2019). Blockchain in Food Traceability. In *Food Traceability* (pp. 133–143). Springer International Publishing. doi:10.1007/978-3-030-10902-8_10

Burnier, P. C., Spers, E. E., & de Barcellos, M. D. (2021). Role of sustainability attributes and occasion matters in determining consumers' beef choice. *Food Quality and Preference*, *88*, 104075. doi:10.1016/j.foodqual.2020.104075

Cao, S., Johnson, H., & Tulloch, A. (2023). Exploring blockchain-based Traceability for Food Supply Chain Sustainability: Towards a Better Way of Sustainability Communication with Consumers. *Procedia Computer Science*, *217*, 1437–1445. doi:10.1016/j.procs.2022.12.342

Carlucci, D., de Gennaro, B., Roselli, L., & Seccia, A. (2014). E-commerce retail of extra virgin olive oil: An hedonic analysis of Italian Smes supply. *British Food Journal*, *116*(10), 1600–1617. doi:10.1108/BFJ-05-2013-0138

Carlucci, D., Nocella, G., de Devitiis, B., Viscecchia, R., Bimbo, F., & Nardone, G. (2015). Consumer purchasing behaviour towards fish and seafood products. Patterns and insights from a sample of international studies. *Appetite*, *84*, 212–227. doi:10.1016/j.appet.2014.10.008 PMID:25453592

Caro, M. P., Ali, M. S., Vecchio, M., & Giaffreda, R. (2018). Blockchain-based traceability in Agri-Food supply chain management: A practical implementation. *2018 IoT Vertical and Topical Summit on Agriculture - Tuscany. IOT Tuscany*, *1–4*, 1–4. doi:10.1109/IOT-TUSCANY.2018.8373021

Carzedda, M., Gallenti, G., Troiano, S., Cosmina, M., Marangon, F., de Luca, P., Pegan, G., & Nassivera, F. (2021). Consumer preferences for origin and organic attributes of extra virgin olive oil: A choice experiment in the italian market. *Foods*, *10*(5), 994. doi:10.3390/foods10050994 PMID:34063198

Chrysochou, P., Tiganis, A., Trabelsi Trigui, I., & Grunert, K. G. (2022). A cross-cultural study on consumer preferences for olive oil. *Food Quality and Preference*, *97*, 104460. doi:10.1016/j.foodqual.2021.104460

Conti, M. (2022). EVO-NFC: Extra Virgin Olive Oil Traceability Using NFC Suitable for Small-Medium Farms. *IEEE Access : Practical Innovations, Open Solutions*, *10*, 20345–20356. doi:10.1109/ACCESS.2022.3151795

Corallo, A., Latino, M. E., Menegoli, M., Pizzi, R., Fanelli, R. M., Pereira-Lorenzo, S., María, A., & Cabrer, R. (2021). *Assuring Effectiveness in Consumer-Oriented Traceability*. Suggestions for Food Label Design. doi:10.3390/agronomy

Erraach, Y., Jaafer, F., Radić, I., & Donner, M. (2021). Sustainability labels on olive oil: A review on consumer attitudes and behavior. In Sustainability (Switzerland) (Vol. 13, Issue 21). MDPI. doi:10.3390u132112310

Flowerdew, R., & Martin, D. (2005). *A guide for students doing a research project*. Pearson Education. www.pearsoned.co.uk

Garaus, M., & Treiblmaier, H. (2021). The influence of blockchain-based food traceability on retailer choice: The mediating role of trust. *Food Control*, *129*, 108082. doi:10.1016/j.foodcont.2021.108082

Giua, C., Materia, V. C., & Camanzi, L. (2022). Smart farming technologies adoption: Which factors play a role in the digital transition? *Technology in Society*, *68*, 101869. Advance online publication. doi:10.1016/j.techsoc.2022.101869

Guido, R., Mirabelli, G., Palermo, E., & Solina, V. (2020). A framework for food traceability: Case study-Italian extra-virgin olive oil supply chain. *International Journal of Industrial Engineering and Management*, *11*(1), 50–60. doi:10.24867/IJIEM-2020-1-252

Gupta, N., Soni, G., Mittal, S., Mukherjee, I., Ramtiyal, B., & Kumar, D. (2023). Evaluating Traceability Technology Adoption in Food Supply Chain: A Game Theoretic Approach. *Sustainability (Switzerland)*, *15*(2), 898. doi:10.3390u15020898

Ismea. (2021). *SCHEDA DI SETTORE: OLIO DI OLIVA giugno 2021*. ISMEA.

Ktari, J., Frikha, T., Chaabane, F., Hamdi, M., & Hamam, H. (2022). Agricultural Lightweight Embedded Blockchain System: A Case Study in Olive Oil. *Electronics (Switzerland)*, *11*(20), 3394. doi:10.3390/electronics11203394

Latino, M. E., Menegoli, M., Lazoi, M., & Corallo, A. (2022). Voluntary traceability in food supply chain: A framework leading its implementation in Agriculture 4.0. *Technological Forecasting and Social Change*, *178*, 121564. doi:10.1016/j.techfore.2022.121564

Leão, P., & da Silva, M. M. (2021). Impacts of digital transformation on firms' competitive advantages: A systematic literature review. *Strategic Change*, *30*(5), 421–441. doi:10.1002/jsc.2459

Liberatore, L., Casolani, N., & Murmura, F. (2018). What's behind organic certification of extra-virgin olive oil? A response from Italian consumers. *Journal of Food Products Marketing*, *24*(8), 946–959. doi:10.1080/10454446.2018.1426513

Likert, R. (1932). A technique for the measurement of attitudes. *Archives de Psychologie*.

Lisienkova, T., N., L., K., & R., K. (2022). A Model for Digital Innovation Assessment and Selection. *IV International Scientific Conference "INTERAGROMASH 2021"*. Springer. 10.1007/978-3-030-81619-3_93

Lozano-Castellón, J., López-Yerena, A., Domínguez-López, I., Siscart-Serra, A., Fraga, N., Sámano, S., López-Sabater, C., Lamuela-Raventós, R. M., Vallverdú-Queralt, A., & Pérez, M. (2022). Extra virgin olive oil: A comprehensive review of efforts to ensure its authenticity, traceability, and safety. *Comprehensive Reviews in Food Science and Food Safety*, *21*(3), 2639–2664. doi:10.1111/1541-4337.12949 PMID:35368142

Majeed, M., Asare, C., Fatawu, A., & Abubakari, A. (2022). An analysis of the effects of customer satisfaction and engagement on social media on repurchase intention in the hospitality industry. *Cogent Business and Management*, *9*(1), 2028331. doi: 10.1080/23311975.2022.2028331

Marozzo, V., Vargas-Sánchez -Tindara, A., Augusto, A., & Amico, D. (2022). Investigating the importance of product traceability in the relationship between product authenticity and consumer willingness to pay 1. *Italian Journal of Management, 40.*

Martini, D., & Menozzi, D. (2021). Food labeling: Analysis, understanding, and perception. *Nutrients*, *13*(1), 1–5. doi:10.3390/nu13010268 PMID:33477758

Mellens, M., Dekimpe, M., & Steenkamp, J. (1996). A review of brand-loyalty measures in marketing. *Tijdschrift Voor Economie En Management*, *4*, 507–533.

Menozzi, D. (2014). Extra-virgin olive oil production sustainability in northern Italy: A preliminary study. *British Food Journal, 116*(12), 1942–1959. doi:10.1108/BFJ-06-2013-0141

MIPAF. (2016). *Piano di settore olivicolo-oleario*. MIPAF.

Monfared, R. (2016). Blockchain ready manufacturing supply chain using distributed ledger. In *Accepted to the International Journal of Research in Engineering and Technology-IJRET* (Issue 09). https://esatjournals.net/ijret/2016v05/i09/IJRET20160509001.pdfMetadataRecord:https://dspace.lboro.ac.uk/2134/22625

Parra-López, C., Reina-Usuga, L., Carmona-Torres, C., Sayadi, S., & Klerkx, L. (2021). Digital transformation of the agrifood system: Quantifying the conditioning factors to inform policy planning in the olive sector. *Land Use Policy*, *108*, 105537. doi:10.1016/j.landusepol.2021.105537

Polenzani, B., Riganelli, C., & Marchini, A. (2020). Sustainability perception of local extra virgin olive oil and consumers' attitude: A new Italian perspective. *Sustainability (Switzerland)*, *12*(3), 920. Advance online publication. doi:10.3390u12030920

Power, M. (2019). Infrastructures of traceability. *Thinking Infrastructures*, *62*, 115–130. doi:10.1108/S0733-558X20190000062007

Rotsios, K., Konstantoglou, A., Folinas, D., Fotiadis, T., Hatzithomas, L., & Boutsouki, C. (2022). Evaluating the Use of QR Codes on Food Products. *Sustainability (Switzerland)*, *14*(8), 4437. doi:10.3390u14084437

Sarfraz, M., Hamid, S., Rawstorne, P., Ali, M., & Jayasuriya, R. (2021). Role of social network in decision making for increasing uptake and continuing use of long acting reversible (LARC) methods in Pakistan. *Reproductive Health*, *18*(1), 96. doi:10.118612978-021-01149-0 PMID:34001169

Schwägele, F. (2005). Traceability from a European perspective. *Meat Science, 71*(1), 164–173. doi:10.1016/j.meatsci.2005.03.002 PMID:22064062

Tharatipyakul, A., & Pongnumkul, S. (2021). User Interface of Blockchain-Based Agri-Food Traceability Applications: A Review. *IEEE Access: Practical Innovations, Open Solutions, 9*, 82909–82929. doi:10.1109/ACCESS.2021.3085982

Theodoridis, P. K., & Zacharatos, T. (2022). Food waste during Covid-19 lockdown period and consumer behaviour – The case of Greece. *Socio-Economic Planning Sciences, 83*, 101338. doi:10.1016/j.seps.2022.101338

Van Rijswijk, W., & Frewer, L. J. (2008). Consumer perceptions of food quality and safety and their relation to traceability. *British Food Journal, 110*(10), 1034–1046. doi:10.1108/00070700810906642

Violino, S., Pallottino, F., Sperandio, G., Figorilli, S., Antonucci, F., Ioannoni, V., Fappiano, D., & Costa, C. (2019). Are the innovative electronic labels for extra virgin olive oil sustainable, traceable, and accepted by consumers? *Foods, 8*(11), 529. doi:10.3390/foods8110529 PMID:31731433

Violino, S., Pallottino, F., Sperandio, G., Figorilli, S., Ortenzi, L., Tocci, F., Vasta, S., Imperi, G., & Costa, C. (2020). A full technological traceability system for extra virgin olive oil. *Foods, 9*(5), 624. doi:10.3390/foods9050624 PMID:32414115

Xue, L., Weiwei, G., Zettan, F., Peng, X., & Weiguang, L. (2007). Traceability and IT: Implications for the future international competitiveness and structure of China's vegetable sector. *New Zealand Journal of Agricultural Research, 50*(5), 911–917. doi:10.1080/00288230709510367

Yin, S., Li, Y., Xu, Y., Chen, M., & Wang, Y. (2017). Consumer preference and willingness to pay for the traceability information attribute of infant milk formula: Evidence from a choice experiment in China. *British Food Journal, 119*(6), 1276–1288. doi:10.1108/BFJ-11-2016-0555

Chapter 7
Study on a Mediation Model of New Brands Entering Competitive Markets Through to the Experience Sharing, Skill Teaching, and Value Perception

Liu Xinyu
Universidade Católica Portuguesa, Portugal

Liu Minghui
Guangzhou College of Technology and Business, China

ABSTRACT

The rapid growing of social media has created many live-influencers and playing an important role to leading consumer for new brand cognition in competitive market. This chapter examines the influence factors of experience sharing, skill teaching and value perception by live-influencer for a new brand enter into a competitive market. The result shows that the live-influencer's experience sharing (H1a), skill teaching (H1b), and value perception (H1c) are positive influences to customer loyalty; the live-influencer are negative influences to consumer brand satisfaction (H2); the live-influencer's customer loyalty are positive influences to consumer brand satisfaction (H3), which indicates that the live-influencer become a new mediation model and playing important role for new brand in consumer loyalty and consumer satisfaction.

DOI: 10.4018/978-1-6684-8351-0.ch007

1. INTRODUCTION

1.1 Research Background

In an era of over-information, a variety of brand information have appeared to confuse consumers (Pascual, P.A.C,2009). The new brands are facing on competitive market challenges nowadays (Wang, 2019). The effective of communication channels are important on brand (Bilgin, Y, 2018). At other hand, the rapid growing of the social media has created many communication channels which bring conveniences communication (López & Francisco,2020). The live-influencer is become a critical guide to the consumer brand cognition in their professional filed, and monopolize some of the major consumer markets. Among live-influencer are the professional musicians, accomplished dancers, elderly computer programmers, experienced lawyers, and engineers whose professional experience has drawn the attention of professionals (Christov et al., 2020). Through the live broadcast was attracted thousands of customers (Shi, 2018). And the customers have learned many special skills from professional experiences, sharing and making them a higher level in the professional field. While sharing their experiences on live, celebrity products recommendations are often lead consumers experience in superiority rather than advertising, because professional followers are feeling its value and they are very expected to reach the professional realm (Sousa et al., 2019). As a result, an intermediary media channel belonging to the live-influencer and consumer's brand cognition has been established, such that the product endorsement of internet celebrities has monopolized the consumer market of some professional products (Xue et al., 2022).

In the past, marketing emphasized how to let more consumers understand the brand and products in a wider and more comprehensive way, just like moveable bus advertisements and TV advertisements. Such accurate and efficient publicity, a better method than aimless publicity?

This article takes influencers as an example to explore whether it is a more efficient marketing method for brands to choose influencers promotions that match the product background when promoting on social media.

1.2 Research Topic

Internet marketing in China has been growing rapidly, bringing $1.1 billion in revenue to the brand market (CB insight 2020, P.P& Albaum 2019). Huge revenue for brand marketing brings a happy win-win situation. On the one hand, brand value is converted, different sales channels are added, sales volume increases greatly, enterprises get working capital, can be more in product development and the brand can have better development prospects. On the other hand, brand value is quickly found by the intermediaries generated by the Internet to direct consumers. As the case, modern Internet technology brings an important role for brands to open the market quickly.

The expeditious development of internet business has driven the phenomenal growth of online marketing in China and has effectively guided consumers in a competitive marketplace, which becoming the new media intermediary (López & Francisco,2020). In today, the age of over information is bringing many marketing messages and anesthetize consumers, and pose a challenge to brand marketing (Pascual, P.A.C,2009). When internet user has reaching to everyone that a new media approach has been born, the live-influencer is becoming one of new intermediary in social media. The emergence of new media intermediaries is bringing revolutionary change, the manufacturers focus on product research without worry about selling, consumers buy satisfactory products without worry about quality, and financial and insurance industries have established new businesses (Christov et al., 2020). Live-influencers have created a new and more directly communicative channel in media intermediary, whereby manufacturers market their products, consumers buy the products they want, and banks build emerging financial businesses especially for online shopping, creating an interactive community medium (Wang, 2019).

The Internet infrastructure connects everyone and spreads information and contents to every corner of the world, so that every mobile phone user can obtain the latest information anytime and anywhere, satisfy in reading information or interesting gossip whether working or off (Xue et al., 2022); The new features of social media have created many colorful pages and convenience functions for everyone present in live-streaming platforms, such as Facebook, Twitter, TikTok, and Kwai. Under the new features, one of the new professions has appeared and called live influencer from emerging industry. As a competitive media market and various incentive programs are promoted, live-influencer has been encouraged to set up his own special program, product team or creative agency (Sousa et al,.2019). Under the promotion, different topic programs are created, such as travel, music, dance, teaching, cooking, healthy, which attract thousands of customers with different interests and addictive hobbies. In business, live influencer cooperate with advertisers or production businesses to present their using experiences and special features of products while broadcasting, such intriguing programs affect the customers' interest and shopping intention (Pascual, P.A.C,2009). As a result, some customers turning into consumers, and live influencer bring benefits to the customers and bring promotions to the merchants.

However, not all the live-influencers are favored by consumers, over-advertising must be displeased customers and will not attract consumers, so the role of live-influencer is extraordinary (López & Francisco,2020). To be successful, of influencer must consider a strong target audience, such as young female makeup lovers or middle-aged people who care about health. With audience who have high demand, strong consumption ability and are more concerned about new things, and these factors drive the live-influencers agency and brand marketing. As the condition, live-influencer as varied and endless just like a team behind a TV station, which it's the key element to keeping survive and attracting customers. This not only relies on the personal ability, but the novelty of program topic, the creative soul of the team and the financial support to successfully bring out the influence of the influencers. Only these exquisite inputs for the content creation that can attract customers, play a role in guiding consumers, and attract advertisers to come to negotiate business cooperation.

1.3 Research Objective

In summary, with the rapid development of social media, a new profession called live-influencer has emerged, and it's playing an increasingly important role in social communication. The live-influencers become a new communication channel and a very important intermediaries to brand marketing, and there is a shortage of research literature on influence factors. Therefore, the paper considers to analyzes the mainly influence factors related to the attraction between live-influencer and customers.

The influence factors of live-influencers are involving psychology, communication and marketing, that we consider from the psychology, the communication from live-influencers to customers, and the overall reaction between live-influencers and customers. As the research objective is to investigate the relationship between experience sharing, skill teaching and value perceptions of webcasters on consumer brand satisfaction.

(The research model is shows in following Figure 1).

Figure 1. Intermediary media

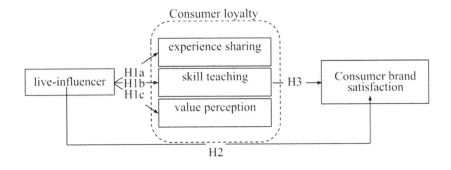

Base to above figure, live-influencer presenting to web customers for the experience sharing (H1a), skill teaching (H1b) and value perception (H1c), these factors are attracts customers who gain useful skill and knowledge, that mean it's an influences relationship; On the other hand, live-influencer are guiding customers to generate first-hand experience and purchase intentions, which means that it's an mutual influence relationship (H2), and the amount of influence determines whether the influence relationship is established; Consumers are satisfied with the brand's understanding, that mean it's another influence relationship between live-influencer, customers loyalty and consumer brand satisfaction (H3). Which indicate that the live-influencer become a new mediation model and playing an important role for brand market.

In the framework, we mainly consider the influencing factors of live-influencer, because there is a shortage of literature review in this emerging phenomenon. The influencing factors are considered on experience sharing (H1a), skill teaching (H1b) and value perception (H1c) as main hypothesis. For the customer loyalty and customer satisfaction are rich literature references (Oliver, R.L., 1999) (Farris, Paul W, et al., 2010), that we are considered as references standard. The consider factors are the reaction of new intermediary media by live-influencer to customer loyalty and satisfaction (H3). The second hypothesis (H2) are considered in general reaction by which excludes experience sharing (H1a), skill teaching (H1b) and value perception (H1c), the consideration are compares that different kind of influences factors, which indicate the live-influencers become a new communication channel and an important intermediary to brand marketing.

2. LITERATURE REVIEW

2.1 The Brand, Intermediaries, and New Media

The brand is defined as the name, symbol, design or feature that distinguishes good or service for seller (Jacoby. J., 1971). In consumer marketing, the brands provide primary differentiation which offerings competitive advantages (Wood, L, 2000). The brand effect can create stronger and higher level in competitive market (Chailan. C., 2008). The intermediary services are helping brand in more successful in competitive market (Moor, L., 2008).

The channel of intermediaries constitutes a key marketing asset in competitive market (Rao, V. R., et al., 1989). The intermediaries enabling brand to reach out direct customers and saving middle cost, some of brand event reliance on channel intermediaries in competitive market (Chung, C., et al., 2012). Therefore, there is a crucial interactive relationship between brands and intermediaries.

The new media is defined as new communication and technologies that reports and commentary events are distributed to the public (McKewon, E., 2012). New media bring new competition between the traditional media and internet media (Dimmick, J; Chen, Y; Li, Z 2004). News media provide a service package to consumers, additionally value added in entertainment and advertising (Baumann, 2015). The media is active and creative attractive information for learners in motivating understander (Indrasari, et al., 2018). With the rapidly development, live-influencer are appeared in new media with promotional condition.

The influencer is defines as third parties with strong influence over an organization (Harris, M. 2000). With the technique updating of news media, live streaming platform become popular features that convenient for the influencers and brands connect with their audience in real-time (Saatchi, S. S., et al.,2007). Live influencers become host live streams while showing off their favorite products (Hayes, N., 2008). Live influencers create live presentation, wonderful video and dramatic story for attract followers, which it is based on attractive volume for seeking cooperation partner from the advertisers, brands or media intermediaries.

In the business model of new media, the new characteristics changing industry and bring new competition (Croteau, D., et al., 2006). The intermediaries' considerations are the effective market respond and hot consumer groups (Feaster, J. C. 2009). For the brand's commercial consideration are the direct marketing and effective publicity rather than expensive advertising (Liao, et al., 2011). As the case, the number of customer becomes the main cooperation condition, and the changes encourage live-influencers to post exclusive content not available on other channels attracts more followers.

Live-influencers have to collect useful knowledge, authority argument or even some of inciting view the helping to increase engagement and retention across the platform (Tan, Y., et al., 2018). Live streaming can direct connection to followers, show off new fashion, fresh gossip, and live questions answer. (Zietek, N., 2016). Live-Influencers can help customers gain more and more trust and authenticity (Backaler, J., et al., 2018). The niche market has makes the media become useful launching pad and brand credibility (Bakshy, E., et al., 2011). Competitive market urges the live-influencers have to keeping creation and attraction, customer loyalty and satisfaction become the main goals.

2.2 Customer Loyalty and Customer Satisfaction

The customer loyalty is defined as a commitment to re-purchasing products or re-services (Oliver, R.L., 1999). Customer loyalty is regarded as crucial management to effective marketing (Migacz, S.J, 2017). In order to holding influences and market efforts, the loyalty extends to emotional relationships and customer satisfaction.

The customer satisfaction is defined as exceeds specified satisfaction goals by the number of customers (Farris, Paul W, et al.,2010). Customer satisfaction is commonly conceptualized as an emotional or cognitive reaction (Giese, J. L., et al., 2000).

Customer satisfaction is one of necessary condition for customer loyalty (Oliver, R.L., 1999). The perceived value of loyalty factor are customers give and receive process (Dick & Basu, 1994). Customer satisfaction and loyalty provide the perceived foundation for high level of customer value (Heskett, J. L, 2002). Therefore, the influencing factors of live-influencer are the basis condition for building fan loyalty, and only these basic conditions can carry out powerful attraction for brand intermediaries.

2.3 The Influence of Live-Influencer on Customer Loyalty

In order to building influencing factors, the live-influence have tried extraordinary to play in different sense (De Jans et al., 2019). Making same level of image and influence as celebs sense (Khamis et al., 2017). In the webcast account pages, live-influencer having great number of followers on one or more platforms (De Veirman, et al., 2019). New media allows online celebrities to broadcast live and set up their own personal online shops, live-influencer can sell "product windows" for more exposure in different platforms (Liao, 2022).

As competition intense, brands have to adjust and changed feature for customers (Ghodeswar, 2008). Social communication aim to user interactive sharing and discussing (Kaplan & Haenlein, 2010).

Due to the pandemic, people spend more time at home and use the internet to connect to the outside world. During the shutdown due to the COVID-19 pandemic, TikTok became the most downloaded app in the world. Everyone put more attention on applications with social properties, like TikTok and DouYin (Chinese version of TikTok). With the entertainment of short videos and live streaming and the ability to socialize with the outside world, more and more people spend more time on them. Applications like TikTok have gained space and importance in human sociality habits, which the Social Sciences cannot ignore (Duarte & Dias, 2021).

The new media creating new features are attracted a number of customers which have become a benefit-chain for manufacturer, brands, intermediaries and services brokers. The customer loyalty and satisfaction become the goal of live-celebrities, the experience sharing, skill teaching and value perception are attractive to customers.

2.3.1 The Experience Sharing

The experience sharing is defined as the process of obtaining core value experience and value creation from those who have experience (Chen., et al., 2012). The brand experience concept can be traced back to Hirschman and Holbrook (1982) with consumption experiences, the experiential view can be based on the symbolic, hedonic, and esthetic nature. Experience sharing bring valuable perception and useful information sources for user, which enabling users to gain advantages in the workplace or professional field (Bae, S. J, et al., 2017).

Experience sharing is the special skill of live-influencer, the creative characters of live-influencer are extraordinary, and the source of attraction starts from the simple story, through a little bit of life process and emotional interpretation, thus attracting the attention of similar people. Then, they share their personal experiences, introduce some key professional skills, and teach the secrets of success to attract many customers in understanding, those detail process are making valuable perception for customs.

Experience sharing enhances customer loyalty, the credibility of internet influencer can moderate the impact of interactivity on emotional attachment and directly impacts brand trustworthiness (Jun & Yi, 2020). On the brand trustworthiness, the increasing acknowledgement of the prominence of brand loyalty in business performance, and the follower's emotional attachment to the influencer's brand have increases brand loyalty through brand trustworthiness (Chinomona, R., et al., 2013). Therefore, experience sharing has a strong influence on the effective attraction of followers.

2.3.2 The Skill Teaching

The teaching skill is defined as special teaching model which pedagogical, technological, and social characteristics increase student learning, achievement, and the ability to apply knowledge (Shavelson, R. J. 1973). The skill teaching is different with teaching skill, and skill teaching defined as one of special teaching facilitate higher levels of understanding between knowledge and skill (Hiebert, J., et al., 1996).

The skill teaching plays in important role for everyone (Henry et al., 2019). Everyone should be positive and aggressive to keep changing and developing, to learn and accept knowledge, and to improve our abilities. The importance of knowledge and useful for professional development in life (Sivarajah, et al., 2019). As human science evolves and knowledge expands, everyone may not have all the knowledge, but learning the key skills in specialized subjects will effectively enhance one's own specialized field.

The experienced teachers is very important to student, teacher skill is an effectively educate and academic taught, where educators typically have the foundational knowledge and key skills to serve trainees based on extensive experience (Henry et al., 2019). The ability to solve problems is a fundamental human cognitive and student process (Rahman, 2019). In particular, teaching key components play an important role for workplace workers, because they can learn and using immediacy. Therefore, experienced teachers and smart teaching methods live up to their reputation.

New media creates convenient teaching to enhance everyone's interest in learning, online teaching is widely used in schools and students can learn useful knowledge from all over the world (Spiteri, M., S. N., 2020). Increased knowledge skills can strengthen self-confidence, improve the acquisition of professional skills, promote research attitudes, (Hardway, C. L., & Stroud, M. (2014).

For those reasons, live influencer provides customers with certain professional knowledge, and that knowledge allows customers to grow in knowledge and forms a good attraction for customers. live-influencer presenting their experience sharing, skill teaching can help customers to gain useful skill and knowledge. When live-influencer teaches customers to focus on attention ways to enhance the professional skills, it will make them gain a lot of knowledge.

2.3.3 The Value Perceptions

The value perception is defined as the perspective or opinion of some thing or factors, in brand marketing, perceived value used to evaluation or expectations for product or service (Doyle, P., 2000). The evaluation or expectations can be dynamic because all people doing is learn about their values in different contexts (Adler, F., 1956).

The value perception is primarily a decision of financial and non-financial factors that drive customer adoption or rejection of the product (Doyle, P., 2000). Value perceptions change due to use of products, service processes, cultural values and regional norms (Overby, J. W., 2005).

The degree of value of a country based on the degree of its cultural and economic development (Aaker et al., 1982). The brand perception in the context of social media market is depends on consumer engagement and the luxury fashion of the brand (Park, et al., 2020).

Summarize the literature, the live-influencer presenting for customers the experience sharing (H1a), skill teaching (H1b) and value perception (H1c) with obvious influence factors, and the factors attract customers who gain useful skill knowledge and become loyal relationships. And also guiding customers generating firsthand experience and purchase intention, and the identity to become consumer. Base on above analysis that the following hypothesis is formulated:

Hypothesis 1 (H1): Live-influencer presenting for customers the experience sharing (H1a), skill teaching (H1b) and value perception (H1c) are positive influence on customers loyalty.

2.4 The Influence of Live-Influencer on Consumer Brand Satisfaction

Customer satisfaction is a necessary condition for marketing (Oliver, 1999). Consumer satisfaction is usually a reflection of customer perception and evaluation (Giese, J. L., et al., 2000). New media brings positive convenience but also has negative effects (Feiz, D., et al., 2013). New media also challenges to traditional communication (Du, R. Y., et al., 2019).

In today's era of over-information, variety advertising has confused to everyone consumers (Pascual, P.A.C.,2009). Information pollution, knowledge overload and mass spam lead to paralysis (Bray, D. A. 2008). The negative discussion will reduce the target evaluation (Pinkleton, B., 1997).

Business sponsorship helps social events grow (Menon, S., et al., 2003). Business sponsorship can be an effective advertising and managing tool to generate a positive reaction toward an advertiser and improve product quality, category leadership, customer responsiveness and even purchase intention (Becker, et al., 2003). Business advertising is the effective force for push of social activity growing (Meenaghan, T., 2001). Business sponsorship is an interaction between culture and economy, and there is a positive correlation between it and market value(Conchar, Crask and Zinkhan 2005). Business sponsorship can effectively support to the development of live-influencer.

Perceived value provides stronger explanation for customer loyalty (Dick and Basu, 1994). Customer satisfaction lays the foundation value for high levels of customer (Heskett, J. L, 2002). In other hand, business advertising and selling behavior of live-influencer are trending to negative impact on customer impression, which directly affects customer satisfaction.

At the same time, Business advertising are the basis condition for survival and development, the live-influencers have to balance opportunities and challenges. As the case, the study proposes a hypothesis to examine the direct advertising-response relationship between live-influencer and consumer brand satisfaction. Based on the analysis that the following hypothesis is advanced:

Hypothesis 2 (H2): Live-influencer are negative influence on consumer brand satisfaction.

2.5 The Influence of Live-Influencer's Customers Loyalty on Consumer Brand Satisfaction

Customer satisfaction is a necessary condition for customer loyalty (Oliver, R.L., 1999). That means its interactive influence factors between live-influencer, customer loyalty and customer satisfaction. The live-influencer playing an extraordinary role.

Consumers' brand loyalty is composed of brand product, quality, service, satisfaction, trust and preference factors (Chinomona. R., et al., 2013). Brand service quality has a direct influences on consumer brand trust and brand satisfaction, and brand trust and brand satisfaction are playing a balancing role in the relationship between brand product, service quality and brand loyalty (Feiz, D., et al., 2013). The consumption experiences can by a phenomenon directed toward the pursuit of fantasies, feelings, and fun (Hirschman, Holbrook, 1982). The brand experience is influence on brand equity and brand satisfaction, and provide unique features and emotional elements that create strong relationship and competitive advantage between brand and customers (Lin, Y. H., 2015).

The influences of brand awareness and social customs on customers perceived online privacy risks (Wang, E.S.Tse., 2019). The experience sharing and skill teaching of live-influencer through to live broadcast is effectively attracts customers and builds loyalty. After the customers perceive the value that generating firsthand experience and purchase intention, they are converted into consumers, guiding consumers is realized, so live-influencer becomes a new media intermediary. And consumer's understanding of the brand and value perception factors make consumers satisfied with the results and maximize consumer brand satisfaction. Hence, the following hypothesis is formulated:

Hypothesis 3 (H3): Live-influencer's customers loyalties are positive influence on consumer brand satisfaction.

In the hypothesis, we mainly consider the key influencing factors of live-influencer because it's lack of literature review. For the customer loyalty and customer satisfaction are rich literature references (Oliver, R.L., 1999) (Farris, Paul W, et al., 2010), that we are considered as references standard. And the consideration is tried to explains that the influencing factors for a new brand enter a competitive market in an era of over-information.

3. METHODOLOGY

3.1 Study Case

In order to test above hypotheses, the study conducts a set of questionnaire interviews with customers through the popular questionnaire survey software Star-Questionnaire. The software provides structured questionnaires to mobile phone users via an Internet link. The test recruits online mobile phone users as participants and answers questions through snowball sampling in the software (Goodman, L. A., 1961). When receiving system information and willing to participate in the questionnaire, the user can click on the link to enter the questionnaire star page, the interface and transfer to the questionnaire system page, and can directly answer the questionnaire questions. Participants who successfully completed the questionnaire were rewarded with 10 e-points as thanks for their responses.

Consider the factors of using the software as it is a new media achievement that fulfills the research needs. Its functionality is connected to each customer (mobile user), which was chosen as the channel to test the customer's reaction, since they are the most common customers on the new medium (Kenney et al., 2000). Mobile users can know the live influencers very well, as well as evaluate what live influencers do to mobile users, and directly obtain the relationship among perceived value (Chen., et al., 2012), loyalty (Hiebert, J., et al., 1996) and satisfaction (Doyle, P., 2000). The purpose of the survey is to broadcast the response parameters among perceived value, loyalty and satisfaction in Live-influencer. 800 questionnaires (100%) were sent out, 132 (16.5%) could not be returned within the specified period, 99 (12.4%) were opened online but had no reply, and 116 (7.6%) had incomplete responses and were considered invalid. Finally, A total of 509 (63.6%) participants completed the online survey.

For the questionnaire design, A three-part survey was designed from above purposes. Part 1 contained two filtering questions: "What are your hobbies in your spare time?" (exclude illegal behavior) and "Who is your live-influencer (idol)?". Part 2 contained items measuring the consumer brand satisfaction with three focal constructs, experience sharing, skill teaching and value perceptions: "Which type of theme live broadcast is your favorite?", "What kind knowledge you learned?" and "Have you ever used the skill in real life?". Part 3 collectes the demographic information, such as gender, age, education, monthly income.

The test constructs were based on the literature, and the construct in the setting of mediation model with some of minor adjustments to more suits the context of influence factors. That are the experience sharing, skill teaching and value perception have been adopted by the above literature. All of the variables were measured by using five-item with Likert scales and measured by means of a five-item scale (Rubin et al., 1985). The consumer brand satisfaction was measured by means of a 10-item scale.

In the present study all variables were measured by using five-point scales (Rubin et al., 1985); which from (1) strongly disagree to (5) strongly agree. The control variables are; Gender (male = 1, female = 2), age (<20 = 1, 21–30 = 2, 31–40 = 3, 41–50 = 4, >51 = 5) educational level (Secondary School = 1, High School = 2, Bachelor's degree = 3, Master's degree = 4, PhD or above= 5) and total income

(CNY3000(USD 462) or less = 1, CNY3001(USD 463) to CNY6000 (USD 924) = 2, CNY6001 (USD 925) to CNY9000 (USD 1386) = 3,CNY9001(USD 1387) or more = 4) were used as control variables. A few of the bivariate correlations between control variables and test results were statistically significant (Table 2).

3.2 Data Collection

Table 1 is providing a detailed summary of the sample characteristics. The sample was almost evenly split between men (50.1%) and women (49.9%), the mean age

Table 1. Sample overview

Variables	n (%), n=509
Gender	
Male	255 (50.1%)
Female	254 (49.9%)
Age	
20 years or younger	49 (9.6%)
21–30 years	193(37.5%)
31–40 years	122(24.0%)
41–50 years	87(19.1%)
51 years or Above	55(9.8%)
Education	
Secondary School or below	46 (9.1%)
High School	129(25.3%)
Bachelor's degree	277(54.4%)
Master's degree	54 (11.2%)
PhD or above	3 (0.6%)
Monthly income	
CNY3000(USD 462) or less	96 (18.9%)
CNY3001(USD 463) to CNY6000 (USD 924)	147(28.9%)
CNY6001 (USD 925) to CNY9000 (USD 1386)	232(45.6%)
CNY9001(USD 1387) or more	34 (6.7%)

Table 2. Descriptive statistics and correlations

	Mean	SD	1	2	3	4	5	6	7
1. Gender	1.52	0.401							
2. Age	32.8	11.23	-.41						
3. Education	3.93	0.792	.028	-1.07					
4. Monthly-income	2.02	1.12	-.91	.39	.09				
5. Experiences-share	2.27	.71	.07	.01	-.05	-.01			
6. Skill-teaching	2.52	.97	.042	**-.29**	**-.08**	-.16	-.03		
7. Value-perception	2.31	.61	.031	**-.12**	**-.09**	-.05	**.51**	**.40**	
8. Customer-satisfaction	1.93	.42	.037	-.03	-.02	-.03	**.53**	**.12**	**.67**

*$P<.05$, **$P<.01$

of participants is 32.2 years old (SD = 11.23) where 9.6% are 20 years or younger, 37.5% are between 21 and 30 years old, 24.0% are between 31 and 40 years old, 19.1% are between 41 and 50 years old, 9.8% are older than 51 years. Regarding to participants' educational level, 9.1% in Secondary School or below, 25.3% are in high school, 54.4% are in Bachelor's degree, 11.2% are in Master's degree, PhD or above are 0.6%. In terms of the monthly income 18.9% ranged between CNY3000(USD 462) or less, 28.9% ranged between CNY3001(USD 463) to CNY6000 (USD 924), 45.6% ranged between CNY6001 (USD 925) to CNY9000 (USD 1386) and 6.7% are more than CNY9001(USD 1387).

3.3 Analysis

IBM SPSS v.27 was used in this case study, the software was used to generate descriptive statistics and perform data analysis, and examine the convergent and discriminant validity of the measures. The reliability result was assessed using Cronbach's alpha and factor loading, the average variance extracted (AVE) values were used to assess convergent validity (Nunnally, 1978; Fornell & Larcker 1981). The more commonly used rule is that when the scale is designed using EFA first, then the confirmatory factor is more significant (Worthington et al., 2006; Norris et al., 2009).

The reliability analysis was based on Cronbach's Alpha, and the test was use for the measure of internal consistency. It was considered for surveys that contain multiple Likert questions and test scales against them (Nunnally, 1978). The average variance extracted (AVE) was used to measure the amount of variance captured by the structure relative to the amount of variance caused by measurement error (Fornell & Larcker 1981). Exploratory factor analysis (EFA) was used to analyze potential relationships between measured variables (Norris et al., 2009). Confirmatory factor analysis (CFA) was used to determine the desired number of factors in the data and the association of measured variables with latent variables (Kline, R. B. 2010).

The analysis using AMOS 25 software to exam the convergent and discriminant validity of these measures. The test provide model fit indices values for assess the model following fit indices, and the results show that the model determined a good fit to the data (CMIN=0.735, CMIN/Df=2.125, GFI=0.921, AGFI=.962, CFI=.913, TLI=.071, RMSEA=.050). The standardized coefficients are significant range in 0.50 to 0.962 which shows the present model fits the data support to the structure.

Above table 2 lists out the means, standard deviations, and correlations for all variables.

4. RESULTS

The above findings indicate that the live-influencer's experience sharing (H1a) ($\beta = .51$, p < .001), skill teaching (H1b) ($\beta = .70$, p < .001) and value perception (H1c) ($\beta = .62$, p < .001) are positively influences to customer loyalty ($\beta = .70$, p < .001) (Table 3), which mean the hypothesis 1 is supported; The live-influencer are negatively influences to consumer brand satisfaction (H2) ($\beta = -.15$, p < .001), which mean the hypothesis 2 is rejected; The live-influencer's customer loyalty are positively influences to consumer brand satisfaction (H3) ($\beta = .61$, p < .001), As a result, the hypothesis 3 is supported.

Table 3. Result of direct and indirect effects

Direct Effects	Std.Beat	SE	Sig	Hypothesis	
Experiences sharing -> SBB	0.51	0.02	P<.001	H1a	Supported
Skill teaching -> SBB	0.70	0.05	P<.001	H1b	Supported
Value perception -> SBB	0.62	0.03	P<.001	H1c	Supported
Mediation paths	**Std.Beat**	**SE**	**Bootstrap 95% Confidence**		
			BootLLCI	BootULCI	
live-influencer -> SBB	-0.15	0.02	0.01	0.01 H2	Rejected
live-influencer -> loyalty-> SBB	0.61	0.03	0.21	0.26 H3	Supported

The result shows that the live-influencer's experience sharing (H1a), skill teaching (H1b) and value perception (H1c) are positive influences to customer loyalty; The live-influencer are negative influences to consumer brand satisfaction (H2); The results are indicated that different kind of influences factors by live-influencer. The live-influencer's customer loyalty are positively influences to consumer brand satisfaction (H3), which indicates the live-influencers playing an important role in social communication and become an important intermediary to brand marketing.

5. DISCUSSION

In today's age of information overload, a flood of brand advertising confuses consumers (Pascual, P.A.C,2009). The new brands are facing on competitive market challenges (Wang, 2019). The market situation is not conducive to brand marketing, making it difficult for brand investment to convert market value, even the aspect is unfavorable to business operation, social development and regional economics.

Therefore, the effective communication and intermediary media are important on brand (Bilgin, Y, 2018).

At other hand, the rapid growing of the social media has created many communications software which bring conveniences communication (López & Francisco,2020). Low Internet charges reduce telephone costs and increase people to use of communications software, thus making social media become a main communication tool for the masses.

Social media has become a common tool in people's lives. It not only accelerates people's direct communication, but also increases people's cognition. In the modern technological environment, traditional and complex works made easy in modern electronic facility. The video creation has become easy and accessible, everyone can easily become a host star or director and create their own film and television themes. A work experience, a simple country song, a story of a life struggle, or moment the neighbors quarreled can all make into short-video, which makes people feel excited, surprised or sad on social media. These outpourings of true feelings are undoubtedly exciting elements and play an important role in cultural communication.

With the rapid development of social media, a new profession called live-influencer has emerged, and it's playing an increasingly important role in social communication. The emergence of Internet celebrities is to directly transmit the elements of true feelings to people.

The live-influencer's live broadcasting has become a new media channel, and transmit the experience sharing, skill and value for people. On the other hand, the merchants are tap the commercial value from this kind of new profession.

Internet celebrities become a media intermediary, not only driving the rapid development of network marketing, but also effectively guiding consumers to understand and recognize brands in the era of over information, and becoming an emerging media intermediary. The rapid growing of social media has created many live-influencers and playing an important role to leading consumer for new brand cognition in competitive market.

This paper analyzes the main influencing factors that affect the attraction between Internet celebrities and customers, but the influence of Internet celebrities is not just a communication intermediary. As mentioned above, short videos spread people's emotions, and it will involve every field of human life. In other hand, Live-influencer can bring a revolutionary change for the industry, includes the third-part merchants are expect to joint and share benefit business, such as bank, logistics, insurances and agency. Because Live-influencer also bring effective benefit business and creates value between brand and consumers, and it can be a business soul to the bank, intermediary, band, internet developer. Live-influencer become new intermediaries are very important to brand marketing, but these still some risks management existing, such as brand quality, delivery guidelines, credit payment, defective product return, after sale services, in case these problems happened, it will be raising seriously affect to the credibility of the influencer and bring a fatal blow to intermediaries. Therefore, there are serious risk for the management of media intermediaries, and the risks need to be further researched and try effective methods to protect the credibility of the media intermediaries.

6. MANAGERIAL IMPLICATIONS

The emergence of Live-influencer is the product of the rapid development in Internet, its benefit has become a new type of media intermediary, which helping brands and consumers achieve goals. On the other hand, the disadvantages are still ubiquitous, its unconstrained behavior and no unified management model are frightening, which will affect consumer loyalty and consumer brand satisfaction. With the further development and evolution of new media intermediaries, the shortage of this rapid development may cause a challenge of cultural overuse and over-commercialization, and thus another phenomenon of over information.

With the Live-influencer's popularization of the new concept and familiarity with the business model, the relationship between its production investment and commercial value will become more and more obvious. The live-influencer will largely consider whether they need to invest in production based on commercial value, and commercial merchants will also make same considerations based on the influence. The attitude of making money and becoming famous influencer have become the main consideration. Under the premise of this commercial driving force, more and more new live-influencer and new commercial merchants be attracted. Advertisers are often using interstitial or imposed advertising on new media channels, which has led to a large number of advertising products, which has led to vicious competition. And new media can lead to over information, therefore, it is necessary to issue relevant guidelines and commercial management.

The consumer loyalty and consumer brand satisfaction are an important indicator of brand marketing, which can help brand marketing formulate strategies that satisfy consumers. Therefore, brands can focus on product development and manufacturing in professional fields, which save unnecessary waste in the middle of products, and focus its product promotion and value contribution. Based on the positive impact of the practicality and guidance of new media intermediaries, the research suggest that new media intermediaries should invest in content that is meaningful to brand consumers. For example, themes such as entertainment, tradition, and people-friendliness, these themes with people's livelihood value should become the first choice between brand marketing and consumers. Therefore, brand marketing, media intermediaries and advertisers should issue relevant guidance and business management based on these factors.

The research has limitation in the context of media intermediary, especially in the risk management of quality. For future research should extend the risk management in quality control, timeliness, after sell services. In other hand, the future research also can compare perceived value from different contexts and different cultures in order to better understand the determinants and barriers of brand mediation in media.

The birth of Internet celebrities is the product of the development of the Internet, and it continues to evolve with human culture. This aspect will cause a challenge of cultural overuse and over-commercialization, and thus another phenomenon of excessive information will erupt.

7. CONCLUSION

This paper studies the influencing factors of live-influencers' experience sharing, skill imparting and value perception as an intermediary model for new brands entering the competitive market. And exposing Internet technology has changed intermediary models in Asia, live-influencers have become one of more effective and more directive intermediary, and play an important guiding role in direct explanation, promotion and value perception between the brand market and consumers, increasing consumer loyalty and consumer satisfaction.

Through to the case study, the influence of live-influencer are extraordinary, and wonderful programme is contained rich experience sharing and vivid skill teaching, so that customers can learn more of rare knowledge and perceived its useful value.

The exam result shows that the live-influencer's experience sharing (H1a), skill teaching (H1b) and value perception (H1c) are positive influences to customer loyalty; the live-influencer are negative influences to consumer brand satisfaction (H2); the live-influencer's customer loyalty are positive influences to consumer brand satisfaction (H3), which indicates that the live-influencer presenting experience sharing and skill teaching of influencer live broadcast attracts the customers and builds up the loyalty of the customers, and the customers perceive the value of purchase and convert into the consumer identity, so that the theory of live-influencer guiding the consumers is realized, and live-influencer become a new mediation model and playing important role for new brand in consumer loyalty and consumer satisfaction.

In the above research, the experience sharing and skill teaching of influencer live broadcast attracts the customers and builds up the loyalty of the customers, and the customers perceive the value of purchase and convert into the consumer identity, so that the theory of live-influencer guiding the consumers is realized, and live-influencer becomes the new media intermediary effect, which has an important role for the brand market.

With the continuous development and growth of live-influencer intermediaries, it is believed that the role of live-influencer intermediaries will effectively attract a large group of customers, who will become their own consumer groups with the guidance of live-influencer, which will have an elevating effect on certain brand marketing and form a brand-specific market share of consumption.

At the same time, live-influencer will become the new intermediary of social media and will establish new industries, such as the banking industry to establish emerging financial business, such as credit guarantee, mobile loan etc.

REFERENCES

Aaker, D. A., Fuse, Y., & Reynolds, F. D. (1982). Is Life-Style Research Limited in its Usefulness to Japanese Advertisers? *Journal of Advertising, 11*(1), 31–36, 48. doi:10.1080/00913367.1982.10672792

Adler, F. (1956). The value concept in sociology. *American Journal of Sociology, 62*(3), 272–279. doi:10.1086/222004

Backaler, J., & Shankman, P. (2018). *Digital influence*. Macmillan. doi:10.1007/978-3-319-78396-3

Bae, S. J., Lee, H., Suh, E. K., & Suh, K. S. (2017). Shared experience in pretrip and experience sharing in posttrip: A survey of Airbnb users. *Information & Management, 54*(6), 714–727. doi:10.1016/j.im.2016.12.008

Bakshy, E., Hofman, J. M., Mason, W. A., & Watts, D. J. (2011). Everyone's an influencer: quantifying influence on twitter. In *Proceedings of the fourth ACM international conference on Web search and data mining* (pp. 65-74). 10.1145/1935826.1935845

Barrick, M. R., Mount, M. K., & Strauss, J. P. (1993). Conscientiousness and performance of sales representatives: Test of the mediating effects of goal setting. *The Journal of Applied Psychology, 78*(5), 715–722. doi:10.1037/0021-9010.78.5.715

Baumann, S. (2015). Media branding from an organizational and management-centered perspective. In *Handbook of media branding* (pp. 65–80). Springer. doi:10.1007/978-3-319-18236-0_5

Becker-Olsen, K. L. (2003). And now, a word from our sponsor—A look at the effects of sponsored content and banner advertising. *Journal of Advertising, 32*(2), 17–32. doi:10.1080/00913367.2003.10639130

Bilgin, Y. (2018). The effect of social media marketing activities on brand awareness, brand image and brand loyalty. *Business & management studies: an international journal, 6*(1), 128-148.

Bray, D. A. (2008). Information pollution, knowledge overload, limited attention spans, and our responsibilities as IS professionals. In *Global Information Technology Management Association (GITMA) World Conference-June.* SSRN.

CB. (2020). *CB insight report.* CB Insights. www.cbinsights.com/research/report/venture-capital-q4-2020/

Chailan, C. (2008). Brands portfolios and competitive advantage: An empirical study. *Journal of Product and Brand Management, 17*(4), 254–264. doi:10.1108/10610420810887608

Chen, T., Drennan, J., & Andrews, L. (2012). Experience sharing. *Journal of Marketing Management, 28*(13-14), 1535–1552. doi:10.1080/0267257X.2012.736876

Chinomona, R. (2013). The Influence Of Brand Experience On Brand Satisfaction, Trust And Attachment In South Africa. [IBER]. *International Business & Economics Research Journal, 12*(10), 1303–1316. doi:10.19030/iber.v12i10.8138

Chinomona, R., Mahlangu, D., & Pooe, D. (2013). Brand service quality, satisfaction, trust and preference as predictors of consumer brand loyalty in the retailing industry. *Mediterranean Journal of Social Sciences, 4*(14), 181. doi:10.5901/mjss.2013.v4n14p181

Christov, A., Verena, H., & Sue, W. (2020. Measuring brand awareness, campaign evaluation and web analytics. Digital and Social Media Marketing. Routledge.

Chung, C., Chatterjee, S. C., & Sengupta, S. (2012). Manufacturers' reliance on channel intermediaries: Value drivers in the presence of a direct web channel. *Industrial Marketing Management, 41*(1), 40–53. doi:10.1016/j.indmarman.2011.11.010

Cronbach, Lee J. (1951). Coefficient alpha and the internal structure of tests. *Sychometrika.* Springer Science and Business Media LLC.

Croteau, D., Hoynes, W., & Hoynes, W. D. (2006). The business of media: Corporate media and the public interest. Pine forge press.

Dimmick, J., Chen, Y., & Li, Z. (2004). Competition Between the Internet and Traditional News Media: The Gratification-Opportunities Niche Dimension. *Journal of Media Economics, 17*(1), 19–33. doi:10.120715327736me1701_2

Doyle, P. (2000). Value-based marketing. *Journal of Strategic Marketing, 8*(4), 299–311. doi:10.1080/096525400446203

Du, R. Y., Xu, L., & Wilbur, K. C. (2019). Immediate responses of online brand search and price search to TV ads. *Journal of Marketing, 83*(4), 81–100. doi:10.1177/0022242919847192

Farris, P. W., Bendle, N. T., Pfeifer, P. E., & Reibstein, D. J. (2010). *Marketing Metrics: The Definitive Guide to Measuring Marketing Performance.* Pearson Education, Inc.

Feaster, J. C. (2009). The repertoire niches of interpersonal media: Competition and coexistence at the level of the individual. *new media & society, 11*(6), 965-984.

Feiz, D., Fakharyan, M., Jalilvand, M. R., & Hashemi, M. (2013). Examining the effect of TV advertising appeals on brand attitudes and advertising efforts in Iran. *Journal of Islamic Marketing, 4*(1), 101–125. doi:10.1108/17590831311306372

Giese, J. L., & Cote, J. A. (2000). Defining consumer satisfaction. *Academy of Marketing Science Review, 1*(1), 1–22.

Hardway, C. L., & Stroud, M. (2014). Using Student Choice to Increase Students' Knowledge of Research Methodology, Improve Their Attitudes toward Research, and Promote Acquisition of Professional Skills. *International Journal on Teaching and Learning in Higher Education, 26*(3), 381–392.

Harris, M. (2000). Life on the Amazon. *The Anthropology of a Brazilian Peasant Village,* 201-216.

Hayes, N. (2008). *Influencer Marketing: Who Really Influences Your Customers?* Taylor & Francis.

Henry, E. O., & Lloyd, M. D. (2019). Reinventing the 'Nwaboi'apprenticeship system: A platform for entrepreneurship promotion in Nigeria. *International Journal of Advanced Research in Management and Social Sciences, 8*(9), 98–130.

Heskett, J. L. (2002). Beyond customer loyalty. *Managing Service Quality, 12*(6), 355–357. doi:10.1108/09604520210451830

Hiebert, J., & Wearne, D. (1996). Instruction, understanding, and skill in multidigit addition and subtraction. *Cognition and Instruction, 14*(3), 251–283. doi:10.12071532690xci1403_1

Holbrook, M. B., & Hirschman, E. C. (1982). The experiential aspects of consumption: Consumer fantasies, feelings, and fun. *The Journal of Consumer Research, 9*(2), 132–140. doi:10.1086/208906

Indrasari, A., Novita, D., & Megawati, F. (2018). Big Book: Attractive media for teaching vocabulary to lower class of young learners. [Journal of English Educators Society]. *JEES, 3*(2), 141–154. doi:10.21070/jees.v3i2.1572

Jacoby, J. (1971). Brand loyalty: A conceptual definition. In *Proceedings of the Annual Convention of the American Psychological Association.* American Psychological Association.

Kaplan, A. M., & Haenlein, M. (2010). Users of the world, unite! The challenges and opportunities of Social Media. *Business Horizons, 53*(1), 59–68. doi:10.1016/j.bushor.2009.09.003

Khan, A. M., & Stanton, J. (2010). A model of sponsorship effects on the sponsor's employees. *Journal of Promotion Management, 16*(1-2), 188–200. doi:10.1080/10496490903574831

King, B. G. (2008). A political mediation model of corporate response to social movement activism. *Administrative Science Quarterly, 53*(3), 395–421. doi:10.2189/asqu.53.3.395

Liao, S. H., Chen, Y. J., & Hsieh, H. H. (2011). Mining customer knowledge for direct selling and marketing. *Expert Systems with Applications, 38*(5), 6059–6069. doi:10.1016/j.eswa.2010.11.007

Lin, Y. H. (2015). Innovative brand experience's influence on brand equity and brand satisfaction. *Journal of Business Research, 68*(11), 2254–2259. doi:10.1016/j.jbusres.2015.06.007

López, M. & Francisco, J. (2020). Influencer marketing: brand control, commercial orientation and post credibility. *Journal of Marketing Management 36.*

Loureiro, S. M., Bilro, R. G., & Japutra, A. (2019). Correia, R.G.Bilro, (2019),"The effect of consumer-generated media stimuli on emotions and consumer brand engagement. *Journal of Product and Brand Management, 29*(3), 387–408. doi:10.1108/JPBM-11-2018-2120

Marx, R. W., Blumenfeld, P. C., Krajcik, J. S., & Soloway, E. (1998). New technologies for teacher professional development. *Teaching and Teacher Education, 14*(1), 33–52. doi:10.1016/S0742-051X(98)00059-6

McKewon, E. (2012). Talking points ammo: The use of neoliberal think tank fantasy themes to delegitimise scientific knowledge of climate change in Australian newspapers. *Journalism Studies, 13*(2), 277–297. doi:10.1080/146167 0X.2011.646403

McKewon, E. (2012). Talking points ammo: The use of neoliberal think tank fantasy themes to delegitimise scientific knowledge of climate change in Australian newspapers. *Journalism Studies, 13*(2), 277–297. doi:10.1080/146167 0X.2011.646403

Meenaghan, T. (2001). Understanding sponsorship effects. *Psychology and Marketing, 18*(2), 95–122. doi:10.1002/1520-6793(200102)18:2<95::AID-MAR1001>3.0.CO;2-H

Menon, S., & Kahn, B. E. (2003). Corporate sponsorships of philanthropic activities: When do they impact perception of sponsor brand? *Journal of Consumer Psychology, 13*(3), 316–327. doi:10.1207/S15327663JCP1303_12

Migacz, S. J., Zou, S., & Petrick, J. F. (2017). The "Terminal" Effects of Service Failure on Airlines: Examining Service Recovery with Justice Theory. *Journal of Travel Research, 57*(1), 83–98. doi:10.1177/0047287516684979

Moor, L. (2008). Branding consultants as cultural intermediaries. *The Sociological Review, 56*(3), 408–428. doi:10.1111/j.1467-954X.2008.00797.x

Nunnally, J. C. (1994). *Psychometric Theory* (2nd ed.). McGraw-Hill.

Oliver, R. L. (1999). Whence consumer loyalty? *Journal of Marketing, 63*(4, suppl1), 33–44. doi:10.1177/00222429990634s105

Overby, J. W., Woodruff, R. B., & Gardial, S. F. (2005). The influence of culture upon consumers' desired value perceptions: A research agenda. *Marketing Theory, 5*(2), 139–163. doi:10.1177/1470593105052468

Park, M., Im, H., & Kim, H. Y. (2020). "You are too friendly!" The negative effects of social media marketing on value perceptions of luxury fashion brands. *Journal of Business Research, 117*, 529–542. doi:10.1016/j.jbusres.2018.07.026

Parsons, A. G., & Schumacher, C. (2012). Advertising regulation and market drivers. *European Journal of Marketing, 46*(11/12), 1539–1558. doi:10.1108/03090561211259970

Pascual, P. A. C. (2009). Ethical controversy over information and communication technology. In *Handbook of Research on Technoethics* (pp. 222–231). IGI Global. doi:10.4018/978-1-60566-022-6.ch015

Pinkleton, B. (1997). The effects of negative comparative political advertising on candidate evaluations and advertising evaluations: An exploration. *Journal of Advertising*, *26*(1), 19–29. doi:10.1080/00913367.1997.10673515

Poon, P., & Albaum, G. (2019). Consumer trust in internet marketing and direct selling in china. *Journal of Relationship Marketing*, *18*(3), 216–232. doi:10.1080/15332667.2019.1589244

Rahman, M. (2019). 21st century skill'problem solving': Defining the concept. Rahman, MM (2019). 21st Century Skill "Problem Solving": Defining the Concept. *Asian Journal of Interdisciplinary Research*, *2*(1), 64–74.

Rao, V. R., & McLaughlin, E. W. (1989). Modeling the decision to add new products by channel intermediaries. *Journal of Marketing*, *53*(1), 80–88. doi:10.1177/002224298905300107

Saatchi, S. S., Houghton, R. A., Dos Santos Alvalá, R. C., Soares, J. V., & Yu, Y. (2007). Distribution of aboveground live biomass in the Amazon basin. *Global Change Biology*, *13*(4), 816–837. doi:10.1111/j.1365-2486.2007.01323.x

Shavelson, R. J. (1973). What is the basic teaching skill? *Journal of Teacher Education*, *24*(2), 144–151. doi:10.1177/002248717302400213

Shi, X., Lin, Z., Liu, J., & Hui, Y. K. (2018). p, (2018), "Consumer loyalty toward smartphone brands: The determining roles of deliberate inertia and cognitive lock-in. *Information & Management*, *55*(7), 866–876. doi:10.1016/j.im.2018.03.013

Sivarajah, R. T., Curci, N. E., Johnson, E. M., Lam, D. L., Lee, J. T., & Richardson, M. L. (2019). A review of innovative teaching methods. *Academic Radiology*, *26*(1), 101–113. doi:10.1016/j.acra.2018.03.025 PMID:30929697

B.Sousa, A.Malheiro, M.Cláudia (2019),"O Marketing Territorial como Contributo para a Segmentação Turística: Modelo conceptual no turismo de shopping." International Journal of Marketing, Communication and New Media 5 (2019).

Spiteri, M., & Chang Rundgren, S. N. (2020). Literature review on the factors affecting primary teachers' use of digital technology. Technology. *Knowledge and Learning*, *25*(1), 115–128. doi:10.100710758-018-9376-x

Tian, Y., Babcock, R., Taylor, C., & Ji, Y. (2018). A new live video streaming approach based on Amazon S3 pricing model. In *2018 IEEE 8th Annual computing and communication workshop and conference (CCWC)* (pp. 321-328). IEEE. 10.1109/CCWC.2018.8301615

Wang, E. S. (2019). Tse. (2019) "Effects of brand awareness and social norms on user-perceived cyber privacy risk. *International Journal of Electronic Commerce*, *23*(2), 272–293. doi:10.1080/10864415.2018.1564553

Wood, L. (2000). Brands and brand equity: Definition and management. *Management Decision*, *38*(9), 662–669. doi:10.1108/00251740010379100

Xue, W., Ma, D., & Hu, J. (2022). Recycling Model Selection for Electronic Products Considering Platform Power and Blockchain Empowerment. *Sustainability 14*.

Zietek, N. (2016). *Influencer Marketing: the characteristics and components of fashion influencer marketing*.

Chapter 8
Digital Branding in the Digital Era

Edna Mngusughun Denga

https://orcid.org/0000-0002-2121-242X
American University of Nigeria, Nigeria

Narasimha Rao Rao Vajjhala

https://orcid.org/0000-0002-8260-2392
Americian University of Nigeria, Nigeria

Sefa Asortse

https://orcid.org/0000-0002-8166-345X
University of Nigeria, Enugu, Nigeria

ABSTRACT

The 21st-century marketplace and its consumers are connected digitally as an innovative and inquisitive technique of information gathering. In the first two decades of this millennium, the proliferation of digital media and increasingly mobile Internet connectivity have undoubtedly had a significant influence on brands and brand management. Innovations have ushered in a brand-new epoch known as "the digital era." This golden age has fostered a few unique challenges that aim to approach branding in novel and interesting ways. Brands are attempting to create a digital identity for their business in today's technology-driven economy to sustain consumer awareness. Maintaining an online presence is essential for businesses to continue being successful and relevant considering the increasing amount of time that customers are spending on digital platforms nowadays.

DOI: 10.4018/978-1-6684-8351-0.ch008

INTRODUCTION

The digital era is a fascinating opportunity to be alive, one brimming with opportunities to expand businesses and build brands online (Ramadhani &Indradjati, 2023). The digital era is an exciting moment to be living since it offers a wealth of chances to expand enterprises and create online brands. Consumer behaviour and buyer-seller connections show a fundamental shift in how customers interact with brands. The "traditional way of doing business" is no longer viable for marketers as the touchpoints have evolved and been restructured. The battle to be relevant exists yet in a society that is overflowing with innovative media channels and borderline aggressive engagement, where information has become the most valuable asset. Not only has the Internet risen in importance as a tool for people and businesses, but it has also become a necessity for everyday living. The Internet is the go-to source for information about virtually anything, with many people spending more time online than offline. Hence, digital branding has emerged as a distinct field with just as many, if not more, specializations and subcategories as traditional branding.

According to recent statistics, 4.88 billion people utilize the internet worldwide nowadays, with the figure rapidly rising by 5% yearly (Ramadhani &Indradjati, 2023). Not only that, but today's internet users spend an astounding 6 hours every day browsing, sharing, and mining information, up from just 2 hours a decade ago. As the influence of the digital world grows, businesses from all niches and ages are being compelled to take their online presence and digital branding seriously. While incorporating any communication strategy, brands today need to understand the significance of the ever-expanding and adaptable digital world. Consumers increasingly seek to connect with brands online as a result of the increasing growth of digital devices.

BACKGROUND

A brand is made up of all the components that set a company apart from competitors, including its logo, colour scheme, typography, taglines, symbols, etc. To distinguish a brand from its rivals in the market, it may be a service, a good, or even just a concept that can be communicated to the public. Branding is the process of creating any product, with the aid of numerous components, with a unique and distinctive personality (Ress, 2022). The necessity of branding in the digital age is as important as branding itself. Digital branding, also known as branding in the digital era, is a brand communication strategy that leverages the internet and digital marketing to strengthen a brand's characteristics, build its presence, and promote the brand (Jerez- Jerez, 2022). Digital branding originates from direct marketing and it is executed through specific digital platforms, including the Internet itself, mobile applications, social media, and most significantly, digital media content. Additionally, it includes all of the components, including the logo, colour palette, typography, taglines, symbols, etc.

Effective branding can solely be viewed as a reflection of how the target consumer perceives a brand, whether it be traditional branding or digital branding (Niculescu et al., 2019). This effective branding will contribute to enhanced brand positioning in consumers' minds. Therefore, it is crucial to strategize communication on digital platforms in a way that resonates with the positioning that brands desire to establish. Digital marketing and social media have simplified the process to communicate with and engage with customers online, but they have also made it simpler for customers to modify their perceptions of brands (Denga & Sandip, 2022b). The brand guidelines, which specify the tone, colour, typography, and general appearance of brands must be adhered to, especially when done digitally to avoid this. Brands must be as consistent as possible across all digital channels to boost their reputation, appeal, and customer loyalty.

The marketing industry has been disrupted by the digital revolution more than any other. After celebrating three decades of the World Wide Web, it is appropriate to examine how branding has evolved in the digital revolution. A thorough evaluation of the digital era seems appropriate since firms are expected to adjust and realign their marketing strategies. The literature on digital branding and the effects of digitalization on brand management, however, is largely in its nascent stage. Thus, the chapter aims to examine the concept, importance, and pillars of digital branding, as well as its elements and evolution in the digital age: challenges and opportunities.

The evolution of digital branding over several decades has been influenced by a range of factors and issues. Technological advancements have been a driving force, providing new platforms and tools for brands to connect with their audience. Shifting consumer behaviour, driven by increased empowerment and connectivity, has necessitated brands to adapt their strategies to meet evolving expectations. The rise of social media has transformed brand-consumer interactions and the importance of user-generated content. Globalization has expanded market reach, requiring brands to consider cultural nuances. Data privacy and security concerns have emerged as critical considerations for brands, demanding transparency and compliance. Content overload and attention span challenges have called for compelling and relevant content creation. Personalization and customer experience have become pivotal in building brand loyalty. Influencer marketing and user-generated content have disrupted traditional approaches, while measurement and analytics have enabled data-driven decision-making. Continuous adaptation and learning have been essential for brands to remain competitive in the dynamic digital landscape. By understanding and addressing these factors, brands can navigate the evolving digital branding landscape successfully and build a strong and impactful digital presence.

THE CONCEPT OF DIGITAL BRANDING

Digital branding is a brand management technique that employs a combination of internet branding and digital marketing to develop a brand over a range of digital channels, including internet-based relationships, device-based applications or media content(Ress,2022). According to Chaffey and Smith (2017), digital branding refers to the process of creating and managing a brand's identity and presence in the digital environment. It involves using digital channels, such as websites, social media, and mobile apps, to communicate the brand's values, establish relationships with customers, and differentiate the brand from competitors. Digital branding aims to forge relationships between customers and the services or products being offered to create brand recognition digitally. Digital branding strives to boost brand awareness, image, and style rather than necessarily generating sales. In turn, digital branding promotes long-term customer loyalty. Four essential elements go into brand establishment: creating a digital brand narrative, digital media and marketing creativity, forming digital relationships and content distribution to channels based on consumer data and habits (Li et al.,2022).

The concept of branding emerged after the advent of competitive markets. This stemmed from a mismatch between supply and demand. The only distinguishing feature that could be detected as supply began to expand and suppliers were offering comparable goods was the branding of their goods. The essence of branding has completely revolutionized with the development of technology. The world of branding has altered significantly as a result of firms attempting to impress customers by telling stories, developing personas, and establishing a distinct brand identity (Mergel et al.,2019).

Branding has undergone tremendous change as a function of the proliferation of digital platforms and is continuously evolving. 25 years ago, branding was quite straightforward. Businesses would generate an enjoyable shopping experience, run TV commercials, advertise on billboards, play radio jingles, and purchase a sizable listing in the Yellow Pages (Ritter & Pedersen,2020). Today's consumers have far higher expectations from brands, therefore they must constantly engage with them. They must put the needs of the customer first, keep an eye out for mentions of their brand online, reply quickly, and employ digital platforms expertly. Businesses that can't keep up with today's quick-moving, constantly growing digital platforms and dwindling customer attention spans will fall behind.

Branding has been redefined in the contemporary day. Contrary to earlier methods of one-sided communication, customers nowadays have a central role in brand co-creation (Lane & Levy, 2019). Digital media has transformed the form of communication from one to many to one to one, as opposed to conventional media's one-to-many. This means buyers now have access to more customized products, which enhances their post-purchase satisfaction. In light of digital trends, the brand promise, brand identity prism, and brand personality are being reinvented. Takeaways from popular culture, knowledge of trending phrases, and social media monitoring have become essential for brands so these things aid in keeping brands relevant.

There are four cornerstones on which brands should base their branding as it evolves to keep abreast with consumers and purchasers in the digital age: **Brand, Technology, Audience,** and **Communication** (Denga et al.,2022d). *Brand-*Consumers are increasingly more adept at identifying what is artificial. The focus ability is deteriorating with advertising spots becoming supersaturated. Brands may redefine their branding for the digital age and achieve success by focusing their attention on three integral domains: Brand identity and unique selling proposition (USP), Visual Branding and Marketing. *Audience-* Creating customer personas alone is not enough for effective digital branding. They ascertain the behaviour of their audiences on the channels they utilize the most. What makes this crucial? primarily because consumers congregate across several digital platforms, each of which serves as a unique touchpoint. Customer personas are insufficient for a thorough digital branding plan in terms of segmentation and mapping unless they expressly identify and define all touchpoints of the consumer's journey (Li et al.,2020). Brands will have a higher opportunity of success in converting prospects into consumers and even advocates if they segment their consumer base and establish focused target groups. To convert consumers into steadfast brand advocates, brands need to have a viable strategy. As keeping existing customers while enticing prospective ones is essential to growth, loyalty aids in attracting potential consumers through word-of-mouth and the creation of favourable online evaluations (Alalwan, 2018).

Communication- A documented communication strategy will enhance brand awareness, engage the audience, and generate sales. However, the market is cutthroat, with rivals vying for the same consumers. If a brand wants to outperform its rivals and effectively reach consumers, all of its marketing strategies must complement one another. A core part of digital branding is often searching and displaying advertising (Trevino & Pineda, 2019). The other is directed at the target demographic on social media and websites wherever they are, whereas the first enables users to find the brand by focusing on keywords entered into search engines. Marketing professionals must keep in mind that online advertising is not a "set and forget" project. It has to be periodically optimized and monitored. Measuring engagement is vital in addition to measures like conversions (Niculescu et al., 2019). Not only are brands competing with one another, but also social media platforms and apps, vying for their users' attention. Users are kept interested through notifications, pushed content, and features like unlimited scrolling. Brands must create content and advertisements that truly engage their audience in the battle for attention.

Technology- Brands may take informed action by using web analytics tools to track and measure insights, results, and customer journey analysis. Brands can make defensible decisions and eliminate uncertainty when every component of the brand is connected to an analytics platform with properly established KPIs (Diaz et al.,2022). One of the foundational elements that successful brands are emphasizing is user experience, a major selling point is having a terrific, quick, and simplified mobile consumer experience. However, it can only be done by monitoring users' activity across the platform and making adjustments based on credible data.

To sum up, in the digital era, the relevance of traditional marketing tactics is dwindling. While traditional marketing channels are still crucial, they are less effective than digital marketing at targeting customers at every stage of their journey (Denga &Sandip, 2022b). Customers anticipate smooth user experiences from brands that are customer-focused. And because technology is constantly developing, brands need to keep up with new trends and improve their offerings if they don't want to fall behind startups that have embraced the most recent developments, whether it's implementing augmented reality or using AI to provide lightning-fast service with no wait times (Diaz et al.,2022). Everything needs to be encapsulated within a single brand with coherent messaging and consistent images.

EVOLUTION OF BRANDING IN THE DIGITAL ERA

Marketing and branding have been significantly influenced by the Internet. Customer and business relationships have evolved in very fundamental ways. Businesses striving to succeed in this modern, dynamic corporate environment where there is so much at stake for them on the Internet, must learn to adapt to several of these innovative business practices. Digital assets, such as website content that are search engine optimized and social media that prioritize speed and accessibility, became the core of digital marketing as word-of-mouth marketing of products and services evolved into the virtual environment (Garzella et al., 2020).

Over the past three decades, digital brand marketing and the usage of information technology have advanced significantly. The readiness to adapt to change became indispensable in the modern web marketing landscape, from marketers striving to capitalize on the enormous potential of the online realm to emerging brand-building strategies and targeted marketing technologies. The myriad innovations wrought by the Internet have a direct effect on brand management processes (Garzella et al., 2020). Businesses have historically conducted branding following the predominant corporate orientation, which placed them in an advantageous position. However, businesses are being driven to update the outdated model due to the opportunities the Internet offers

Here are a few ways digitalization has altered branding:

Instant communication and customer service that never sleeps: Always essential has been the buyer-seller relationship. The Internet, on the other hand, has stripped control away from the marketer and transferred it to the customer, granting them a voice and an opportunity to be heard. Brands are no longer pushing impersonal mass communication down a one-way street; instead, they are driving a two-way, consumer-driven freeway. There is now a discussion that is more customer-centric than ever before, rather than one-way advertising (Edelman, 2010). The "always-on" mentality is an additional intriguing phenomenon that emerged from the era of digital technology, internet traffic, new customer touchpoints, and rapid communication. In the digital age, customer service does not get much sleep. Customers want businesses to respond swiftly to their complaints and resolve them, developing an "always-on" relationship with them (Press et al.,2021).

Being more human and fostering intimacy as brands' biggest asset: Businesses no longer engage their customers directly. The decades-old marketing strategy that eliminated any chance for interactions between customers and sellers is no longer effective in the digital era (Press et al.,2021). Through social media, brands have the opportunity to interact with their customer base and speak to them rather than at them. Although brands are not people, they are people-powered. Let some of that emerge. Consumers of today are knowledgeable enough to avoid being tricked by marketing that lacks any morals or authenticity and will be perceived as being superficial (Yu & Yuan, 2019). Success for brands goes beyond the surface level. It goes beyond attractive colours, a fantastic logo, or a catchy catchphrase, and despite the significant influence social media has played in this, it also extends farther than likes and followers. The key to success is to encourage intimacy and authenticity so that businesses may become more human.

Brand loyalty has taken a historic plunge: Nowadays, there are more options than ever for businesses to monitor outcomes in real time and gather quantifiable information on consumer behaviour. However, there has been a paradigm shift in customer retention, and strangely, there is a historic plunge in brand loyalty. Brand loyalty and the latest digital marketing trends are not supposed to be mutually exclusive concepts (Yu & Yuan, 2019). However, marketers should not expect well-informed, empowered, and spoiled-for-choice consumers to remain loyal customers. They are more inclined to value money, accessibility, and convenience over loyalty. A traditional marketing strategy's cornerstone has been eroded by the variations within the customer base. To enhance the relationship and make their presence more enticing while preserving some of the "traditional" values, businesses must alter their business models and marketing strategies.

Brand consistency across all channels, online and offline: To maintain brand consistency, all brand representations and marketing assets must adhere to a set of predetermined guiding principles, such as the company's identity, values, and guidelines. Consistency in messaging, core values, tone of voice, and style components across all mediums is paramount to mastering the art of effective branding (Yu & Yuan, 2019). Making brands immediately recognized in the evolving consumer landscape is the ultimate aim. However, it's challenging to stay "on-brand" when firms have "traditional" and "digital" marketing teams operating out of sync rather than creating a cohesive strategy with consistent messaging. Through all platforms and touchpoints, online and off, brands must communicate the same, consistent message precisely. This is how to establish a pattern of consistency that will evoke in customers' sentiments of authenticity and familiarity. Given that customer trust in brands is at an all-time low, businesses cannot afford to have even the slightest branding inconsistencies.

Demand for total transparency as the new normal: The hyper-connected digital world, which is rife with fake news, data breaches, and privacy worries - the era of mistrust - has put marketers up against a steep uphill battle to earn the trust of customers. Customers and clients in the modern day expect absolute transparency as the new norm. Customers who aspire to know everything about brands, from manufacturing to ways it contributes to society, are highlighted by the transformation in the consumer profile (Makri et al.,2019). The pressure of this rapidly evolving conversation, which progresses from unintentional revelations to complete and utter transparency, is felt by almost every firm and the entire industry. Making transparency a marketing tactic is one-way companies may respond to this and capitalize on the moral component of consumers' purchasing decisions. Brands that "get it" have a prospect to win over customers' trust and profit from their greater propensity for complete accountability and transparency.

Leverage customer and social networks: Customers have been able to build a robust network of virtual connections like brand tribes thanks to the Internet's interconnectedness. With the aid of such a network, users can share their online experiences with others while also feeling a sense of community and enjoying all the advantages of an online community. Depending on the type of connectivity and its intended use, these networks improve word-of-mouth marketing, the spread of innovative ideas, real-time customer feedback on product development, and tracking of current and emerging trends across a wide range of industries, including fashion and consumer electronics (Li et al ., 2022). Brands have access to priceless resources through such information that can be leveraged to develop effective strategies.

Large marketing budgets no longer equal success: Marketing used to be a fairly simple, understandable concept, at least in the sense that whoever had the biggest marketing budget typically controlled the terrain. Simply put, a company was more likely to succeed if it could expand its market reach through marketing initiatives and improve brand awareness (Mergel et al.,2019). With the burgeoning usage of social media and the Internet, brands are experiencing a new era when anybody can participate in the marketing environment. That is not to imply that having a large budget does not offer a company a competitive edge; it does. It is no longer a deciding factor, though. It is feasible for even the smallest businesses to participate in the race as businesses are vying based on marketing strategy, expertise, and service.

Tremendous amounts of data allow for highly relevant interactions: Everyone is familiar with the adage "content is king." Audiences are engaged by great content in the digital era. Brands that can fully grasp who their users, viewers, and customers are tend to end up with the chuck of the market share. Technology has altered how businesses promote their services and products. Marketing campaigns have transitioned beyond traditional channels of customers' point of contact and into the world of social media, Search engine optimization, and digital technologies (Ritter & Pederson, 2020). There is insufficient time for extensive research and long evaluation. Marketing professionals acquire data on consumers, track engagement in real-time, and depend on analytics to monitor the success of these digital marketing initiatives.

A level playing field: Brands can instantly connect with their target audience and communicate with them attributable to digital marketing platforms and advancements in consumer behaviour that have evolved alongside it. The playing field is more level than it has ever been as a direct outcome of that. It is fascinating to highlight how what was once regarded as the inherent value of a well-known brand name has somewhat eroded in the contemporary era of digital marketing (Svarc et al.,2020). The likelihood of a small business becoming a success story is now on par with that of a "large," well-known brand. Small businesses receive the same amount of coverage from digital marketing channels and communication innovations as larger ones, offering them a decent opportunity to get a piece of the marketing action. Marketing professionals have their work cut out for them as being a major firm is no longer sufficient to witness a surge in sales.

Management of brand identity: A brand's identity communicates to its target market the values, perceptions, and connotations of the brand. As a result, it is one of those corporate activities that is managed with the utmost caution, consistency and diligence. Brand identity management will have to transition into a collaborative process with less control and constant change as a function of the novel dynamics that have emerged between brands and their customers.

The evolution of branding in the digital era has brought about significant changes and opportunities for businesses. Traditional branding principles have been reshaped by the digital landscape, requiring brands to adapt and leverage new strategies to stay relevant. The digital era has expanded the reach and impact of branding, allowing businesses to engage with global audiences in real time through various digital platforms. The rise of social media and online communities has empowered consumers to actively participate in brand conversations, influencing brand perception and reputation. Brands now need to prioritize transparency, authenticity, and meaningful engagement to build trust and loyalty with their digital-savvy customers. Overall, the evolution of branding in the digital era necessitates a dynamic and customer-centric approach. Brands must embrace technology, leverage data insights, and adopt agile strategies to create meaningful connections, deliver personalized experiences, and maintain a positive brand reputation. By embracing the opportunities presented by the digital era, brands can thrive, grow, and remain competitive in an ever-evolving digital landscape.

PILLARS OF DIGITAL BRANDING

The operation and control of brand identity, visibility, and credibility constitute what is commonly referred to as digital brand management (Niculescu et al.,2019). It creates an opportunity for the brands to reach their capabilities by establishing the business online, differentiating it from the competitors, and fostering an emotional connection with the target audience. Digital branding also refers to a collection of strategies and techniques employed to establish a brand's recognition, reputation, and presence across a variety of digital platforms, such as websites, emails, apps, social media, blogs, videos, etc.

Figure 1. Digital branding pillars

Visual Identity

A brand's visual identity is made up of all the images and graphics that represent its unique characteristics and set it apart from competitors. In other words, it refers to everything that customers can physically see, including Logo. Typography, colours, imagery styles, and compositional techniques. These elements create a visible, instantly recognizable, and memorable relationship between the brand and its ideology by successfully visualizing and identifying the company's philosophy and values (Lipiainen & Karjaluoto,2015). These elements combine to form a visual brand identity, but they incorporate more than just outward characteristics. The images convey a more comprehensive message and theme. They establish the tone for the entire branding.

A brand's visual identity is a potent tool for interacting with consumers and expressing its narrative. The wrong message can have disastrous effects because of how effective it is at communication. Visual identity typically translates to the creation of a brand style guide, which offers standardized guidelines on how the brand should be visually portrayed at all times and in any circumstance. The purpose of visual identity is to:

- elicit an emotional impression from target audiences.
- enlighten consumers on the nature of the business and its available services and products.
- utilize consistent visuals to harmonize the various components of a business.

Credibility

Building a customer-centric brand with strong connections to the target market is the responsibility of credibility. Similar to a reputation, it requires effort to build and maintain a solid one, but it has a big impact as it strengthens reputation, authority, and trustworthiness. Successful brands and a business's online activities are built on digital credibility (Lipiainen & Karjaluoto,2015). Without credibility, trust cannot be established, persuasion cannot take place, and communication cannot take place. Simply put, if customers don't want to interact with a brand, they won't. On top of that, when it is high:

- It aids the business in effectively battling competition.
- Without much investment, it attracts potential customers.
- It fosters loyal customers, boosting the average revenue per person,
- It strengthens retention campaigns while significantly reducing costs.

Visibility

Brand visibility is defined as a brand's proportion of exposure in comparison to its competitors and industry (Kozinets,2022). It's a part of brand awareness, a broad phrase that denotes a variety of techniques for gauging consumer opinion and total brand coverage in a market. Brand visibility is a component of the process of creating brand awareness. It is best to think about it as the frequency with which the target market is exposed to the brand through various marketing channels (Li et al.,2022). This is particularly pertinent now that the majority of our lives have moved entirely online. It matters immensely how and where this is measured because brand visibility gauges, quite literally, how "visible" a brand is to target consumers (Lipiainen & Karjaluoto,2015). A company may have the best website in the world, but if customers are unable to locate or access it online, it won't be as valuable as it may be. SEO has grown to be a crucial tool for enhancing online exposure because search traffic can only redirect so many distinctive visitors (also known as new daily visitors). Elements of digital brand visibility include SEO, content marketing, social media etc.

The pillars of digital branding serve as the foundation for building a strong and impactful brand presence in the digital landscape. Each pillar plays a crucial role in shaping the brand's image, engaging with the target audience, and driving business growth. By embracing and implementing these pillars, brands can establish a strong and influential digital presence, engage with their audience effectively, deliver personalized experiences, and drive business success in the digital era.

ELEMENTS OF SUCCESSFUL DIGITAL BRANDING

Digital branding has been dubbed the cornerstone of contemporary marketing, with novel opportunities for digital branding continually developing attributable to the dynamic nature of the digital world (Diaz et al.,2022). A successful brand is the outcome of a series of actions undertaken to establish a brand, supported by a set of characteristics that shape and solidify its identity through time. A powerful digital brand must sustain this momentum and ensure it remains relevant in the mind of the target audience. Here are some strategies for successful digital branding:

Logo

A good logo delivers the owner's intended message and is distinctive, appropriate, practical, graphic, and simple in design. An effective logo typically has an idea or "meaning" that conveys the desired message. The only image that the consumer should associate with the brand is the logo, logos are extremely significant because they serve as a company's visual identity. Products will be easier to identify and recall with a logo. It is the pillar that reflects the company's identity and personality (Aly, 2020). Since it is a trigger that makes a brand memorable, it is vital to get it right. On all of the marketing channels and platforms that brands employ, the logo must take on the role of the primary identity. It is fundamental to design a logo that captures the essence and personality of a brand.

An effective branding strategy and a well-designed logo work together to enable firms to reach their customers more efficiently, and also forge an enduring, market-dominating brand (Bala & Verma, 2018). Never undervalue the value of a well-designed logo that is in line with an overall branding strategy. In the long run, a brand or organization will benefit from the investment. A logo must reflect a business's personality and core principles as well as its industry and target audience. A logo is an essential element in developing a successful digital brand.

Website

The most pivotal component of a digital marketing strategy may be a website. People go to websites to buy things from a brand, schedule services, read about a business, receive contact information, and, in general, learn anything they might need to know about a business (Casidy et al., 2022). For this reason, a website must be designed with the customer in mind. A website must effectively communicate a company's brand. The website must perform properly, look professional, and make every effort to attract prospective customers and leads. A successful website evokes emotions in viewers and aids in opinion formation about the company.

There are a few key elements that any website must have, yet the architecture of a website can be uniquely tailored to a brand and the type of business it is. Websites that are most successful stick to a brand's colour scheme, typography, and general look and feel. A website must also be easily "crawlable," which refers to having everything on the site easily accessible to both users and search engines. The user experience is invaluable here; the website design has to be straightforward but comprehensive and, of course, flawless (Das, 2021). Otherwise, website visitors can become dissatisfied and choose another option

Brand Messaging

Whether a brand is creating a new design from scratch, undergoing a rebrand, or simply adapting an established one for digital spaces, the brand message is pertinent. A mission statement and a value proposition are both components of brand messaging. A value proposition describes what a firm offers to customers from their perspective, whereas a mission statement describes what and who the organization is. These statements must be written out in internal documents even if they are not explicitly declared on a website (Bonnim & Alfonso, 2019). Every person in a firm can benefit from embracing a mission statement and value proposition to govern their decision-making, writing, and interactions with customers and potential customers.

The intangibles, such as the subtext, the overall vibe, and the values that are expressed between the lines, are also essential elements of a brand's messaging. These elusive elements of brand messaging emerge gradually over time as businesses strengthen their reputation and ties to their clients and customers (Bonnim & Alfonso, 2019). The success of a brand's messaging depends on its brand voice. Making a brand persona is a fantastic approach to giving a brand voice extra substance. In other words, who would a brand be if it were a person? How would they interact with other people? What are their values, interests, aspirations, and goals? Early in the 20th century, Swiss psychiatrist Carl Jung postulated that archetypes—classified symbols and roles that we perform in our own lives and the lives of those around us—are something that all humans contain inside themselves and also recognize in others. Modern marketers have developed a set of 12 distinct brand archetypes from Jung's presumption that may be leveraged to represent a brand's persona and voice. To establish, develop, and execute a brand's voice inside its messaging, it might be advantageous to identify where a brand falls among these 12 archetypes: ruler, caregiver, creator, innocent, sage, explorer, hero, magician, rebel, citizen, jester and lover.

SEO

SEO, also known as search engine optimization, is an integral part of every brand's digital strategy. The technique of making a website increasingly visible to all of the web traffic originating from search engines is known as SEO (Denga et al.,2022a) SEO strives to boost organic, unpaid search traffic. The prime purpose of SEO is to position the brand site as highly as possible in search results on Google, Bing, and Yahoo. SEO is fundamental to digital branding because it empowers a business to reach a much larger target audience and accelerates conversions. The creation and dissemination of relevant content on the website is a terrific technique to enhance a brand's SEO (Denga et al.,2022a). Even though they may not be in the writing or idea-sharing profession, many brands include a blog or news section on their websites. These sections frequently contain articles and thought pieces addressing current trends and information in the brand's industry that are written from the viewpoint of the brand. A link to additional websites that are regarded as credible authorities on the topics should be included in each of these pieces of content. The credibility of a brand will strengthen as a function of the website (Bonnim & Alfonso, 2019).

Brand Story

A brand story is a coherent narrative that includes both the facts and the emotions that a brand evokes (Bonnim & Alfonso, 2019). A story aims to evoke an emotional response in the audience, unlike conventional advertising, which focuses on showing and informing about a business. Product, price, history, quality, marketing, in-store experience, purpose, values, location, and most importantly what other people say about the brand can all have an impact on a brand. A company's branding is the concept and perception that consumers have of its goods, services, or business. Storytelling has a visceral impact on your audience by connecting the idea and the visual. Brands can champion a narrative to get people talking about their business. Keeping in mind that oral histories and folklore have endured because of communities like telling their experiences. With the help of a compelling narrative, an audience can transform from admirers to loyal customers that speak favourably of a brand and have faith in it (Bonnim & Alfonso, 2019). However, by fostering word-of-mouth, storytelling can even reduce marketing expenses. Great design and narrative are remembered by the majority of people. Branding is most effective when a company's name, logo, and graphics elicit a variety of emotional and physical responses that conjure feelings of how a product or service should make a customer feel.

Content Marketing

A strategic marketing method known as "content marketing" concentrates on generating and disseminating valuable, timely, and consistent content to attract and retain the attention of a target audience and, ultimately, stimulate profitable customer behaviour (Denga et al.,2022c). Nowadays, merely advertising products is insufficient. Engagement is essential to developing a base of repeat customers. That's where content marketing comes in. It represents the brand's human side. Customers should be intrigued by a brand and enthusiastic about its products and message for content marketing to be effective. It aims to create long-lasting, fruitful partnerships and contributes to building trust between brands and users. While digital marketing introduces a customer to a business, effective content marketing should retain their interest and convert one-time users into ardent supporters. Blog posts, infographics, podcasts, and videos are a few examples of content marketing (Denga et al.,2022d).

Social Media

Social media is a relatively novel but rapidly evolving facet of any company's branding. A brand's goal and values can be effectively communicated to everyone on the platform by having a strong social media presence, especially to prospective and current customers. If handled properly, social media is a great technique to expose a digital brand to potential customers (Jacobson et al.,2020). But if it's not done correctly, it may also be a significant waste of time, money, and resources. Facebook, YouTube, WhatsApp, Instagram, TikTok, Snapchat, and Twitter are the most utilized social media platforms worldwide. Customers are increasingly leveraging social media as a direct channel for brand communication. They may post unfavourable opinions on particular goods, services, or brands in addition to positive comments and product reviews (Jacobson et al.,2020).

The days of campaigns lasting more than two months are long gone. Brands must pay attention to consumer feedback and almost immediately adapt to real-time. Social media offers an effective avenue for doing this. Brands can adapt their messaging more quickly than ever and create communication that best resonates with their customer thanks to social listening and authentic brand experience that is conveyed through social channels. Social media listening, also known as social listening, is the process of identifying and evaluating online comments made about a business, person, product, or brand (Jacobson et al.,2020). Brands employ social media strategy and fresh content creation techniques to engage all audiences and stay abreast. Brands must be ready to produce "ephemeral" content or material with a very short shelf life. To keep audiences interested, brands essentially need to continuously provide bite-sized information. Social media communication also has a technical component (Jacobson et al.,2020). Brands have found success through the adoption of adaptable chatbots on social media to answer questions from customers, offer general customer assistance, or launch innovative products. Particularly for B2C brands where there is a significant level of user engagement.

Email Marketing

Email marketing is one of the most versatile strategies a company can adopt to expand: it can be leveraged for branding, engagement, acquisition, retention, direct sales, reactivation, generating traffic, and acquiring referrals (Guenzi & Habel, 2020). It is a strategy for reaching out to customers through email marketing. Email marketing is less expensive than other forms of marketing when promoting a company's products or services. Creating a lead-filled email list is the first step in creating a successful email marketing campaign. A successful campaign may provide exclusive discounts on products and services to foster consumer loyalty (Guenzi & Habel, 2020). An efficient email campaign must be simple to read, professionally planned, and explicitly identify the goals it is intended to accomplish.

Influencer Marketing

Influencer marketing, a digital marketing tactic that is closely related to social media marketing, is swiftly surging in popularity. Influencer marketing is described by Sprout Social as "a form of social media marketing that employs endorsements and product mentions from influencers — people who have a dedicated social following and are recognized as experts in their niche." Influencer marketing has become a full-time, highly lucrative career for individuals with large followings. Influencer marketing benefits brands immensely by boosting sales and highlighting their unique personality (Garzella et al., 2020). Influencers demonstrate how their principles and the brand's ideals are compatible when they promote goods or services.

Paid Digital Advertising

In paid digital advertising, businesses pay a publisher (such as a search engine or website owner) each time a user clicks or views one of their adverts in a search result, on a website, on social media, or a variety of other digital platforms (Bonnim & Alfonso, 2019). Instead of the (sometimes slow) process of garnering attention organically, brands can now practically buy it. It is frequently adopted by marketers who place bids to take part in live auctions so that their ads will appear on a certain search engine, platform, or network. Pay-Per-Click (PPC) advertising is the common name for this type of internet advertising, which is done to drive traffic to websites. Numerous platforms, including Google Ads, Bing, Facebook, Instagram, Twitter, and LinkedIn, can be utilized for paid advertising. Each of these platforms offers a variety of choices for paid advertising, and they might include one or several of the following ad types: search, display, remarketing, shopping, and social media ads.

IMPORTANCE OF BRANDING IN THE DIGITAL ERA

Customers are more likely to become emotionally invested in a brand or product when it has a strong online presence. Well-designed branding enables brands to communicate directly with consumers through everyday experiences on the digital platforms they are utilizing, which strengthens relationships with customers. Here are some benefits of digital branding and how they impact firms that adopt it:

Intensify customer experience: No matter the environment digital or not, tactics without a viable strategy fall short of achieving company objectives. Executing a brand promise is where the business strategy starts. As a result, the emphasis of marketing strategy must be on continually delivering on this pledge to enhance the consumer experience across all digital platforms. The remarkable approach to enticing prospects into a brand experience is to engage them across all digital touch points in their everyday routines (Denga, 2022a). It still takes seven times for someone to see a message for them to remember it. Consumers want consistent experiences across several channels (web, mobile, in-person, and social), and if they don't get them, 73% of them are inclined to switch brands. Each customer encounter affects consumer loyalty and attrition A study revealed that 76 per cent of consumers stated it is now simpler than ever to switch brands in pursuit of an experience that measures up to their expectations and takes their business elsewhere (Hardey, 2014). A gorgeous logo and catchy tagline have never been the only components of branding. It's about using tried-and-true techniques that deliver on promises across all of the various channels that the target audience accesses daily (Kozinets, 2022). Brands must ensure that their messaging not only reflects the interests of their target audience throughout the consumer decision-making process but also that it is appropriate for the specific medium to enhance the customer experience.

Improve competitive advantage: While maintaining a consistent appearance and feel across digital channels is crucial, the best entity businesses can offer to specific customers is their brand promise. This is the emotionally charged takeaway that will motivate clients, keep them returning for more, and ultimately persuade them to purchase more goods or services. A brand's promise guarantees a competitive edge in the market. It consists of basic elements like quality, variety, prestige, inspiration, or even speedy delivery(Glyynn,2011). Everything that matters most to the target audience must be communicated through all touch points and channels, as well as how the brand intends to fulfil its promise. A company's promise and core values are more important to a brand than the goods or services it offers. Although only partially true, this is extremely crucial. In reality, a brand is how potential clients and customers perceive it. The overall impression—the remaining resonance of feelings—is what motivates customers or leads them to interact with a company. A powerful brand creates a lasting impression and raises standards for a service or product(Herhausen et al.,2020). If branding is weak, customers may engage with other brands instead, which can force tactical elements of digital marketing efforts, such as social media, SEO/SEM, email marketing, behavioural targeting, and programmatic, to become extremely unconnected and fragmented across vehicles (Edelman, 2010). An advantage over competitors in the market is always provided by a strong brand. Enhancing trust, ease of conversion, and earned media will inevitably follow with a lower cost-per-conversion when a brand has significant market weight.

Increase credibility and trust: Customers prefer to transact with brands they can trust. Businesses establish credibility and an affinity to their customers' core values through branding efforts. Brands provide customers with more than just content; they also provide emotional experiences. Building a strong, distinctive, and relatable offering that endures across all of the diverse channels is what differentiates brands from their competitors and ultimately strengthens brand trust (Bonnim & Alfonso, 2019). Customers place a higher value on trust than a lower price of goods or services. A recent study indicated that customers prioritize brand to trust when making purchases, with 81 per cent of survey participants stating that they "must be able to trust the brand to do what is right"(Casidy et al.,2022) Most customers said they would generally prefer to purchase from a well-known, reputable brand. Increased personal interactions between brands and their prospects are made possible by consumer-trusted digital platforms like social media and online reviews.

Showcase shared value: Company-branded "content" must align with customers' core values and motivate them to re-engage with them when prospects and customers are ready to make a purchase decision (Aly, 2020). Customers want brands to be consistent in their messaging at all consumer decision-making touchpoints. Furthermore, the messaging must be suitable for each touch point. Customers also want brands to value the same things they do.

Autonomous Consumers: Consumers are frequently left in perplexing situations as a function of the vast amounts of information that are constantly flowing on the digital platform, particularly when it comes to goods and services. Since consumers are frequently "spoilt for choice," marketers must differentiate their brands from those of their rivals in terms of the products and services they offer (Casidy et al.,2022). The accessibility of information on all products and services has empowered the average consumer smarter than ever before.

To sum it up, when it comes to branding, little has changed in either the digital or "real world" era. Customers expect brand promises to be consistent. But there have been massive alterations in how it is delivered. Similarly, branding's role in digital marketing is constantly evolving (Jacobson et al.,2020). A brand's creation never truly ends. The process of enhancing and expanding a company's or offering's distinctive qualities is continual. Even so, the effort is worth it. Strong digital branding guarantees that businesses are constantly in the consideration stage as prospects and customers view and engage with their online content. (Denga et al.,2022c)

MAINTAINING A BRAND IN A DIGITAL ERA

It is now essential for brands to leverage digital technology to market and sell their products and services given the rapid technological advancements. The digital realm has continued to challenge tenacious brands in their effort to stay competitive amongst all the internet noise, from building online platforms for consumer engagement to packaging information about products and services for digital marketing. Maintaining a brand in the digital era requires a strategic and adaptive approach to effectively engage with consumers in the online landscape. Here is a summary of key considerations for maintaining a brand in the digital era:

Create mobile-friendly content: Better digital marketing techniques are still essential as an outcome of the evolution of mobile phone technology and the proliferation of smartphones, particularly among millennials (Svarc et al.,2020). Brands are now compelled to optimize their websites for mobile users with faster load times. In reality, websites that make it simple for visitors to navigate across mobile devices are rewarded by Google and other Search Engine Result Pages (SERPs) with a higher organic position on SERPs. Consumers are empowered to be informed about product and service promotions through the usage of mobile apps, and notably mobile messaging.

Embrace Internet marketing techniques: Notable online marketing strategies include search engine optimization and paid search marketing. Paid search marketing makes use of Google AdWords, which utilizes a set budget for brands to rank highly on SERPs like Google, Yahoo, and Bing, in addition to Pay Per Click Marketing (PPC), which costs brands for each click on a link that drives target audience to their product or service homepage.

Improve online brand engagement: Although creating social media profiles on sites like Facebook, Twitter, and LinkedIn, to name a few, is simple, online engagement entails much more effort. A prompt response to online inquiries serves to retain customers loyal to a brand. It is not always appropriate to have formal, business-like conversations. Brands can decide to mention the user's username and concentrate on having a friendly and interesting chat. Brands have increased their online engagement with this tactic, which has increased their visibility on social media sites(Ritter & Pederson, 2020). For customers to continue utilizing digital platforms, consistency in content creation is also pivotal. Brands can offer information about their products and consumer reviews of their services. Engaging online also entails responding to the negative publicity that surfaced on social media platforms.

Leverage infographics and video content: Online text content is so abundant that more people are reading less of it. Statistics show that the average person only retains 20% of what they read and 65% of what they watch. This is due to how effortless it is to follow and comprehend visual content. Leading businesses are embracing short videos that highlight their societal impact and customer testimonials as they attract a wider audience than text-based information since YouTube's advent (Ritter & Pederson, 2020).

In conclusion, maintaining a brand in the digital era requires a proactive and adaptive approach to engaging with customers effectively. A strong online presence, supported by a well-designed website and active participation on social media platforms, is crucial. Crafting a compelling content strategy that resonates with the target audience and leveraging social media engagement helps to build meaningful relationships and enhance brand awareness. Personalization techniques and influencer collaborations contribute to delivering tailored experiences and expanding brand reach. Prioritizing customer experience, leveraging data-driven decision-making, and staying adaptable to digital trends are key factors for success. Effective online reputation management and continuous learning help to safeguard and improve brand perception. By implementing these strategies, brands can thrive in the digital era, foster customer loyalty, and achieve sustainable growth in an ever-evolving digital landscape.

BRANDING CHALLENGES AND OPPORTUNITIES IN THE DIGITAL ERA

The manner people are consuming branded content has been fundamentally revolutionized by the information age. Brands are increasingly more preoccupied with creating an identity and a symbol for the user than with serving a function. Brands now face a particularly challenging drawback as they strive to rebuild their brands and marketing strategies and adapt to contemporary demands as a result of developments like soaring mobile device usage (including tablets and smartphones), advertising algorithms, and programmatic buying. The effects of digitalization on branding strategies are multifaceted. For brand managers, innovations in technologies, market trends, and communication techniques present both opportunities and challenges.

In the digital era, brands face enormous challenges, the most crucial one among them is digital consumer journeys. Consumers interact with brands frequently, both online and offline employing a multitude of communication channels. The plethora of information available online has culminated in exceptionally well-informed consumers nowadays who can evaluate the quality of the products, the variety of options available in the market, and price comparisons. One dilemma is that customers have easy access to vast volumes of online brand information as a result of their digital consumer journeys. This information is readily available on consumers' smartphones with a simple swipe. The availability of information has transformed, and one could readily assume that brands are no longer as important. However, it is precisely because of this abundance of information that branding remains important. Customers require a mechanism to sort through the clutter of information, uncover trends, and make sense of it.

Brand awareness and distinct brand positioning are vital mechanisms in this process (Keller, 1993). When making a purchase, customers will choose well-known brands that are easily remembered and recalled as well as those that can offer practical and useful benefits (Olsen, 2011, for a discussion). In a digital age characterized by information overload, this forecast is even more accurate (Trevino & Pineda, 2019).

This has also spurred "showrooming." Such informed buyers won't be converted by false promises and inaccurate content. This presents a challenge to marketers, forcing them to consistently maintain information symmetry.

The fragile brand image is another problem. The power is in the customers' hands attributable to digital media. A two-way communication between brands has ensued from this transition. Even one unfavourable review on social media platforms has the potential to harm a brand's reputation. The image can be irreparably damaged once digital media picks up on that trend. Online opinions of contemporary brands are not entirely under their control (Lane &Levy, 2019). Customers create brands and shape public perception of them, particularly on social media. While interacting with their clients, brands need to be transparent and extremely cautious as all it takes is one unpleasant instance to become viral and have a significant negative effect.

As there are more consumer touchpoints in the digital age, branding becomes increasingly challenging. It is pertinent to have an Omni-channel strategy so that branding is consistent across all of these channels without resorting to cross-posting as some target groups are present in some media while others are in others. Simply creating a website for a brand is insufficient. Every day, customers interact with a variety of devices and channels, including social media, blogs, mobile apps, and search engines in addition to websites. For any brand to keep its recall, establishing a strong presence across all of these platforms is indispensable (Ress, 2022). There is a considerable amount of information about markets, customers, purchasing trends, and similar topics available in the world of the Internet. Every brand must collect and evaluate information on consumer purchasing habits, strategy performance metrics, A/B testing outcomes, etc. The secret to creating the ideal strategy and unveiling each market's untapped potential is data.

The opportunities for brands have proliferated with the advent of digital media, to the point that certain businesses could not have survived without the advent of the digital age. Amazon is one such organization. Without the introduction of the digital era or technology, the E-Commerce sector could not have been exploited. The efficiency to engage consumers in a more personalized fashion is one of the primary branding opportunities in the digital age. With the rapid growth of digital media, brands' reach has broadened. Market penetration has surged because of platforms like Facebook and WhatsApp, which have made branding and marketing easier. social media has pioneered the concept of earned and shared media while heretofore brands wrote content in the form of owned and paid media. Today, their existing (and satisfied) customers are their strongest advocates because potential customers are more influenced by them than by any brochure or website. In the modern world, reviews are relevant.

Furthermore, customers collaborate with businesses to co-create brands. As a reflection of how vital customer feedback and opinions are, firms are investing millions of dollars in research to better understand consumer needs and preferences. Leveraging the opportunities that the digital era offers and being flexible to respond to change has so clearly become essential as Only businesses that adapt to the times will survive; otherwise, even the most well-known brands, like Nokia, might become obsolete in a short period. It's necessary to break the inertia of adhering to outdated guidelines. Brands that will survive in the foreseeable future are those that adapt to emerging trends and strive hard to remain relevant.

CONCLUSION

Consumers in the digital age obsessively search for interesting content to interact with. This has transformed the way consumers think and act, as well as the way brands communicate with them. Regardless of the brand's offerings, a digital presence has become extremely essential. Branding is altered by emerging digital technologies, media platforms, and online consumption behaviours. The chapter explores how innovations brought on by digitalization impact brand management and branding strategies. Although there are challenges with branding in the digital era, these hurdles don't diminish the significance of brands; rather, they change the practice of branding and offer brand managers new opportunities. These issues emphasize the importance of in-depth consumer insight, a thorough grasp of digital customer journeys, and the significance of well-known and strategically positioned brands. Brand managers should undoubtedly seize new digital opportunities, explore emerging media, experiment with novel branding strategies, and implement the most effective ones. However, the fundamentals of branding and brand management remain crucial and will continue to be central in the future. Fundamental concepts like brand positioning, differentiation, and identification will rarely go out of trend and are becoming more crucial in the age of digital marketing, (Samuelsen et al.,2016).

REFERENCES

Alalwan, A. A. (2018). Investigating the impact of social media advertising features on customer purchase intention. *International Journal of Information Management*, *42*, 65–77. doi:10.1016/j.ijinfomgt.2018.06.001

Aly, H. (2020). Digital transformation, development and productivity in developing countries: is artificial intelligence a curse or a blessing? Review of Economics and Political Science. doi:10.1108/REPS-11-2019-0145

Anusha, G. (2016). Effectiveness of online advertising. *International Journal of Research*, *4*(3), 14–21.

Bala, M., & Verma, D. (2018). A Critical Review of Digital Marketing. *International Journal of Management. IT & Engineering*, *8*(10), 321–339.

Baum, D., Spann, M., Füller, J., & Thürridl, C. (2019). The impact of social media campaigns on the success of new product introductions. *Journal of Retailing and Consumer Services*, *50*, 289–297. doi:10.1016/j.jretconser.2018.07.003

Bonnin, G., & Alfonso, M. R. (2019). The narrative strategies of B2B technology brands. *Journal of Business and Industrial Marketing*, *34*(7), 1448–1458. doi:10.1108/JBIM-03-2019-0112

Casidy, R., Leckie, C., Nyadzayo, M. W., & Johnson, L. W. (2022). Customer brand engagement and co-production: An examination of key boundary conditions in the sharing economy. *European Journal of Marketing*, *56*(10), 2594–2621. doi:10.1108/EJM-10-2021-0803

Das, S. (2021). A Systematic Study of integrated marketing communication and content management system for millennial consumers. *Innovations in Digital Branding and Content Marketing*, 91-112. . doi:10.4018/978-1-7998-4420-4.ch005

Denga, E. M & Sandip Rakshit (2022b). Digital Marketing and the Sustainable Performance of Small and Medium Enterprises. In R. Mourly Potluri & N. R Vajjhala (Eds), Advancing SMEs Toward E-Commerce Policies for Sustainability (pp235-247). IGI Global. doi:10.4018/978-1-6684-5727-6.ch011

Denga, E. M., Vajjhala, N. R., & Rakshit, S. (2022c). Relationship Selling as a Strategic Weapon for Sustainable Performance. In J. D. Santos (Ed.), *Sales Management for Improved Organizational Competitiveness and Performance* (pp. 78–101). IGI Global. doi:10.4018/978-1-6684-3430-7.ch005

Denga, E. M., Vajjhala, N. R., & Rakshit, S. (2022d). The Role of Digital Marketing in Achieving Sustainable Competitive Advantage. In O. Yildiz (Ed.), *Digital Transformation and Internationalization Strategies in Organizations* (pp. 44–60). IGI Global. doi:10.4018/978-1-7998-8169-8.ch003

Denga Edna Mngusughun. (2022a). Implementing E-Marketing in Small and Medium-Sized Enterprises for Enhanced Sustainability. In R. Mourly Potluri & N. R. Vajjhala (Eds.), *Advancing SMEs Toward E-Commerce Policies for Sustainability* (pp. 88–110). IGI Global. doi:10.4018/978-1-6684-5727-6.ch005

Diaz, E., Esteban, Á., Carranza Vallejo, R., & Martín-Consuegra Navarro, D. (2022). Digital tools and smart technologies in marketing: A thematic evolution. *International Marketing Review*, *39*(5), 1122–1150. doi:10.1108/IMR-12-2020-0307

Edelman, D. C. (2010). Branding in the Digital Age. *Harvard Business Review*, *88*, 62–69.

Garzella, S., Fiorentino, R., Caputo, A., & Lardo, A. (2020). Business model innovation in SMEs: The role of boundaries in the digital era. *Technology Analysis and Strategic Management*, 1–13.

Glynn, M. (2011). Brands and Branding: The Economist Series. *Journal of Consumer Marketing, 28,* 161-162. doi:10.1108/07363761111116024

Guenzi, P., & Habel, J. (2020). Mastering the Digital Transformation of Sales. *California Management Review*, *62*(4), 57–85. doi:10.1177/0008125620931857

Hardey, M. (2014). Marketing Narratives: Researching Digital Data, Design and the In/Visible Consumer. Emerald Group Publishing Limited, Bingley. doi:10.1108/S1042-319220140000013008

Herhausen, D., Miočević, D., Morgan, R. E., & Kleijnen, M. H. P. (2020). The digital marketing capabilities gap. *Industrial Marketing Management*, *90*, 276–290. doi:10.1016/j.indmarman.2020.07.022

Jacobson, J., Gruzd, A., & Hernández-García, Á. (2020). Social media marketing: Who is watching the watchers? *Journal of Retailing and Consumer Services*, *53*, 53. doi:10.1016/j.jretconser.2019.03.001

Jerez-Jerez, M. J. (2022). Digital Transformation and Corporate Branding: Opportunities and Challenges for Identity and Reputation Management. Foroudi, P., Nguyen, B. and Melewar, T.C. (Ed.) The Emerald Handbook of Multi-Stakeholder Communication. Emerald Publishing Limited, Bingley. doi:10.1108/978-1-80071-897-520221014

Kozinets, R. V. (2022). Algorithmic branding through platform assemblages: Core conceptions and research directions for a new era of marketing and service management. *Journal of Service Management*, *33*(3), 437–452. doi:10.1108/JOSM-07-2021-0263

Lane, K., & Levy, S. J. (2019). Marketing in the Digital Age: A Moveable Feast of Information. Marketing in a Digital World (Review of Marketing Research, Vol. 16), Emerald Publishing Limited, Bingley. doi:10.1108/S1548-643520190000016004

Li, Y., Song, X. & Zhou, M. (2022). Impacts of brand digitalization on brand market performance: the mediating role of brand competence and brand warmth. *Journal of Research in Interactive Marketing*, 1-18. . doi:10.1108/JRIM-03-2022-0107

Lipiäinen, H. S. M., & Karjaluoto, H. (2015). Industrial branding in the digital age. *Journal of Business and Industrial Marketing*, *30*(6), 733–741. doi:10.1108/JBIM-04-2013-0089

Makri, K., Papadas, K.-K., & Schlegelmilch, B. B. (2019). Global-local consumer identities as drivers of global digital brand usage. *International Marketing Review*, *36*(5), 702–725. doi:10.1108/IMR-03-2018-0104

Mergel, I., Edelmann, N., & Haug, N. (2019). Defining digital transformation: Results from expert interviews. *Government Information Quarterly*, *36*(4), 101385. doi:10.1016/j.giq.2019.06.002

Niculescu, A., Dumitriu, D., Purdescu, C., & Popescu, M. A. M. (2019). Enhancing Brand Value of Modern Organizations through Digital Marketing Tools and Techniques: A Study on Top Ten Romanian Companies. *TEM Journal*, *8*(1), 171.

Press, J., Bellis, P., Buganza, T., & Magnanini, S. (Rami) Shani, A.B., Trabucchi, D., Verganti, R. & Zasa, F.P. (2021). Innovation in the Digital Era. IDeaLs (Innovation and Design as Leadership). Emerald Publishing Limited, Bingley, 13-34. doi:10.1108/978-1-80071-833-320211002

Ramadhani, I. S., & Indradjati, P. N. (2023). Toward contemporary city branding in the digital era: conceptualizing the acceptability of city branding on social media. Open House International. doi:10.1108/OHI-08-2022-0213

Rees, S. (2022). Authentic Sports Branding in the Digital Age. Heřmanová, M., Skey, M. & Thurnell-Read, T. (Ed.) Cultures of Authenticity. Emerald Publishing Limited, Bingley. doi:10.1108/978-1-80117-936-220221009

Ritter, T., & Pedersen, C. L. (2020). Digitization capability and the digitalization of business models in business-to-business firms: Past, present, and future. *Industrial Marketing Management*, *86*, 180–190. doi:10.1016/j.indmarman.2019.11.019

Švarc, J., Lažnjak, J., & Dabić, M. (2020). The role of national intellectual capital in the digital transformation of EU countries. Another digital divide? *Journal of Intellectual Capital*. . doi:10.1108/JIC-02-2020-0024

Treviño, T., & Pineda Garelli, J. L. (2019). Understanding digital moms: Motivations to interact with brands on social networking sites. *Qualitative Market Research*, *22*(1), 70–87. doi:10.1108/QMR-01-2017-0013

Yu, X., & Yuan, C. (2019). How consumers' brand experience in social media can improve brand perception and customer equity. *Asia Pacific Journal of Marketing and Logistics*, *31*(5), 1233–1251. doi:10.1108/APJML-01-2018-0034

ADDITIONAL READING

Bamm, R., Helbling, M., & Joukanen, K. (2018). Online Branding and the B2B Context. Koporcic, N., Ivanova-Gongne, M., Nyström, A.-G. and Törnroos, J.-Å. (Ed.) Developing Insights on Branding in the B2B Context. Emerald Publishing Limited, Bingley. doi:10.1108/978-1-78756-275-220181009

Frechette, B. G. (2010). Brand Digital: Simple Ways Top Brands Succeed in the Digital World. *Journal of Consumer Marketing*, *27*(3), 293–293. doi:10.1108/07363761011038374

Rowley, J. (2004). Online branding. *Online Information Review*, *28*(2), 131–138. doi:10.1108/14684520410531637

Travis, D. (2001). Branding in the digital age. *The Journal of Business Strategy*, *22*(3), 14–18. doi:10.1108/eb040166

KEY TERMS AND DEFINITIONS

Brand: A concept employed in business and marketing to assist consumers to recognize a specific organization, product, or person.

Branding: A process of instilling a strong, favourable image of a business, its goods or its services in the minds of the public by fusing features such as a logo, design, mission statement, and a recurring theme throughout all marketing communications.

Digital Branding: The act of leveraging digital assets to develop a brand identity that can be conveyed on any digital channel, such as a website, social media profiles, digital advertising, and content marketing.

Digital Era: A period in history that started in the middle of the 20th century and is marked by a quick transition from traditional industries developed during the Industrial Revolution to an economy focused on information technology.

Chapter 9
Brand Activertising:
From Profit–Purpose to Social Positioning

Alexandre Duarte

https://orcid.org/0000-0002-2665-864X
ICNOVA, Universidade NOVA de Lisboa, Portugal

Simão Chambel
FCSH/UNL, Universidade NOVA de Lisboa, Portugal

ABSTRACT

In an era of highly polarized public opinion, organizations all over the world are now facing a great dilemma, as brand activism and CSR strategies have a stronger influence on consumer behaviors than the traditional marketing campaigns. With marketing changing from purpose to action, and consumers becoming more belief driven, companies are being asked to take a stand, and choose a side on controversial sociopolitical issues. Advertising, the spearhead of organizational communication, which has always appropriated the social codes in force in society to persuade its target audience to carry out certain actions, nowadays, can no longer be dissociated from the moral concerns of consumers who increasingly demand corporate responsibility from organizations. This chapter explores the evolution of advertising's role, in a historical and contextual approach, analyzed from the new relationship model that citizens and consumers demand from companies and the reflection that it has on the advertising message.

ORGANIZATIONS AND THE PUBLIC SPACE

Whenever people needed to produce something too complex for the individual task, they created organizations, which can be seen as human associations built for the fulfillment of a certain objective. But they are more than that. According to Ruão (2016, p.63), organizations can be understood as a "cultural phenomena, centered

DOI: 10.4018/978-1-6684-8351-0.ch009

on the production of systems of meanings, or as socially constructed realities, based on physical and mental structures". And it is precisely in this production of meaning that organizations have been changing the way they relate to their various audiences.

Parallel to this change in the communicational behavior of organizations, another significant change has been happening, in front of us, in recent times: the awareness and consequent focus and importance given to social causes (Chan, 2023). Indeed, much has been debated about global community problems (Robins & Dowty, 2008) that have been progressively and consistently invading the public space, often accompanied by long spectrums of positions and arguments that create rich debates around them. In fact, "today's culture of political unrest, protest and populist sentiment is prime opportunity for advertisers to connect with audiences in new ways" (Benner, 2018, p. 1). According to Vredenburg et al. (2020), in the increasingly polarized society that we're living, several controversial issues are serving as catalysts for many brands to define problems of social interest and refocus on doing social good (p. 456). Some of the main drivers of its assiduity in modernity have been the movements of affirmation and empowerment of ethnic, cultural, religious minorities, but also of class, sexual orientation, and gender, among others, related to movements of anti-precariousness and dignified conditions. And whatever position, whether citizens, individually, or organizations, as social groups, take or not on these issues, the inevitability of their presence in everyday life is a reality that cannot be ignored.

From an *Habermasian* perspective, the political sphere, namely liberal democracies, given their natural and inevitable public nature, have the inescapable duty to address these issues, creating legislation or opinions that affect or concern defenders or opponents of a certain cause. On the other hand, it is not just citizens, grouped or individually, who form civil society and are in permanent contact with various social issues. Also, companies and corporations, namely private ones – derived from the bourgeois public sphere (Habermas, 1962) – have been progressively asserting themselves as a third domain with its own interests, sometimes collective and corporate, clearly demarcated from those of the State. Its distance from government authorities and its clear interest in the autonomy of its instruments of power guarantee it a simultaneously integrated, but truly specific role in civil society. These corporations, which we will call private from now on (as opposed to public, statal) maintain, therefore, relations both with single individuals and with the State, but traditionally with a "selfish" perspective.

From an historical and even legal point of view, companies have always had the option of participating in the public debate on social issues – with the possibility of publicly pronouncing or not on certain situations. However, with a closer look at the beginnings of commercial communication, we can see that the exemption of positions and comments on social causes was not only the norm, but we can even say that it was desirable, prudent, and wise. It turns out that today, considering developments in what consumers ethically expect from the companies whose products and services they consume, the decision to comment on social and political aspects - and to do so "correctly" - is less and less a choice. As Paris (2022, p.3) stated, "as cultural controversies arise, brands are under pressure from consumers, and even competitors, to take a stand". In this everyday more polarized world (Mukherjee & Althuizen, 2020), brands are being pushed to stand out, to take a stance, and show some responsibility on the most important social causes. One of the key reasons why companies engage in brand activism is to appeal to consumers who are increasingly conscious of social and environmental issues. By aligning their brand with a particular cause, companies can differentiate themselves from their competitors and tap into the growing market of socially conscious consumers. If the values and causes that a brand express are aligned with those of consumers, it is very likely that they will choose it, since the brand speaks or is actively committed to a cause that is important to them. This can also help to build a sense of trust and loyalty among consumers, as they see the company as being more than just a profit-driven entity (Eyada, 2020). Nevertheless, in very comprehensive research, Hydock et al. (2020) found that when a brand's customers are politically heterogeneous, a brand activist strategy (or Corporate Political Advocacy (CPA), as the authors called it) is likely to benefit small-share brands and harm large-share brands (p.1149).

Even though brand activism involves uncertainty and risks, the potential pay-off could worth it (Mukherjee & Althuizen, 2020). In the introduction to the annual Global Communications report (2022), which analyzes the challenges, opportunities, risks and rewards of corporate activism, Fred Cook, Director of the Center for Public Affairs at the School for Communication and Journalism at the University of Southern California ANNENBERG, stated that:

In the past few years, societal discord has become a significant risk factor for global business, posing a threat to corporate reputation, employee recruitment, and organizational morale. In response, CEOs, who have embraced stakeholder capitalism, are now recognizing they have the responsibility—and the platform—to engage with controversial topics outside of their normal comfort zones. (p.2)

This social pressure gave rise to the so-called "CEO activism", a topic addressed by Kathy Bloomgarden (2019), on the World Economic Forum website, questioning whether CEOs – whom she dubbed activists – should talk about social causes. For the author, "corporate activism" is no longer something relegated to the Corporate Social Responsibility (CSR) department, ethics, or the back-office, with the leader himself now taking center stage, causing a real impact on society. Regarding this, Marc Benniof (2018), Chairman and Co-CEO of Salesforce, stated on Twitter that

"CEO activism is not a choice of leaders, but a modern – and evolved – expectation". In the same vein, the CEO of Bank of America, Brian Moynihan, said that "our jobs as CEOs now include driving what we think is right. It's not exactly political activism, but it's taking a stand on issues beyond business" (Bloomgarden, 2019, p.18).

Indeed, leaders increasingly take public positions on political, social, and environmental causes that are not directly related to the organization's core business they lead, on topics ranging from climate change to respect for sexual orientation, from racial issues to gender equality, among others (Chatterji & Toffel, 2019). Examples abound, such as the cases of Starbucks CEO Kevin Johnson, who closed all his stores to conduct training on racial prejudice, the decision of Nike CEO Mark Parker to create and run advertisements featuring the controversial ex-football player Colin Kaepernick, or Disney CEO Bob Iger, who canceled Roseanne Barr's show after she made a derogatory comment about President Barak Obama's former top aide (Bloomgarden, 2019).

Branicki et al. (2020) recall the great public interest that the social and environmental activism of CEOs attracts, essentially due to their extreme influence, a consequence of their huge public visibility and positional power. The authors questioned, however, the morality of these "new" CEOs and concluded that, although CEO activism is a new, important, and potent phenomenon, one cannot universally consider all CEOs as moral leaders. Rather, one should first question the motives and effects of what CEOs do in the name of morality (p.269).

Even so, and despite the growing number of so-called activist CEOs, this is often a true double-edged sword, since organizations are made up of people, who are citizens above all else, and the border between what is private and what is public often becomes diffuse, as seen in the case[1] with the CEO of Prozis[2], who issued a controversial personal opinion, by publicly welcoming the decision of the US Supreme Court to revoke the protection of the right to abortion. As a result, the company he leads has suffered consequences, having been the target of numerous censorships, cancellations of contracts with influencers and personalities who did not want to be associated with these statements, as well as thousands of ordinary people who unfollowed the brand on social networks and publicly assumed that would stop consuming products from that company. In fact, this "cancel culture" is one of the biggest challenges that modern organizations are facing now-a-days, since companies, brands and even people can no longer be neutral, without being seen as accomplices (Paris, 2022).

One of the most prominent references to the importance of the social role of organizations, in this context of high scrutiny and demand for their responsibility, was made by Debora Doane, in an article published in the book "O Mundo das Marcas", edited by Rita Clifton and John Simmons (2005). This book, which appears somehow in defense of brands and as a counterargument to the book "No Logo" by Naomi

Klein (2002), compiles texts by various authors on brands and brand management in the context of globalization (Ruão, 2005). In this text, the author seeks a realistic understanding of the actions of brands, fleeing radical extremisms both for and against, finding a middle ground in its definition. Focusing on the social value of brands, Doane presents and clearly explains the concept of "social leadership". This construct assumes that brands, as important economic agents, but also social ones, have a duty towards society and their action must be guided by a logic of balance between corporate objectives and social concerns. For the author, more than mere "social responsibility", brands should really commit to leading social change, aiming a fairer and more sustainable society, as a response to consumer demands.

This ethical concern of consumers, especially in this participatory culture (Jenkins, 1992), portrays a trend that organizations quickly noticed, mobilizing new communication approaches that adapt to business models and operations that consider the concept CSR, increasingly fundamental in the survival and competitiveness of companies that have, however, gained their own "corporate citizenship", which therefore presupposes a set of rights and duties. Indeed, as societal expectations of corporate behavior have changed, so has the concept of "corporate responsibility has evolved from the simple generation of profit to the more recent belief that the primary responsibility of companies should be to generation of shared value" (Agudelo et al., 2019, p. 1). The World Business Council for Sustainable Development, defines CSR as:

the continuous commitment, by companies, to act ethically and contribute to economic development along with improvements in the quality of life of workers, their families, the local community, and society in general. (WBCSD, 2000, p.10).

This definition introduces a shift in the traditional conception of a firm as an entity whose sole maxim is the creation of monetary value - profit - and the commitment and satisfaction of shareholders, for an organization with several responsibilities towards society, with an emphasis on communities it affects (Cornelissen, 2014, p. 359). As Holt (2002) timely noted, brands are now seen as powerful social actors, as they embody important ideas and meanings for society. This way, the social issues that affect and mobilize populations also concern companies that intend to establish and maintain relationships with them, in a balanced symbiosis between the objectives of communities and corporations.

For Sarkar and Kotler (2018), brand activism is an evolution of CSR, although they have different characteristics, goals, and consequences. CSR differs from brand activism in the sense that the first concept is usually seen as beneficial for the whole society, so generally accepted and non-divisive, that only elicits negative feedback from consumers if perceived as an unauthentic marketing trick (Mukherjee & Althuizen, 2020). The second one, defined as "a purpose- and values-driven strategy in which a brand adopts a nonneutral stance on institutionally contested sociopolitical issues, to create social change and marketing success" (Vredenburg et al., 2020, p.446), chooses one side on controversial sociopolitical issues, lacking this way any type of consensus (Hydock et al., 2020; Miguel & Miranda, 2022; Sarkar & Kotler, 2018). On top of that, Daniel Korschun (2021) adds two other distinctive characteristics between both constructs: first, brand activism involves a public stated position, spread through visible means; and second, it implies advocacy, meaning that more than "doing's one part", it proactively seeks to change people's opinions and behavior regarding divisive causes by persuading individuals and other organizations to join their side.

SOCIOPOLITICAL CAUSES IN ADVERTISING: AN EXPONENTIAL REALITY

Without the Creative Revolution of the 1960s, led by David Ogilvy and Bill Bernbach, which gave rise to the so-called Modern Advertising Era (Castro, 2002), it would not make much sense to speak of a focus on social and political issues that are mobilized with that, going beyond the simple promotion of a product and its benefits. The personality, values, image and positioning that organizations strive to build and maintain in the consumer's minds, results, strongly, from communication efforts that include, in addition to the remaining elements of the communication mix, all advertising campaigns.

Advertising, as a form of paid communication, which aims to persuade a given audience to perform a certain action (Wells et al., 2000), has always resorted to a persuasive argument that also aims to build, in consumer's minds, a desired image for the products or services advertised. Parallel to this intention, this form of communication has gained, in recent decades, such a decisive importance, to the point of constituting itself as the very form of culture (Lipovetsky & Serroy, 2010), so that it can no longer be dissociated from the moral and ethical concerns of consumers who increasingly demand corporate responsibility from the organizations. Until the mid-1960s, advertising creation lived as if somewhat distant from the sociopolitical reality (Estrela, 2005), a fact that has changed radically in recent years. Although "the general perception is that advertising, as a form of commercial communication, is inherently misleading, following a particular interest, as opposed to what could be - and usually is - considered public interest" (Hazaparu, 2014, p.312), the truth is consumers increasingly expect companies to enter the sociopolitical domain (Eyada, 2020) and "brands are now seemingly comfortable alienating some consumers to address contested and polarizing sociopolitical issues" (Vredenburg et al., 2020, p.445). Until now, the risk of taking public positions on polarizing issues did not seem to outweigh the possibility of a negative response from consumers who, generally, were not interested in invading the political dimension under the harmless prime time television advertising, which consoled the viewer with its idyllic scenarios, familiar, and with a comforting simplicity.

Between an urban world and a media scenario that increasingly accompanied its tragedies and upheavals, advertising intended to remain in the sphere of an "out-of-the-real reality", whereby any political stand was usually avoided and hidden. In this way, advertising would fulfill its maximum effectiveness, taking the maximum psychological advantage of a consumer vulnerable to the effects of primary emotions, without social concerns entering the basic stimulus-response equation intended by the argumentative narrative of advertising. But things changed. The incorporation of public and political affairs into advertising started to become a recurring issue in critical theory and cultural studies (Manfredi-Sánchez, 2019). Since ever, advertising shaped mentalities and taked advantage of social trends for the commercial benefit and the creation of new business opportunities. What's new, nowadays, is the appropriation of polarized, activist causes by companies, spread out to society through advertising, phenomenon that the authors coined as *brand activertising*. According to Kumar (2020, p. 2013), this new communication paradigm "may actually contribute to the bullying or preaching of an advertising by consumers". After all, controversial sociopolitical issues are often focus of intense public debate so it's almost impossible for a consumer to ignore a brand's stand or dismiss the moral relevance of the brand's actions (Mukherjee & Althuizen, 2020). One of the first and most evoked disruptions against the old standard of corporate communication was the public relations campaign of the American Tobacco Company, in the promotion of Lucky Strike brand cigarettes. In 1929, the company organized a march for gender equality, where women paraded smoking brand's cigarettes, symbol of their emancipation and "feminist choice" to participate in an action that until then was always seen as exclusive to the male sphere (Simkovitch, 2019, p. 5). After this event, the emergence of advertising campaigns that made use of feminist causes did not stop increasing. Today, they remain up to date, accompanying contemporary issues and demands, such as access to legal and safe abortion, the #MeToo movement or the end of wage inequality, just to name a few.

In addition to the issue of expectations regarding corporate citizenship, there is another main reason for the political turn to which advertising has been undergoing – the consolidation of political consumerism among the remaining models of political participation (Clarke, 2008; Manfredi-Sánchez, 2019; van Deth, 2014, Vázquez, 2014). After all, as former Portuguese Secretary of State for Culture, Nuno Artur Silva, told newspaper Expresso (2022, October, 21 p.14), "any public act is a political act". The term "political consumerism" can be defined as the specific consumer involvement and behavior in the market, consequence of social concerns, which purchase behavior is determined by moral concerns related to social, legal, business, economic, political, and environmental issues, among others (Sarkar & Kotler, 2018). To Lipovetsky (2022) "for the [actual] committed consumer, purchasing a product is much more than just a behavior focused on seeking private pleasure, it is adopting and defending a set of values, affirming a vision of the world, contributing to improving the present, preparing a better future. (…) the act of consuming becomes (...) a way of acting for the common good" (p.264). The truth is that consumer-citizens demand diversity, inclusion, and positioning of brands in relation to social and political values (Canclini, 2006), and this reality cannot just be seen as a tendency of an activist minority. A good example is the so-called "pink money", which is increasingly coveted by companies that lose fear and prejudice of having their brands associated with gay, lesbian, bisexual and transgender communities (Mozdzenski, 2019).

Studies such as those by Stolle and Micheletti (2005) conclude that the use of buycotting and boycotting – actions with political significance – has been increasing among consumers, indicating that more and more consumers equate the moral and ethical image they have of a certain brand, product, or company in your purchasing process. Eyada (2020) remember us that buying a product has become a way to express an opinion, to make a statement, as consumers view the products they buy as an extension of their beliefs, values, and lifestyles and, therefore, an opportunity to make an impact and exercise their power. Nevertheless, while brand activism can positively affect purchase intentions (buycotting), the flip side can also happen. In that case, if consumers don´t relate to the cause or see it as a gimmick, boycotting the brand can bring a decrease in sales, cash flow and stock prices, can affect the reputation and brand image, and can negatively affect consumer's attitude towards the brand (Shetty et al., 2019). For Neureiter and Bhattacharya (2021), the increase or decrease in sales of a company or brand depends, on the one hand, on the controversial subject itself and, on the other hand, on the level of involvement with the political beliefs of its main customer base.

THE TRUMP ERA OF ADVERTISING

One of the traits that characterizes liberal democracies today is general discontent and distrust of political institutions (Bertsou, 2019). In this sense, it would be expected that external communication, specifically advertising, would mobilize in the construction of a corporate image that exploits this discontent to participate in the political scene, encouraging potential consumers to join the cause (Simkovitch, 2019, p. 5). This trend has seen growth over the last decade, due essentially to the culmination of globalization, the network society, and the popular massification of social and political phenomena.

Taking as an example the election of the former president of the United States, Donald Trump, in 2016, a planetary scale political phenomenon, it is pertinent to mention what Jennings (2018) called "the Trump Age of advertising" – a time when that "woke ads" are privileged (Mirzaei et al., 2022) – an informal way of calling the co-option process that advertising makes of social causes. The submission of advertising trends and rules to the American paradigm, however, projected this phenomenon worldwide and defined new standards in advertising production. In his article, Jennings (2018) marked 2017 as the year for companies to take a stand and pointed out examples of advertising campaigns during events such as the Oscars or the *Super Bowl*[3] that used or mentioned social causes – Coca-Cola, Airbnb, Cadillac, among others.

As mentioned, an organization that, in its advertising, co-opts social movements, assumes an enormous risk, as this decision can bring enormous gains, if successful, or catastrophic losses, of customers, financial and often of its own reputation, in the opposite scenario. And for every good example of advertising campaigns that knew how to make skillful use of these themes, there are twice as many organizations that have been hit by an avalanche of criticism and negative reactions – the so-called backlash.

However, in the "Trump Era", the space where organizations must avoid causes that speak to the general population has become increasingly narrow. Jennings (2018) states that rule number one is that something must be said, since leaders sometimes seem almost obliged to make public statements about political events and social issues. Now, in a decade marked by anti-racist movements like Black Lives Matter, feminists like #MeToo, queer like Pride, body positivity movements, criticism of toxic masculinity and an understanding and desire for greater social inclusion and smaller disparities between minorities and majority, the divergence between progressivism and conservatism has never been more visible.

It is commonly accepted that the racial justice protests during the summer of 2020 changed the dynamics of corporate activism forever. The millions of citizens who got out to the streets to protest against the murder of George Floyd have awakened corporate America. Hundreds of companies, which had never spoken publicly about race, issued statements, made commitments, and donated money (USC, 2022, p.22).

Of course, the social and political positioning of a company, based on its advertising communication, must always consider the target audience it intends to reach. For most companies, it is normal to use this knowledge in the construction of advertising campaigns, extensively studied regarding the effects they will have on their communication target, since they are extremely familiar with this information. As summarized by Simkovitch (2019, p. 3),

[Companies] must truly know their target, who is currently buying their products, and what kind of company they want to be in the future. It is more complex than simply "taking a stance" on a popular current issue. Any social media campaign can turn any decision into a larger social statement, so companies and CEOs must be more selective about why and how they address these issues.

Still, eighty-five percent of communication officers believe that the number of companies advocating for a cause will increase over the next five years, and seventy-three percent say their own companies and customers will increase their public engagement already this year (USC, 2022, p.15).

ADVERTISING AND SOCIAL MOVEMENTS: A RISKY BUT INEVITABLE GAMBLE

In an article published by the *Thinking with Google* blog, Google's Brazil Marketing Director Susana Ayarza (2020) argues that brands should also be agents of equality, equity, and inclusion, even asking: "What, after all, is our purpose?" and adding:

It has been time to retrace our plans and think about what we want to defend. And that includes the way we communicate with people, with customers, advertisers, and entrepreneurs. The responsibility that brands and companies, like Google itself, have with their communication has become more urgent and important. To make a difference, we must consider social and cultural urgencies, avoiding reinforcing stereotypes.

Mukherjee and Althuizen (2020, p.773) remember us that consumers tend to consider their own moral beliefs to be superior or sacrosanct and, therefore, prefer brands aligned with their values. This self-brand identification increases favorable attitudes towards the brand, purchase intentions and the levels of advocacy.

An advertising campaign that has mastered the use of social movements to communicate its position will obviously captivate an audience that identifies with these causes. And if the company is consistent and authentic when it comes to its moral sensibilities, it will probably be able to retain this public more easily, as is the case of well-known brands and veterans of activism, Ben & Jerry's, and Patagonia, which, according to the Communication report USC Global (2022), lead the list of companies with the greatest involvement with social causes (p. 26). The same report also adds that PR strategists are, more than ever, focused on purposeful communication, and realize that an effective corporate activism campaign must be more than a mere statement of support or an image on a Facebook page. To be effective, it must be authentic and relevant to customers and involve employees. But this is not an easy recipe for companies to follow, and sometimes the result lacks substance (p.24). This is what happens when an advertising campaign addresses sociopolitical issues in an insensitive, contradictory, visibly manipulative, or inauthentic and forced way. The consequences can, indeed, be disastrous and permanently tarnish a good reputation. Sometimes the result and impact are far worse, proportionately, than certain campaigns that have proven to be successful. There are several cases that have become famous, such as Pepsi, Dove, Uber, or Burger King, among others, whose campaigns were met with severe criticism and calls for boycotts, particularly on social media, using hashtags such as #BoycottPepsi, #BoycottDove or #DeleteUber which dominated social media trends for several weeks. About the famous case[4] of the advertising commercial that featured a smiling Kendall Jenner handing a can of Pepsi to a policeman, in a clear attempt to appropriate the feeling of resolution and appeasement, during what seemed to be a harmless demonstration against police violence, even after a declaration of a public apology, Pepsi saw its image and reputation suffer a heavy blow that even today leaves visible scars (Taylor, 2017; Meister, 2019). In other words, the famous maxim that "all publicity is good publicity" should perhaps be rethought. While it is true that, although we could have said this several years ago, it is now certain that political consumerism is here to stay and will not so easily allow obvious and performative appropriations of social issues such as violence, gender issues, police racism, or environmental issues, among others, are received without harsh disapproval from consumers. In recent times, we've seen the birth of several anti-brand movements and anti-brand communities (Miguel & Miranda, 2022), and even websites and mobile apps such as www.boycott.com with the purpose to "encourage Social Responsibility, Social Engagement, to democratize the Internet, and to give back the power and voice to the people".

It is, therefore, necessary that business leaders understand, and choose well, how and which issues they should address. That is, if on the one hand there is no shortage of topics, choosing the right one is a critical decision that must be based on the organization's values and the nature of its business. On the other hand, as we know, the means/channel of delivery is also crucial in the impact and effectiveness of the messages. And if it is true that most communication professionals find value in promoting corporate activism, it is also a fact that they continue to use the typical dissemination tools, such as websites, relationships with traditional media and social media. And social media is a perfect training ground that allows people to become activists, as kids in high school are already capable of having a voice in society (Kozinets & Jenkins, 2022, p. 277). This specific audience, young people, must be understood as more than simple consumers, as they are the decision-makers of the future. As Shetty et al. (2019, p. 164) stated, millennials prefer brands that are socially responsible and have a high ethical and moral standard, and that's why some brands look to brand activism as "a way to target a coveted young audience who is far more progressive and political than their parents". For Pelosa and Shang (2011) brand activism and cause marketing are one of the best ways to reach out millennials, and to reach them, "brands must tap into the political energy that generation created and show young people that they can take a stand" (Benner, 2018, p.2). This is a generation that places a greater emphasis on being politically active and honest than those that preceded them. Also, they are socially, culturally, and environmentally more conscious than older generations. In addition, they have many more career options, they want meaningful jobs (Moorman, 2020) where they can express themselves fully (Korschun, 2021), and prefer to choose a company that is more in line with their values, than a company with a lot of value. They can work out of a van instead of an office. They can get news through TikTok instead of The Times. And they care more about climate change than the stock market. One thing is certain: the next generation will judge their future profession by its contribution to society and will measure the success of their professional career by the change it will be able to create (USC, 2022, p.36), so this paradigm shift must be considered in the future strategic decisions of organizations.

From the point of view of commercial communication, from the moment of the creative briefing, the path of the messages - from the creation to the reception by the target audiences - is full of choices that entail several opportunities, but also risks. For an advertising campaign that intends to use and take advantage of social issues to avoid a dangerous failure, it is necessary not to underestimate each of these risks. First, everyone involved must be properly informed about the topic they intend to address, and, on the other hand, it is of the utmost important to know the opinion and sensitivity that the organization's target audience has about it. Finally, it is essential that the company's actions, such as its *modus operandi*, its business and relationships with other corporations, the treatment of its employees and respect for human rights translate what the campaign intends to criticize or support. Any discrepancy between what the company does and what it says becomes an easy target for criticism that will surely lead to campaign failure and, worse, to the development of a feeling of revolt by its various stakeholders.

In this context of intense scrutiny to which business communication is subject by the public sphere - namely in social networks, either by activists, groups, and organizations, but also by the media - all advertising that resorts to practices such as *greenwashing*, *pinkwashing*, *diversitywashing*, or others, will be promptly flagged and moved to the center of many and proliferating debates. To avoid an advertising tragedy, Simkovitch (2019, p. 16) identifies 3 factors that influence the success of a campaign that co-opts social movements: authenticity; the level of commitment to the issue; and transparency. These principles, worked in symbiosis, not only avoid possible criticism related to the motives behind a certain campaign, but also enhance the reach and impact of the messages.

Vredenburg et al. (2020) argues that authenticity is enhanced by the alignment of the corporate's activist messages with brand purpose, values, messages, and a prosocial corporate practice (p. 449). Also, it is to be expected that the public will point the finger at a company that, for example, for years showed no interest in environmental issues, and now does so only for financial reasons, or to ride the wave of social trends. This point leads to the second factor – the level of commitment. An advertising campaign that communicates how "green" a certain company is, will not be enough without concrete and real actions by that organization that show up on other occasions in which its social responsibility in the face of climate change is consistent with what is advertised. Finally, transparency plays an indispensable role in the triad proposed by the author because it is necessary for the flow of communication between the organization and its audiences to occur without noise that compromises the effectiveness and good understanding of the proposals. Transparency should therefore not be seen as an unnecessary burden or obligation, but rather as an added value. A company that is really committed to changing something will certainly have no problem being transparent about this domain.

CONCLUSION

Advertising is an important tool that organizations have, to more than merely informing about the advantages of their products and building a desired image in the minds of the target audiences, also communicate what is expected of organizations - currently placed in the sphere of public debate, through the appropriation of causes and social movements, to identify themselves for or against certain issues, creating what Duarte (2023) coined the "social positioning", defined as the perception that consumers have in their minds about the symbolic identification of brands related to social causes. In other words, it's the way a brand positions itself in the minds of consumers in relation to a particular issue or cause. Additionally, social positioning can also play a crucial role in building a brand's reputation, by aligning with a particular theme, that resonates with a specific group of consumers. Consequence of an intricate network of symbolic meanings with which consumers identify, this positioning must be authentic, long-term, action-oriented, and meaningful for all the organization's stakeholders.

This symbolic identification translates into the direction that political consumerism has been taking towards becoming an action with potential for political participation. The inevitability of adapting to the reality of a new advertising paradigm, which is very different from the one that governed Madison Avenue in the years preceding contemporary times, entails new risks, but also creates new opportunities for organizations that intend to adapt to it. Risks can be harmful in certain cases, as insincerity can lead to a loss of trust and credibility among consumers, but good advertising communication, created with transparency, authenticity and commitment to the cause can be excellent success factors in building and consolidating a desired good reputation, with a civic, ethical, and moral sense.

REFERENCES

Agudelo, M. A., Jóhannsdóttir, L., & Davídsdóttir, B. (2019). A literature review of the history and evolution of corporate social responsibility. *International Journal of Corporate Social Responsibility*, *4*(1), 1–23. doi:10.118640991-018-0039-y

Ayarza, S. (2020), *Por que – e como – as marcas podem ser agentes de igualdade, equidade e inclusão*. Think With Google. https://www.thinkwithgoogle.com/intl/pt-br/futuro-do-marketing/gestao-e-cultura-organizacional/por-que-e-como-as-marcas-podem-ser-agentes-de-igualdade-equidade-e-inclusao/

Benioff, M. (2018). *CEO activism is not a leadership choice, but a modern — and an evolving — expectation.* [tweet] (@benioff. https://twitter.com/benioff/status/977033953835143170?lang=de

Benner, R. E. (2018). *Brand Activism: Working Toward Progressive Representations of Social Movements in Advertsing* [Doctoral dissertation, University of Oregon].

Bertsou, E. (2019). Rethinking political distrust. *European Political Science Review*, *11*(2), 213–230. doi:10.1017/S1755773919000080

Bloomgarden, K. (2019). *CEOs as activists: should leaders speak up about social causes?* We Forum. https://www.weforum.org/agenda/2019/02/3-reasons-why-we-need-ceo-activists/

Boström, M., Micheletti, M., & Oosterveer, P. (2019). *The Oxford Handbook of Political Consumerism*. Oxford University Press. doi:10.1093/oxfordhb/9780190629038.001.0001

Branicki, L., Brammer, S., Pullen, A., & Rhodes, C. (2021). The Morality of "new" CEO Activism. *Journal of Business Ethics*, *170*(2), 269–285. doi:10.100710551-020-04656-5

Canclini, N. G. (2006). El consumo cultural: una propuesta teórica. *El consumo cultural en América Latina. Construcción teórica y líneas de investigación*, 25-50.

Castro, J. (2002). *Comunicação de Marketing*. Ed. Sílabo.

Chan, T. H. (2023). How brands can succeed communicating social purpose: Engaging consumers through empathy and self-involving gamification. *International Journal of Advertising*, *42*(5), 801–834. doi:10.1080/02650487.2022.2116846

Chatterji, A. K., & Toffel, M. W. (2019). Assessing the Impact of CEO Activism. *Organization & Environment*, *32*(2), 159–185. doi:10.1177/1086026619848144

Clarke, N. (2008). From ethical consumerism to political consumption. *Geography Compass*, *2*(6), 1870–1884. doi:10.1111/j.1749-8198.2008.00170.x

Clifton, R., & Simmons, J. (2005). *O Mundo das Marcas*. Actual Editora.

Cornelissen, J. (2014). *Corporate Communication: A Guide to Theory and Practice* (4th ed.). SAGE.

Duarte, A. (2023). The relationship between Brands and Consumers. In P. Dias & A. Duarte (Eds.), *Social Brand Management in a Post Covid-19 Era* (pp. 3–16). Routledge., doi:10.4324/9781003382331-2

Estrela, R. (2005). *A Publicidade no Estado Novo*. Lisboa: Coleção Comunicando.

Eyada, B. (2020). Brand activism, the relation and impact on consumer perception: A case study on nike advertising. *International Journal of Marketing Studies*, *12*(4), 30–42. doi:10.5539/ijms.v12n4p30

Gray, A. (2019). *Brands take a stand for good: The effect of brand activism on social media engagement.* [Honors Theses and Capstones, University of New Hampshir]. University of New Hampshir Scholars' Repository. https://scholars.unh.edu/honors/440

Habermas, J. (1962). *The Structural Transformation of the Public Sphere: an Inquiry into a Category of Bourgeois Society*. The MIT Press.

Hazaparu, M. A. (2014). Setting the agenda in advertising: Understanding ethical dilemmas from a communicative perspective. *Comunicação e Sociedade*, *25*, 328–343. doi:10.17231/comsoc.25(2014).1878

Holt, D. B. (2002). Why do brands cause trouble? A dialectical theory of consumer culture and branding. *The Journal of Consumer Research*, *29*(1), 70–90. doi:10.1086/339922

Hydock, C., Paharia, N., & Blair, S. (2020). Should your brand pick a side? How market share determines the impact of corporate political advocacy. *JMR, Journal of Marketing Research*, *57*(6), 1135–1151. doi:10.1177/0022243720947682

Jenkins, H. (1992). *Textual poachers: Television fans and participatory cultures.* Routledge.

Jennings, R. (2018). How Nike's Colin Kaepernick ad explains branding in the Trump era. *Vox.* https://www.vox.com/2018/9/4/17818222/nike-colin-kaepernick-ad

Klein, N. (2002). *No Logo. O poder das marcas.* Relógio d'Água.

Korschun, D. (2021). Brand Activism Is Here to Stay: Here's Why. *NIM Marketing Intelligence Review*, *13*(2), 11–17. doi:10.2478/nimmir-2021-0011

Kotler, P., Kartajaya, H., & Setiawan, I. (2017). *Marketing 4.0: Moving from traditional to digital.* Wiley.

Kozinets, R. V., & Jenkins, H. (2022). Consumer movements, brand activism, and the participatory politics of media: A conversation. *Journal of Consumer Culture*, *22*(1), 264–282. doi:10.1177/14695405211013993

Kumar, N. (2020). Study the impact of brand activism and political activism on marketing trends. *European Journal of Molecular & Clinical Medicine*, *7*(10), 2010–2021.

Lipovetsky, Gilles (2022). A sagração da Autenticidade. Edições 70.

Lipovetsky, G. & Serroy, J. (2010). *A Cultura-Mundo. Resposta a uma sociedade desorientada.* Lisboa: Edições.

Manfredi-Sánchez, J. L. (2019). El activismo político de las marcas. *Comunicación y Sociedad (Guadalajara)*, *32*(4), 343–359. doi:10.15581/003.32.4.343-359

Meister, A. R. (2019). The Power of Apology: How Crisis Communication Practices Impact Brand Reputation. [Thesis].

Miguel, A., & Miranda, S. (2022). The role of social media in the proliferation and promotion of Brand Activism. *Comunicação Pública, 17.*

Mirzaei, A., Wilkie, D. C., & Siuki, H. (2022). Woke brand activism authenticity or the lack of it. *Journal of Business Research*, *139*, 1–12. doi:10.1016/j.jbusres.2021.09.044

Moorman, C. (2020). Commentary: Brand activism in a political world. *Journal of Public Policy & Marketing*, *39*(4), 388–392. doi:10.1177/0743915620945260

Mozdzenski, L. (2019). A publicidade-documentário e a construção discursiva do efeito de real em prol da causa LGBTQ. *Revista Ícone, Recife*, *17*(2), 107–124. doi:10.34176/icone.v17i2.238965

Mukherjee, S., & Althuizen, N. (2020). Brand activism: Does courting controversy help or hurt a brand? *International Journal of Research in Marketing, 37*(4), 772–788. doi:10.1016/j.ijresmar.2020.02.008

Neureiter, M., & Bhattacharya, C. B. (2021). Why do boycotts sometimes increase sales? Consumer activism in the age of political polarization. *Business Horizons, 64*(5), 611–620. doi:10.1016/j.bushor.2021.02.025

Paris, C. (2022). *Achieving Brand Authenticity in the Age of Cancel Culture: Why Brands Can No Longer Be Neutral Without Being Seen as Complicit.* [Theses, University of Arkansas]. https://scholarworks.uark.edu/mktguht/54

Peloza, J., & Shang, J. (2011). How can corporate social responsibility activities create value for stakeholders? A systematic review. *Journal of the Academy of Marketing Science, 39*(1), 117–135. doi:10.100711747-010-0213-6

Robbins, R. H., & Dowty, R. (2008). *Global problems and the culture of capitalism.* Pearson/Allyn & Bacon.

Ruão, T. (2005). Clifton, Rita; Simmons, John (2005) O Mundo das Marcas, Lisboa: Actual Editora. *Comunicação e Sociedade, 8,* 323–327. doi:10.17231/comsoc.8(2005).1204

Ruão, T. (2016). *A Organização Comunicativa: Teoria e Prática em Comunicação Organizacional.* CS Edições.

Shetty, A. S., Venkataramaiah, N. B., & Anand, K. (2019). Brand activism and millennials: An empirical investigation into the perception of millennials towards brand activism. *Problems and Perspectives in Management, 17*(4), 163–175. doi:10.21511/ppm.17(4).2019.14

Sibai, O., Mimoun, L., & Boukis, A. (2021). Authenticating brand activism: Negotiating the boundaries of free speech to make a change. *Psychology and Marketing, 38*(10), 1651–1669. doi:10.1002/mar.21477

Simkovitch, A. (2019). *Political Consumerism and Branding: An Analysis of the Exploitation of Political Movements for Brand Equity and Profit. Honors College Theses.* Ace University.

Stolle, D., Hooghe, M., & Micheletti, M. (2005). Politics in the Supermarket: Political Consumerism as a Form of Political Participation. *International Political Science Review, 26*(3), 245–269. doi:10.1177/0192512105053784

Stolle, D., & Micheletti, M. (2013). *Political consumerism: global responsibility in action.* Cambridge University Press. doi:10.1017/CBO9780511844553

Taylor, C. R. (2017). How to avoid marketing disasters: Back to the basic communications model, but with some updates illustrating the importance of e-word-of-mouth research. *International Journal of Advertising*, *36*(4), 515–519. doi:10.1 080/02650487.2017.1323406

USC Annenberg Center for Public Relations. (2022). The future of Corporate Activism. *Global Communication Report*. USC Annenberg. https://annenberg.usc. edu/research/center-public-relations/global-communication-report

van Deth, J. W. (2014). A conceptual map of political participation. *Acta Politica*, *49*(3), 349–367. doi:10.1057/ap.2014.6

Vázquez, A. N. (2014). "Consumocracia". El consumo político como forma de participación de la ciudadanía. *Política y Sociedad*, *51*(1), 121–146.

Vredenburg, J., Kapitan, S., Spry, A., & Kemper, J. A. (2020). Brands taking a stand: Authentic brand activism or woke washing? *Journal of Public Policy & Marketing*, *39*(4), 444–460. doi:10.1177/0743915620947359

Wells, W., Burnett, J., & Moriarty, S. (2000). Advertising: Principles and Practice, 5th edition, Pearson World Business Council for Sustainable Development (WBCSD).

ENDNOTES

[1] https://observador.pt/2022/06/29/fundador-da-prozis-assumiu-se-contra-o-aborto-e-influencers-ja-estao-a-cortar-vinculo-com-a-marca/

[2] Prozis is a Portuguese brand that operates in the field of sports supplements (www.prozis.pt).

[3] Super Bowl is the final game of the NFL (National Football League) championship, the main American football league in the USA, which decides the champion of the season, and is the biggest sporting event and with the highest television audience in the country, watched annually by millions of people.

[4] https://www.youtube.com/watch?v=OjgHdCRgymY

Compilation of References

Aaker, D. (1991). *Managing Brand Equity*. Free Press.

Aaker, D. A., Fuse, Y., & Reynolds, F. D. (1982). Is Life-Style Research Limited in its Usefulness to Japanese Advertisers? *Journal of Advertising*, *11*(1), 31–36, 48. doi:10.1080/00913367.1982.10672792

Aaker, D. A., Stayman, D. M., & Hagerty, M. R. (1986). Warmth in advertising: Measurement, impact, and sequence effects. *The Journal of Consumer Research*, *12*(4), 365–381. doi:10.1086/208524

Aaker, D., & Joachimsthaler, E. (2000). *Brand Leadership*. Free Press.

Abela, A. (2003). *When Brand is a promise*. [Unpublished master's thesis. The Darden Graduate School of Business Administration, University of Virginia] doi:10.1186/s12889-020-10103-x

Adachi, N., Yamashita, R., & Matsuoka, H. (2022). How does spectator marketing in women's leagues differ from that in men's leagues? *International Journal of Sport Management and Marketing*, *22*(1–2), 1–18. doi:10.1504/IJSMM.2022.121259

Aditya, D., & Sarno, R. (2018). Neuromarketing: State of the arts. *Advanced Science Letters*, *24*(12), 9307–9310. doi:10.1166/asl.2018.12261

Adler, F. (1956). The value concept in sociology. *American Journal of Sociology*, *62*(3), 272–279. doi:10.1086/222004

Agudelo, M. A., Jóhannsdóttir, L., & Davídsdóttir, B. (2019). A literature review of the history and evolution of corporate social responsibility. *International Journal of Corporate Social Responsibility*, *4*(1), 1–23. doi:10.118640991-018-0039-y

Akbarov, S. (2018). Antecedents of Customer Based Brand Equity-Research in Azerbaijan. *Journal of Business and Management Sciences*, *6*(2), 54–58. doi:10.12691/jbms-6-2-5

Akoglu, H. E., & Özbek, O. (2022). The effect of brand experiences on brand loyalty through perceived quality and brand trust: A study on sports consumers. *Asia Pacific Journal of Marketing and Logistics*, *34*(10), 2130–2148. doi:10.1108/APJML-05-2021-0333

Alalwan, A. A. (2018). Investigating the impact of social media advertising features on customer purchase intention. *International Journal of Information Management*, *42*, 65–77. doi:10.1016/j.ijinfomgt.2018.06.001

Aldayel, M., Ykhlef, M., & Al-Nafjan, A. (2020). Deep learning for EEG-based preference classification in neuromarketing. *Applied Sciences (Basel, Switzerland)*, *10*(4), 1525. doi:10.3390/app10041525

Alexander, S. (2005). Trail-blazers who pioneered women's football. *BBC News*. http://news.bbc.co.uk/sport2/hi/football/women/4603149.stm

Alexander, J., Shenoy, V., & Yadav, A. (2019). Ethical challenges in neuromarketing: A research agenda. *Indian Journal of Marketing*, *49*(3), 36–49. doi:10.17010/ijom/2019/v49/i3/142145

Allison, R. (2018). Women's soccer in the United States: Introduction. *Sport in Society*, *21*(7), 993–995. doi:10.1080/17430437.2018.1401361

Alsharif, A. H., Salleh, N. Z. M., & Baharun, R. (2021). Neuromarketing: The popularity of the brain-imaging and physiological tools. *Neuroscience Research Notes*, *3*(5), 13–22. doi:10.31117/neuroscirn.v3i5.80

Alsharif, A. H., Salleh, N. Z., & Khraiwish, A. (2022). Biomedical Technology in Studying Consumers' Subconscious Behavior. *International Journal of Online & Biomedical Engineering*, *18*(8).

Aly, H. (2020). Digital transformation, development and productivity in developing countries: is artificial intelligence a curse or a blessing? Review of Economics and Political Science. doi:10.1108/REPS-11-2019-0145

Amaro, E. Jr, & Barker, G. J. (2006). Study design in fMRI: Basic principles. *Brain and Cognition*, *60*(3), 220–232. doi:10.1016/j.bandc.2005.11.009 PMID:16427175

Ambach, W., & Gamer, M. (2018). Physiological measures in the detection of deception and concealed information. In *Detecting concealed information and deception* (pp. 3–33). Academic Press. doi:10.1016/B978-0-12-812729-2.00001-X

Andre, F. E., Booy, R., Bock, H. L., Clemens, J., Datta, S. K., John, T. J., Lee, B. W., Lolekha, S., Peltola, H., Ruff, T. A., Santosham, M., & Schmitt, H. J. (2008). Vaccination greatly reduces disease, disability, death and inequity worldwide. *Bulletin of the World Health Organization*, *86*(2), 140–146. doi:10.2471/BLT.07.040089 PMID:18297169

Angelmar, R., Angelmar, S., & Kane, L. (2007). Building strong condition brands. *Journal of Medical Marketing*, *7*(4), 341–351. doi:10.1057/palgrave.jmm.5050101

Anongdeh, A., & Barre, H. I. (2019). Instagram profile's effect on influencer credibility. *Jönköping International Business School*. https://hj.diva- portal.org/smash/get/diva2:1321148/FULLTEXT01.pdf

Anusha, G. (2016). Effectiveness of online advertising. *International Journal of Research*, 4(3), 14–21.

Aparicio-Ruiz, R., Tena, N., & García-González, D. L. (2022). An International Survey on Olive Oils Quality and Traceability: Opinions from the Involved Actors. *Foods*, *11*(7), 1045. doi:10.3390/foods11071045 PMID:35407132

Arai, A., Ko, Y. J., & Ross, S. (2014). Branding athletes: Exploration and conceptualization of athlete brand image. *Sport Management Review*, *17*(2), 97–106. doi:10.1016/j.smr.2013.04.003

Atulkar, S. (2020). Brand trust and brand loyalty in mall shoppers. *Marketing Intelligence & Planning*, *38*(5), 559–572. doi:10.1108/MIP-02-2019-0095

Aubrey, J. S., Olson, L., Fine, M., Hauser, T., Rhea, D., Kaylor, B., & Yang, A. (2012). Investigating personality and viewing-motivation correlates of reality television exposure. *Communication Quarterly*, *60*(1), 80–102. doi:10.1080/01463373.2012.641830

Aureliano-Silva, L., Spers, E. E., Lodhi, R. N., & Pattanayak, M. (2022). Who loves to forgive? The mediator mechanism of service recovery between brand love, brand trust and purchase intention in the context of food-delivery apps. *British Food Journal*, *124*(12), 4686–4700. doi:10.1108/BFJ-07-2021-0819

Ayarza, S. (2020), *Por que – e como – as marcas podem ser agentes de igualdade, equidade e inclusão*. Think With Google. https://www.thinkwithgoogle.com/intl/pt-br/futuro-do-marketing/gestao-e-cultura-organizacional/por-que-e-como-as-marcas-podem-ser-agentes-de-igualdade-equidade-e-inclusao/

B.Sousa, A.Malheiro, M.Cláudia (2019),"O Marketing Territorial como Contributo para a Segmentação Turística: Modelo conceptual no turismo de shopping." International Journal of Marketing, Communication and New Media 5 (2019).

Baalbaki, S. (2012). *Consumer perception of brand equity measurement: A new scale*. [Doctoral Dissertation, University of North Texas]. UNT Digital Library. https://digital.library.unt.edu/ark:/67531/metadc115043/

Backaler, J., & Shankman, P. (2018). *Digital influence*. Macmillan. doi:10.1007/978-3-319-78396-3

Bae, S. J., Lee, H., Suh, E. K., & Suh, K. S. (2017). Shared experience in pretrip and experience sharing in posttrip: A survey of Airbnb users. *Information & Management*, *54*(6), 714–727. doi:10.1016/j.im.2016.12.008

Bakshy, E., Hofman, J. M., Mason, W. A., & Watts, D. J. (2011). Everyone's an influencer: quantifying influence on twitter. In *Proceedings of the fourth ACM international conference on Web search and data mining* (pp. 65-74). 10.1145/1935826.1935845

Bala, M., & Verma, D. (2018). A Critical Review of Digital Marketing. *International Journal of Management. IT & Engineering*, *8*(10), 321–339.

Balconi, M., Stumpo, B., & Leanza, F. (2014). Advertising, brand and neuromarketing or how consumer brain works. *Neuropsychological Trends*, *16*(16), 15–21. doi:10.7358/neur-2014-016-balc

Ballester, E. D., & Aleman, J. L. M. (2001). Brand trust in the context of consumer loyalty. *European Journal of Marketing*, *35*(11), 1238–1258. doi:10.1108/EUM0000000006475

Barrick, M. R., Mount, M. K., & Strauss, J. P. (1993). Conscientiousness and performance of sales representatives: Test of the mediating effects of goal setting. *The Journal of Applied Psychology*, *78*(5), 715–722. doi:10.1037/0021-9010.78.5.715

Batra, R., & Keller, K. L. (2016). Integrating marketing communications: New findings, new lessons, and new ideas. *Journal of Marketing*, *80*(6), 122–145. doi:10.1509/jm.15.0419

Baumann, S. (2015). Media branding from an organizational and management-centered perspective. In *Handbook of media branding* (pp. 65–80). Springer. doi:10.1007/978-3-319-18236-0_5

Baum, D., Spann, M., Füller, J., & Thürridl, C. (2019). The impact of social media campaigns on the success of new product introductions. *Journal of Retailing and Consumer Services*, *50*, 289–297. doi:10.1016/j.jretconser.2018.07.003

Becerra, E. P., & Badrinarayanan, V. (2013). The influence of brand trust and brand identification on brand evangelism. *Journal of Product and Brand Management*, *22*(5/6), 371–383. doi:10.1108/JPBM-09-2013-0394

Becker-Olsen, K. L. (2003). And now, a word from our sponsor—A look at the effects of sponsored content and banner advertising. *Journal of Advertising*, *32*(2), 17–32. doi:10.1080/00913367.2003.10639130

Belanche, D., Casaló, L. V., Flavián, M., & Ibáñez-Sánchez, S. (2021, July). Building influencers' credibility on Instagram: Effects on followers' attitudes and behavioral responses toward the influencer. *Journal of Retailing and Consumer Services*, *61*, 102585. doi:10.1016/j.jretconser.2021.102585

Ben-Ayed, R., Kamoun-Grati, N., & Rebai, A. (2013). An overview of the authentication of olive tree and oil. *Comprehensive Reviews in Food Science and Food Safety*, *12*(2), 218–227. doi:10.1111/1541-4337.12003

Benioff, M. (2018). *CEO activism is not a leadership choice, but a modern — and an evolving — expectation.* [tweet] (@benioff. https://twitter.com/benioff/status/977033953835143170?lang=de

Benner, R. E. (2018). *Brand Activism: Working Toward Progressive Representations of Social Movements in Advertsing* [Doctoral dissertation, University of Oregon].

Bertsou, E. (2019). Rethinking political distrust. *European Political Science Review*, *11*(2), 213–230. doi:10.1017/S1755773919000080

Bilgin, Y. (2018). The effect of social media marketing activities on brand awareness, brand image and brand loyalty. *Business & management studies: an international journal, 6*(1), 128-148.

Binder, A., Naderer, B., & Matthes, J. (2020). A "forbidden fruit effect": An eye-tracking study on children's visual attention to food marketing. *International Journal of Environmental Research and Public Health*, *17*(6), 1859. doi:10.3390/ijerph17061859 PMID:32183015

Biswas, A., & Roy, M. (2015). Green products: An exploratory study on the consumer behaviour in emerging economies of the East. *Journal of Cleaner Production*, *87*(1), 463–468. doi:10.1016/j.jclepro.2014.09.075

Biswas, D., Jalali, H., Ansaripoor, A. H., & de Giovanni, P. (2023). Traceability vs. sustainability in supply chains: The implications of blockchain. *European Journal of Operational Research*, *305*(1), 128–147. doi:10.1016/j.ejor.2022.05.034

Bloomgarden, K. (2019). *CEOs as activists: should leaders speak up about social causes?* We Forum. https://www.weforum.org/agenda/2019/02/3-reasons-why-we-need-ceo-activists/

Bočková, K., Škrabánková, J., & Hanák, M. (2021). Theory and practice of neuromarketing: Analyzing human behavior in relation to markets. *Emerging Science Journal*, *5*(1), 44–56. doi:10.28991/esj-2021-01256

Bonnin, G., & Alfonso, M. R. (2019). The narrative strategies of B2B technology brands. *Journal of Business and Industrial Marketing*, *34*(7), 1448–1458. doi:10.1108/JBIM-03-2019-0112

Borge, S. (2015). An agon aesthetics of football. *Sport, Ethics and Philosophy*, *9*(2), 97–123. doi:10.1080/17511321.2015.1061045

Boström, M., Micheletti, M., & Oosterveer, P. (2019). *The Oxford Handbook of Political Consumerism*. Oxford University Press. doi:10.1093/oxfordhb/9780190629038.001.0001

Bowen, G. A. (2009). Document analysis as a qualitative research method. *Qualitative Research Journal*, *9*(2), 27–40. doi:10.3316/QRJ0902027

Branicki, L., Brammer, S., Pullen, A., & Rhodes, C. (2021). The Morality of "new" CEO Activism. *Journal of Business Ethics*, *170*(2), 269–285. doi:10.100710551-020-04656-5

Bray, D. A. (2008). Information pollution, knowledge overload, limited attention spans, and our responsibilities as IS professionals. In *Global Information Technology Management Association (GITMA) World Conference-June*. SSRN.

Brechman, J. M., & Purvis, S. C. (2015). Narrative, transportation and advertising. *International Journal of Advertising*, *34*(2), 366–381. doi:10.1080/02650487.2014.994803

Brennen, J., Simon, F., Howard, P., & Nielsen, R. (2020). *Types, sources, and claims of COVID-19 misinformation*. The Reuters Institute for the Study of Journalism. https://reutersinstitute.politics.ox.ac.uk/typessources-and-claims-covid-19-isinformation

Brierley, G., Ozuem, W., & Lancaster, G. (2020). Subconscious marketing communication techniques and legal implications. *Journal of Decision Systems*, *29*(2), 69–78. doi:10.1080/12460125.2020.1752047

Briesemeister, B. B., & Trebbe, J. (2022). Welcome to the Real World: Neuromarketing for the Stationary Point of Sale to Quantify the Customer Experience. *Neuromarketing in Business: Identifying Implicit Purchase Drivers and Leveraging them for Sales,* 91-108.

Brito, K. D. S., Filho, R. L. C. S., & Adeodato, P. J. L. (2021). A Systematic Review of Predicting Elections Based on Social Media Data: Research Challenges and Future Directions. In IEEE Transactions on Computational Social Systems (Vol. 8, Issue 4, pp. 819–843). Institute of Electrical and Electronics Engineers Inc. doi:10.1109/TCSS.2021.3063660

Burgess, J., & Jones, C. (2020). Exploring the forced closure of a brand community that is also a participatory culture. *European Journal of Marketing, 54*(5), 957–978. doi:10.1108/EJM-01-2019-0075

Burgess, J., & Jones, C. (2021). Exploring lack of closure as a brand transgression. *Journal of Consumer Marketing, 38*(3), 241–250. doi:10.1108/JCM-07-2020-3937

Burke, T. (2019). Blockchain in Food Traceability. In *Food Traceability* (pp. 133–143). Springer International Publishing. doi:10.1007/978-3-030-10902-8_10

Burnier, P. C., Spers, E. E., & de Barcellos, M. D. (2021). Role of sustainability attributes and occasion matters in determining consumers' beef choice. *Food Quality and Preference, 88,* 104075. doi:10.1016/j.foodqual.2020.104075

Cacioppo, J. T., & Petty, R. E. (1983). *Social psychophysiology*. The Guilford Press.

Calvert, G. A., Pathak, A., Ching, L. E. A., Trufil, G., & Fulcher, E. P. (2019). Providing excellent customer service is therapeutic: Insights from an implicit association neuromarketing study. *Behavioral Sciences (Basel, Switzerland), 9*(10), 109. doi:10.3390/bs9100109 PMID:31615003

Camarrone, F., & Van Hulle, M. M. (2019). Measuring brand association strength with EEG: A single-trial N400 ERP study. *PLoS One, 14*(6), e0217125. doi:10.1371/journal.pone.0217125 PMID:31181083

Campanella, S., Bourguignon, M., Peigneux, P., Metens, T., Nouali, M., Goldman, S., Verbanck, P., & De Tiège, X. (2013). BOLD response to deviant face detection informed by P300 event-related potential parameters: A simultaneous ERP–fMRI study. *NeuroImage, 71,* 92–103. doi:10.1016/j.neuroimage.2012.12.077 PMID:23313569

Canclini, N. G. (2006). El consumo cultural: una propuesta teórica. *El consumo cultural en América Latina. Construcción teórica y líneas de investigación,* 25-50.

Cao, S., Johnson, H., & Tulloch, A. (2023). Exploring blockchain-based Traceability for Food Supply Chain Sustainability: Towards a Better Way of Sustainability Communication with Consumers. *Procedia Computer Science, 217,* 1437–1445. doi:10.1016/j.procs.2022.12.342

Carlucci, D., de Gennaro, B., Roselli, L., & Seccia, A. (2014). E-commerce retail of extra virgin olive oil: An hedonic analysis of Italian Smes supply. *British Food Journal, 116*(10), 1600–1617. doi:10.1108/BFJ-05-2013-0138

Carlucci, D., Nocella, G., de Devitiis, B., Viscecchia, R., Bimbo, F., & Nardone, G. (2015). Consumer purchasing behaviour towards fish and seafood products. Patterns and insights from a sample of international studies. *Appetite*, *84*, 212–227. doi:10.1016/j.appet.2014.10.008 PMID:25453592

Caro, M. P., Ali, M. S., Vecchio, M., & Giaffreda, R. (2018). Blockchain-based traceability in Agri-Food supply chain management: A practical implementation. *2018 IoT Vertical and Topical Summit on Agriculture - Tuscany. IOT Tuscany*, *1–4*, 1–4. doi:10.1109/IOT-TUSCANY.2018.8373021

Carzedda, M., Gallenti, G., Troiano, S., Cosmina, M., Marangon, F., de Luca, P., Pegan, G., & Nassivera, F. (2021). Consumer preferences for origin and organic attributes of extra virgin olive oil: A choice experiment in the italian market. *Foods*, *10*(5), 994. doi:10.3390/foods10050994 PMID:34063198

Casaló, L. V., Flavián, C., & Ibáñez-Sánchez, S. (2020). Influencers on Instagram: Antecedents and consequences of opinion leadership. *Journal of Business Research*, *117*, 510–519. doi:10.1016/j. jbusres.2018.07.005

Casidy, R., Leckie, C., Nyadzayo, M. W., & Johnson, L. W. (2022). Customer brand engagement and co-production: An examination of key boundary conditions in the sharing economy. *European Journal of Marketing*, *56*(10), 2594–2621. doi:10.1108/EJM-10-2021-0803

Castillo, D., & Fernández, R. (2019). The role of digital influencers in brand recommendation: Examining their impact on engagement, expected value and purchase intention. *International Journal of Information Management*, *49*, 366–376. doi:10.1016/j.ijinfomgt.2019.07.009

Castro, J. (2002). *Comunicação de Marketing*. Ed. Sílabo.

CB. (2020). *CB insight report*. CB Insights. www.cbinsights.com/research/report/venture-capital-q4-2020/

Chahal, H., & Rani, A. (2017). How trust moderates social media engagement and brand equity. *Journal of Research in Interactive Marketing*, *11*(3), 312–335. doi:10.1108/JRIM-10-2016-0104

Chailan, C. (2008). Brands portfolios and competitive advantage: An empirical study. *Journal of Product and Brand Management*, *17*(4), 254–264. doi:10.1108/10610420810887608

Chandwaskar, P. (2019). A Review on: Neuromarketing as an emerging field in consumer research., International Journal of Management. *Technology And Engineering*, *8*(11), 2281–2287.

Chan, T. H. (2023). How brands can succeed communicating social purpose: Engaging consumers through empathy and self-involving gamification. *International Journal of Advertising*, *42*(5), 801–834. doi:10.1080/02650487.2022.2116846

Chatterji, A. K., & Toffel, M. W. (2019). Assessing the Impact of CEO Activism. *Organization & Environment*, *32*(2), 159–185. doi:10.1177/1086026619848144

Chaudhuri, A., & Holbrook, M. B. (2001). The chain of effects from brand trust and brand affect to brand performance: The role of brand loyalty. *Journal of Marketing*, *65*(2), 81–93. doi:10.1509/jmkg.65.2.81.18255

Chen, T., Drennan, J., & Andrews, L. (2012). Experience sharing. *Journal of Marketing Management*, 28(13-14), 1535–1552. doi:10.1080/0267257X.2012.736876

Chen, X., & Qasim, H. (2021). Does E-Brand experience matter in the consumer market? Explaining the impact of social media marketing activities on consumer-based brand equity and love. *Journal of Consumer Behaviour*, 20(5), 1065–1077. doi:10.1002/cb.1915

Chernatony, L. (2001). Succeeding with Brands on the Internet. *Journal of Brand Management*, 8(3), 186–195. doi:10.1057/palgrave.bm.2540019

Chinomona, R. (2013). The Influence Of Brand Experience On Brand Satisfaction, Trust And Attachment In South Africa. [IBER]. *International Business & Economics Research Journal*, 12(10), 1303–1316. doi:10.19030/iber.v12i10.8138

Chinomona, R., Mahlangu, D., & Pooe, D. (2013). Brand service quality, satisfaction, trust and preference as predictors of consumer brand loyalty in the retailing industry. *Mediterranean Journal of Social Sciences*, 4(14), 181. doi:10.5901/mjss.2013.v4n14p181

Choi, N. H., Qiao, X., & Wang, L. (2020). Effects of multisensory cues, self-enhancing imagery and self-goal achievement emotion on purchase intention. *Journal of Asian Finance. Economics and Business*, 7(1), 141–151. doi:10.13106/jafeb.2020.vol7.no1.141

Cho, J. Y., & Lee, E. J. (2017). Impact of interior colours in retail store atmosphere on consumers' perceived store luxury, emotions, and preference. *Clothing & Textiles Research Journal*, 35(1), 33–48. doi:10.1177/0887302X16675052

Christodoulides, G. (2009, March). Branding in the post-internet era. *Marketing Theory*, 9(1), 141–144. doi:10.1177/1470593108100071

Christov, A., Verena, H., & Sue, W. (2020. Measuring brand awareness, campaign evaluation and web analytics. Digital and Social Media Marketing. Routledge.

Chrysochou, P., Tiganis, A., Trabelsi Trigui, I., & Grunert, K. G. (2022). A cross-cultural study on consumer preferences for olive oil. *Food Quality and Preference*, 97, 104460. doi:10.1016/j.foodqual.2021.104460

Chung, C., Chatterjee, S. C., & Sengupta, S. (2012). Manufacturers' reliance on channel intermediaries: Value drivers in the presence of a direct web channel. *Industrial Marketing Management*, 41(1), 40–53. doi:10.1016/j.indmarman.2011.11.010

Clarke, E., Geurin, A. N., & Burch, L. M. (2022). Team identification, motives, and behaviour: A comparative analysis of fans of men's and women's sport. *Managing Sport and Leisure*, 1–24. doi:10.1080/23750472.2022.2049455

Clarke, N. (2008). From ethical consumerism to political consumption. *Geography Compass*, 2(6), 1870–1884. doi:10.1111/j.1749-8198.2008.00170.x

Clifton, R., & Simmons, J. (2005). *O Mundo das Marcas*. Actual Editora.

Cohen, J. (1992). Quantitative methods in psychology: A power primer. *Psychological Bulletin*, *112*(1), 155–159. doi:10.1037/0033-2909.112.1.155 PMID:19565683

Conti, M. (2022). EVO-NFC: Extra Virgin Olive Oil Traceability Using NFC Suitable for Small-Medium Farms. *IEEE Access : Practical Innovations, Open Solutions*, *10*, 20345–20356. doi:10.1109/ACCESS.2022.3151795

Cooky, C., Council, L. D., Mears, M. A., & Messner, M. A. (2021). One and done: The long eclipse of women's televised sports, 1989–2019. *Communication & Sport*, *9*(3), 347–371. doi:10.1177/21674795211003524

Corallo, A., Latino, M. E., Menegoli, M., Pizzi, R., Fanelli, R. M., Pereira-Lorenzo, S., María, A., & Cabrer, R. (2021). *Assuring Effectiveness in Consumer-Oriented Traceability*. Suggestions for Food Label Design. doi:10.3390/agronomy

Cornelissen, J. (2014). *Corporate Communication: A Guide to Theory and Practice* (4th ed.). SAGE.

Cronbach, Lee J. (1951). Coefficient alpha and the internal structure of tests. *Sychometrika*. Springer Science and Business Media LLC.

Croteau, D., Hoynes, W., & Hoynes, W. D. (2006). The business of media: Corporate media and the public interest. Pine forge press.

Cuesta-Cambra, U., Niño-González, J. I., & ve Rodríguez-Terceño, J. (2017). The Cognitive Processing of an Educational App with EEG and'Eye Tracking'. Comunicar. *Media Education Research Journal, 25*(2).

Cunningham, N. R., & Eastin, M. S. (2017). Second screen and sports: A structural investigation into team identification and efficacy. *Communication & Sport*, *5*(3), 288–310. doi:10.1177/2167479515610152

Dam, T. (2020). Influence of Brand Trust, Perceived Value on Brand Preference and Purchase Intention. *The Journal of Asian Finance. Economics and Business*, *7*(10), 939–947. doi:10.13106/jafeb.2020.vol7.no10.939

Das, S. (2021). A Systematic Study of integrated marketing communication and content management system for millennial consumers. *Innovations in Digital Branding and Content Marketing*, 91-112. . doi:10.4018/978-1-7998-4420-4.ch005

Dator, J. (2019). *A short history of the banning of women's soccer*. SB Nation. https://www.sbnation.com/soccer/2019/7/6/18658729/banning-womens-soccer-world-cup-effects

Davis, P. (2015). Football is football and is interesting, very interesting. *Sport, Ethics and Philosophy*, *9*(2), 140–152. doi:10.1080/17511321.2015.1020855

De Veirman, M., Cauberghe, V., & Hudders, L. (2017, July 14). Marketing through Instagram influencers: The impact of number of followers and product divergence on brand attitude. *International Journal of Advertising*, *36*(5), 798–828. doi:10.1080/02650487.2017.1348035

Delgado-Ballester, E. (2020). Effect of underdog (vs topdog) brand storytelling on brand identification: Exploring multiple mediation mechanisms. *Journal of Product and Brand Management*. Advance online publication. doi:10.1108/JPBM-11-2019-2639

Delgado-Ballester, E., Munuera-Alemán, J., & Yagüe-Guillén, M. (2003). Development and Validation of a Brand Trust Scale. *International Journal of Market Research*, *45*(1), 1–18. doi:10.1177/147078530304500103

DelVecchio, D., & Smith, D. (2000). Moving beyond fit: The role of brand portfolio characteristics in consumer evaluations of brand reliability. In A. Menon & A. Sharma (Eds.), *Proceedings of the 2000 Ama Winter Educators Conference: Marketing Theory & Applications* (p. 59). Amer Marketing Assn., https://www.proquest.com/scholarly-journals/moving-beyond-fit-role-brand-portfolio/docview/199493969/se-2?accountid=177838 doi:10.1108/10610420010351411

Denga Edna Mngusughun. (2022a). Implementing E-Marketing in Small and Medium-Sized Enterprises for Enhanced Sustainability. In R. Mourly Potluri & N. R. Vajjhala (Eds.), *Advancing SMEs Toward E-Commerce Policies for Sustainability* (pp. 88–110). IGI Global. doi:10.4018/978-1-6684-5727-6.ch005

Denga, E. M & Sandip Rakshit (2022b). Digital Marketing and the Sustainable Performance of Small and Medium Enterprises. In R. Mourly Potluri & N. R Vajjhala (Eds), Advancing SMEs Toward E-Commerce Policies for Sustainability (pp235-247). IGI Global. doi:10.4018/978-1-6684-5727-6.ch011

Denga, E. M., Vajjhala, N. R., & Rakshit, S. (2022c). Relationship Selling as a Strategic Weapon for Sustainable Performance. In J. D. Santos (Ed.), *Sales Management for Improved Organizational Competitiveness and Performance* (pp. 78–101). IGI Global. doi:10.4018/978-1-6684-3430-7.ch005

Denga, E. M., Vajjhala, N. R., & Rakshit, S. (2022d). The Role of Digital Marketing in Achieving Sustainable Competitive Advantage. In O. Yildiz (Ed.), *Digital Transformation and Internationalization Strategies in Organizations* (pp. 44–60). IGI Global. doi:10.4018/978-1-7998-8169-8.ch003

Deng, L., & Wang, G. (2019). Application of EEG and interactive evolutionary design method in cultural and creative product design. *Computational Intelligence and Neuroscience*, *2019*, 2019. doi:10.1155/2019/1860921 PMID:30733799

Diaz, E., Esteban, Á., Carranza Vallejo, R., & Martín-Consuegra Navarro, D. (2022). Digital tools and smart technologies in marketing: A thematic evolution. *International Marketing Review*, *39*(5), 1122–1150. doi:10.1108/IMR-12-2020-0307

Dimmick, J., Chen, Y., & Li, Z. (2004). Competition Between the Internet and Traditional News Media: The Gratification-Opportunities Niche Dimension. *Journal of Media Economics*, *17*(1), 19–33. doi:10.120715327736me1701_2

Ding, Y., Robinson, N., Zhang, S., Zeng, Q., & Guan, C. (2021). Tsception: Capturing temporal dynamics and spatial asymmetry from EEG for emotion recognition. arXiv preprint arXiv:2104.02935.

Djamasbi, S. (2014). Eye tracking and web experience. *AIS Transactions on Human-Computer Interaction, 6*(2), 37–54. doi:10.17705/1thci.00060

Dlacic, J., & Kezman, E. (2014). Exploring relationship between brand equity and customer loyalty on pharmaceutical market. *Economic and Business Review for Central and South - Eastern Europe, 16*(2), 121-131.

dos Santos, R. L., Petroll, M. D. L. M., Boeing, R., & Scussel, F. (2021). Let's play a new game: The drivers of eSports consumption. *Research. Social Development, 10*(5), e40710515188. Advance online publication. doi:10.33448/rsd-v10i5.15188

Doyle, P. (2000). Value-based marketing. *Journal of Strategic Marketing, 8*(4), 299–311. doi:10.1080/096525400446203

Duarte, A. (2023). The relationship between Brands and Consumers. In P. Dias & A. Duarte (Eds.), *Social Brand Management in a Post Covid-19 Era* (pp. 3–16). Routledge., doi:10.4324/9781003382331-2

DuBose, B. (2020). *As part owner, James Harden celebrates NWSL title by Houston Dash.* https://rocketswire.usatoday.com/2020/07/26/as-part-owner-james-harden-celebrates-nwsl-title-by-houston-dash/

Du, R. Y., Xu, L., & Wilbur, K. C. (2019). Immediate responses of online brand search and price search to TV ads. *Journal of Marketing, 83*(4), 81–100. doi:10.1177/0022242919847192

Dwivedi, A., Johnson, L. W., Wilkie, D. C., & de Araujo Gil, L. (2019). Consumer emotional brand attachment with social media brands and social media brand equity. *European Journal of Marketing, 53*(6), 1176–1204. doi:10.1108/EJM-09-2016-0511

Ebrahim, R. (2019). The Role of Trust in Understanding the Impact of Social Media Marketing on Brand Equity and Brand Loyalty. *Journal of Relationship Marketing, 19*(3), 1–22. doi:10.1 080/15332667.2019.1705742

EBU. (2022). *EBU members on a high after record UEFA Women's EURO TV viewing figures.* https://www.ebu.ch/news/2022/08/ebu-members-on-a-high-after-record-uefa-womens-euro-tv-viewing-figures

Edelman, D. C. (2010). Branding in the Digital Age. *Harvard Business Review, 88*, 62–69.

Editorial. (2000). 21st century brand knowledge — towards the ADEP*T standard for brands' promise and trust. *Journal of Brand Management, 7*(4), 220-231. doi:10.1057/bm.2000.8

Elliott, R., & Yannopoulou, N. (2007). The nature of trust in brands: A psychosocial model. *European Journal of Marketing, 41*(9), 988–998. doi:10.1108/03090560710773309

Elouadifi, S., & Essakallı, M. (2022). Conceptual model of the factors impacting the adoption of Neuromarketing Technologies. *International Journal of Accounting, Finance, Auditing, Management and Economics, 3*(4-2), 1-23.

Erraach, Y., Jaafer, F., Radić, I., & Donner, M. (2021). Sustainability labels on olive oil: A review on consumer attitudes and behavior. In Sustainability (Switzerland) (Vol. 13, Issue 21). MDPI. doi:10.3390u132112310

Estrela, R. (2005). *A Publicidade no Estado Novo*. Lisboa: Coleção Comunicando.

Eyada, B. (2020). Brand activism, the relation and impact on consumer perception: A case study on nike advertising. *International Journal of Marketing Studies, 12*(4), 30–42. doi:10.5539/ijms.v12n4p30

Farris, P. W., Bendle, N. T., Pfeifer, P. E., & Reibstein, D. J. (2010). *Marketing Metrics: The Definitive Guide to Measuring Marketing Performance*. Pearson Education, Inc.

Feaster, J. C. (2009). The repertoire niches of interpersonal media: Competition and coexistence at the level of the individual. *new media & society, 11*(6), 965-984.

Feiz, D., Fakharyan, M., Jalilvand, M. R., & Hashemi, M. (2013). Examining the effect of TV advertising appeals on brand attitudes and advertising efforts in Iran. *Journal of Islamic Marketing, 4*(1), 101–125. doi:10.1108/17590831311306372

FIFA. (2019). *FIFA Women's World Cup 2019 watched by more than 1 billion*. FIFA. https://www.fifa.com/tournaments/womens/womensworldcup/france2019/news/fifa-women-s-world-cup-2019tm-watched-by-more-than-1-billion

Fisher, C. E., Chin, L., & Klitzman, R. (2010). Defining neuromarketing: Practices and professional challenges. *Harvard Review of Psychiatry, 18*(4), 230–237. doi:10.3109/10673229.2010.496623 PMID:20597593

Flowerdew, R., & Martin, D. (2005). *A guide for students doing a research project*. Pearson Education. www.pearsoned.co.uk

Folse, J., Burton, S., & Netemeyer, R. (2013). Defending brands: Effects of alignment of spokes character personality traits and corporate transgressions on brand trust and attitudes. *Journal of Advertising, 42*(4), 331–342. doi:10.1080/00913367.2013.795124

Fournier, S. (1998). Consumers and their brands: Developing relationship theory in consumer research. *The Journal of Consumer Research, 24*(4), 343–353. doi:10.1086/209515

Frost, R., & Stauffer, J. (1987). The effects of social class, gender, and personality on physiological responses to filmed violence. *Journal of Communication, 37*(2), 29–45. doi:10.1111/j.1460-2466.1987.tb00981.x

Fuan, L., Zhou, N., Kashyap, R., & Yang, Z. (2008). Brand Trust as a Second-Order Factor. *International Journal of Market Research, 50*(6), 817–839. doi:10.2501/S1470785308200225

Gantz, W. (1981). An exploration of viewing motives and behaviors associated with television sports. *Journal of Broadcasting & Electronic Media, 25*(3), 263–275. doi:10.1080/08838158109386450

Garaus, M., & Treiblmaier, H. (2021). The influence of blockchain-based food traceability on retailer choice: The mediating role of trust. *Food Control, 129*, 108082. doi:10.1016/j.foodcont.2021.108082

Garczarek-Bąk, U., & Disterheft, A. (2018). EEG frontal asymmetry predicts product purchase differently for national brands and private labels. *Journal of Neuroscience, Psychology, and Economics, 11*(3), 182–195. doi:10.1037/npe0000094

Garzella, S., Fiorentino, R., Caputo, A., & Lardo, A. (2020). Business model innovation in SMEs: The role of boundaries in the digital era. *Technology Analysis and Strategic Management*, 1–13.

Gecti, F., & Zengin, H. (2013). The relationship between brand trust, brand affect, attitudinal loyalty and behavioral loyalty: A field study towards sports shoe consumers in Turkey. *International Journal of Marketing Studies, 5*(2), 111–119. doi:10.5539/ijms.v5n2p111

Giese, J. L., & Cote, J. A. (2000). Defining consumer satisfaction. *Academy of Marketing Science Review, 1*(1), 1–22.

Gill, R., & Singh, J. (2020, December). A review of Neuromarketing techniques and emotion analysis classifiers for visual-emotion mining. In *2020 9th International Conference System Modeling and Advancement in Research Trends (SMART)* (pp. 103-108). IEEE. 10.1109/SMART50582.2020.9337074

Gilliam, D. A., Preston, T., & Hall, J. R. (2017). Frameworks for consumers' narratives in a changing marketplace: Banking and the financial crisis. *Marketing Intelligence & Planning, 35*(7), 892–906. doi:10.1108/MIP-01-2017-0005

Giua, C., Materia, V. C., & Camanzi, L. (2022). Smart farming technologies adoption: Which factors play a role in the digital transition? *Technology in Society, 68*, 101869. Advance online publication. doi:10.1016/j.techsoc.2022.101869

Glynn, M. (2011). Brands and Branding: The Economist Series. *Journal of Consumer Marketing, 28*, 161-162. doi:10.1108/07363761111116024

Goel, V., & Ember, S. (2015). Instagram to Open Its Photo Feed to Ads. *New York Times*. https://www.nytimes.com/2015/06/03/technology/instagram-to-announce-plans-to-expand-advertising.html

Gotham, F. C. (2022). *Steven Temares*. Gotham FC. https://www.gothamfc.com/steven-temares

Gray, A. (2019). *Brands take a stand for good: The effect of brand activism on social media engagement*. [Honors Theses and Capstones, University of New Hampshir]. University of New Hampshir Scholars' Repository. https://scholars.unh.edu/honors/440

Grossmann, T., & Friederici, A. D. (2012). When during development do our brains get tuned to the human voice? *Social Neuroscience*, *7*(4), 369–372. doi:10.1080/17470919.2011.628758 PMID:22017313

Guenzi, P., & Habel, J. (2020). Mastering the Digital Transformation of Sales. *California Management Review*, *62*(4), 57–85. doi:10.1177/0008125620931857

Guido, R., Mirabelli, G., Palermo, E., & Solina, V. (2020). A framework for food traceability: Case study-Italian extra-virgin olive oil supply chain. *International Journal of Industrial Engineering and Management*, *11*(1), 50–60. doi:10.24867/IJIEM-2020-1-252

Gupta, N., Soni, G., Mittal, S., Mukherjee, I., Ramtiyal, B., & Kumar, D. (2023). Evaluating Traceability Technology Adoption in Food Supply Chain: A Game Theoretic Approach. *Sustainability (Switzerland)*, *15*(2), 898. doi:10.3390u15020898

Habermas, J. (1962). *The Structural Transformation of the Public Sphere: an Inquiry into a Category of Bourgeois Society*. The MIT Press.

Hakim, A., & Levy, D. J. (2019). A gateway to consumers' minds: Achievements, caveats, and prospects of electroencephalography-based prediction in neuromarketing. *Wiley Interdisciplinary Reviews: Cognitive Science*, *10*(2), e1485. doi:10.1002/wcs.1485 PMID:30496636

Hamari, J., & Sjöblom, M. (2017). What is eSports and why do people watch it? *Internet Research*, *27*(2), 211–232. doi:10.1108/IntR-04-2016-0085

Hannah, R., Edouard, M., Rodés-Guirao, L., Appel, C., Giattino, C., Ortiz-Ospina, E., Hasell, J., Macdonald, B., Beltekian, D., & Roser, M. (2020). *Coronavirus Pandemic (COVID-19)*. Our World in Data. https://ourworldindata.org/coronavirus

Hardey, M. (2014). Marketing Narratives: Researching Digital Data, Design and the In/Visible Consumer. Emerald Group Publishing Limited, Bingley. doi:10.1108/S1042-319220140000013008

Hardway, C. L., & Stroud, M. (2014). Using Student Choice to Increase Students' Knowledge of Research Methodology, Improve Their Attitudes toward Research, and Promote Acquisition of Professional Skills. *International Journal on Teaching and Learning in Higher Education*, *26*(3), 381–392.

Haridakis, P. M. (2010). Rival sports fans and intergroup communication. In H. Giles, S. Reid, & J. Harwood (Eds.), *The dynamics of intergroup communication* (pp. 249–262). Peter Lang.

Harris, M. (2000). Life on the Amazon. *The Anthropology of a Brazilian Peasant Village*, 201-216.

Haudi, H., Handayani, W., Musnaini, M., Suyoto, Y., Prasetio, T., Pitaloka, E., & Cahyon, Y. (2022). The effect of social media marketing on brand trust, brand equity and brand loyalty. *International Journal of Data and Network Science*, *6*(3), 961–972. doi:10.5267/j.ijdns.2022.1.015

Hayes, N. (2008). *Influencer Marketing: Who Really Influences Your Customers?* Taylor & Francis.

Hazaparu, M. A. (2014). Setting the agenda in advertising: Understanding ethical dilemmas from a communicative perspective. *Comunicação e Sociedade, 25,* 328–343. doi:10.17231/comsoc.25(2014).1878

Hazlett, R. L., & Hazlett, S. Y. (1999). Emotional response to television commercials: Facial EMG vs. self-report. *Journal of Advertising Research, 39*(2), 7–7.

Henry, E. O., & Lloyd, M. D. (2019). Reinventing the 'Nwaboi' apprenticeship system: A platform for entrepreneurship promotion in Nigeria. *International Journal of Advanced Research in Management and Social Sciences, 8*(9), 98–130.

Herbst, J. (2022). *How Natalie Portman and her Angel City FC cofounders are changing the game for women's soccer.* FastCompany. https://www.fastcompany.com/90739855/how-natalie-portman-and-her-angel-city-fc-cofounders-are-changing-the-game-for-womens-soccer

Herhausen, D., Miočević, D., Morgan, R. E., & Kleijnen, M. H. P. (2020). The digital marketing capabilities gap. *Industrial Marketing Management, 90,* 276–290. doi:10.1016/j.indmarman.2020.07.022

Heskett, J. L. (2002). Beyond customer loyalty. *Managing Service Quality, 12*(6), 355–357. doi:10.1108/09604520210451830

Hess, J. (1995). Construction and Assessment of a Scale to Measure Consumer Trust. In Stern, B., & Zinkhan, G. (Eds.), Enhancing Knowledge Development in Marketing, AMA Educators' Proceedings (pp. 20-26). American Marketing Association.

Hess, E. H. (1965). Attitude and pupil size. *Scientific American, 212*(4), 46–54. doi:10.1038cientificamerican0465-46 PMID:14261525

Hess, E. H. (1968). Pupillometrics. In *F. M. Bass, C. W. King, & E. A. Pessemier Applications of the sciences in marketing management.* John Wiley & Sons.

Hess, E. H., & Polt, G. M. (1960). Pupil size as related to interest value of visual stimuli. *Science, 132*(3423), 349–350. doi:10.1126cience.132.3423.349 PMID:14401489

Hesterberg, K. (2022, July 13). *13 Influencer Marketing Campaigns to Inspire and Get You Started With Your Own.* Hubspot. https://blog.hubspot.com/marketing/examples-of-influencer-marketing- campaigns

Hiebert, J., & Wearne, D. (1996). Instruction, understanding, and skill in multidigit addition and subtraction. *Cognition and Instruction, 14*(3), 251–283. doi:10.12071532690xci1403_1

Hinson, R., Boateng, H., Renner, A., & Kosiba, J. P. B. (2019). Antecedents and consequences of customer engagement on Facebook: An attachment theory perspective. *Journal of Research in Interactive Marketing, 13*(2), 204–226. doi:10.1108/JRIM-04-2018-0059

Holbrook, M. B., & Hirschman, E. C. (1982). The experiential aspects of consumption: Consumer fantasies, feelings, and fun. *The Journal of Consumer Research, 9*(2), 132–140. doi:10.1086/208906

Holt, D. B. (2002). Why do brands cause trouble? A dialectical theory of consumer culture and branding. *The Journal of Consumer Research*, *29*(1), 70–90. doi:10.1086/339922

Hopp, J. J., & Fuchs, A. F. (2004). The characteristics and neuronal substrate of saccadic eye movement plasticity. *Progress in Neurobiology*, *72*(1), 27–53. doi:10.1016/j.pneurobio.2003.12.002 PMID:15019175

Hsieh, L. W., Wang, C. H., & Yoder, T. W. (2011). Factors associated with professional baseball consumption: A cross-cultural comparison study. *International Journal of Business and Information*, *6*(2), 135–159.

Hsu, H. Y., & Tsou, H. T. (2011). Understanding customer experiences in online blog environments. *International Journal of Information Management*, *31*(6), 510–523. doi:10.1016/j.ijinfomgt.2011.05.003

Hsu, M. (2017). Neuromarketing: Inside the mind of the consumer. *California Management Review*, *59*(4), 5–22. doi:10.1177/0008125617720208

Huang, R., Ha, S., & Kim, S.-H. (2018). Narrative persuasion in social media: An empirical study of luxury brand advertising. *Journal of Research in Interactive Marketing*, *12*(3), 274–292. doi:10.1108/JRIM-07-2017-0059

Hubert, M., & Kenning, P. (2008). A current overview of consumer neuroscience. *Journal of Consumer Behaviour: An International Research Review*, *7*(4-5), 272–292. doi:10.1002/cb.251

Hussein, I., Chams, N., Chams, S., El Sayegh, S., Badran, R., Raad, M., Gerges-Geagea, A., Leone, A., & Jurjus, A. (2015). Vaccines Through Centuries: Major Cornerstones of Global Health. *Frontiers in Public Health*, *3*, 1–16. doi:10.3389/fpubh.2015.00269 PMID:26636066

Hydock, C., Paharia, N., & Blair, S. (2020). Should your brand pick a side? How market share determines the impact of corporate political advocacy. *JMR, Journal of Marketing Research*, *57*(6), 1135–1151. doi:10.1177/0022243720947682

Iloka, B. C., & Anukwe, G. I. (2020). Review of eye-tracking: A neuromarketing technique. *Neuroscience Research Notes*, *3*(4), 29–34. doi:10.31117/neuroscirn.v3i4.61

Iloka, B. C., & Onyeke, K. J. (2020). Neuromarketing: A historical review. *Neuroscience Research Notes*, *3*(3), 27–35. doi:10.31117/neuroscirn.v3i3.54

Im, H., Lennon, S. J., & Stoel, L. (2010). The perceptual fluency effect on pleasurable online shopping experience. *Journal of Research in Interactive Marketing*, *4*(4), 280–295. doi:10.1108/17505931011092808

Indrasari, A., Novita, D., & Megawati, F. (2018). Big Book: Attractive media for teaching vocabulary to lower class of young learners. [Journal of English Educators Society]. *JEES*, *3*(2), 141–154. doi:10.21070/jees.v3i2.1572

Isa, S. M., & Mansor, A. A., & Razali, K. (2019). Ethics in neuromarketing and its implications on business to stay vigilant. *KnE Social Sciences*, 687-711.

Isa, S. M., & Mansor, A. A. (2020). Rejuvenating the marketing mix through neuromarketing to cultivate the green consumer. *International Journal of Information Management, 5*, 66–75.

Ismea. (2021). *SCHEDA DI SETTORE: OLIO DI OLIVA giugno 2021*. ISMEA.

Jacob, J., & Chestnut, R. (1978). *Brand Loyalty Measurement and Management*. John Wiley & Sons.

Jacobson, J., Gruzd, A., & Hernández-García, Á. (2020). Social media marketing: Who is watching the watchers? *Journal of Retailing and Consumer Services, 53*, 53. doi:10.1016/j.jretconser.2019.03.001

Jacoby, J. (1971). Brand loyalty: A conceptual definition. In *Proceedings of the Annual Convention of the American Psychological Association*. American Psychological Association.

Jenkins, H. (1992). *Textual poachers: Television fans and participatory cultures*. Routledge.

Jennings, R. (2018). How Nike's Colin Kaepernick ad explains branding in the Trump era. *Vox*. https://www.vox.com/2018/9/4/17818222/nike-colin-kaepernick-ad

Jerez-Jerez, M. J. (2022). Digital Transformation and Corporate Branding: Opportunities and Challenges for Identity and Reputation Management. Foroudi, P., Nguyen, B. and Melewar, T.C. (Ed.) The Emerald Handbook of Multi-Stakeholder Communication. Emerald Publishing Limited, Bingley. doi:10.1108/978-1-80071-897-520221014

Jerritta, S., Murugappan, M., Wan, K., & Yaacob, S. (2014). Emotion recognition from facial EMG signals using higher order statistics and principal component analysis. *Zhongguo Gongcheng Xuekan, 37*(3), 385–394. doi:10.1080/02533839.2013.799946

Jing, C., Liu, G., & Hao, M. (2009, July). The research on emotion recognition from ECG signal. In *2009 international conference on information technology and computer science* (*Vol. 1*, pp. 497-500). IEEE.

Jose, S. (2021). COVID vaccine and generation Z – a study of factors influencing adoption. *Young Consumers*. doi:10.1108/YC-01-2021-1276

Kapferer, J. (1991). *Strategic brand management*. Free Press.

Kaplan, A. M., & Haenlein, M. (2010). Users of the world, unite! The challenges and opportunities of Social Media. *Business Horizons, 53*(1), 59–68. doi:10.1016/j.bushor.2009.09.003

Kassouf, J. (2022). *As expansion race heats up, NWSL faces tough questions about its future with Utah expected to join in 2024*. ESPN. https://www.espn.com/soccer/united-states-nwsl/story/4692534/as-expansion-race-heats-upnwsl-faces-tough-questions-about-its-future-with-utah-expected-to-join-in-2024s

Kavisankar, L., Balasubramani, S., Arvindhar, D. J., & Krishan, R. (2021). Scenario based vaccine status monitoring and recommendation system for Covid-19 Vaccination. *Journal of Management Information and Decision Sciences, 24*, 1–7.

Kehri, V., Ingle, R., Patil, S., & Awale, R. N. (2019). Analysis of facial EMG signal for emotion recognition using wavelet packet transform and SVM. In *Machine intelligence and signal analysis* (pp. 247–257). Springer Singapore. doi:10.1007/978-981-13-0923-6_21

Kejariwal, M., & Bhat, R. (2022). Marketing Strategies for Pharmaceutical Industry-A Review. *Journal of Pharmaceutical Negative Results*, *13*(8), 3602–3606.

Keller, K. (1993). Conceptualizing, Measuring, and Managing Customer- Based Brand Equity. *Journal of Marketing*, *57*(1), 1–22. doi:10.1177/002224299305700101

Kemp, S. (2021, February 11). *Digital in Lithuania: All the Statistics You Need in 2021.* DataReportal – Global Digital Insights. https://datareportal.com/reports/digital-2021-lithuania

Kemp, S. (2022, February 15). *Digital 2022: Estonia.* DataReportal – Global Digital Insights. https://datareportal.com/reports/digital-2022- estonia

Kerstetter, D., & Cho, M. H. (2004, October). Prior knowledge, credibility and information search. *Annals of Tourism Research*, *31*(4), 961–985. doi:10.1016/j.annals.2004.04.002

Khan, A. M., & Stanton, J. (2010). A model of sponsorship effects on the sponsor's employees. *Journal of Promotion Management*, *16*(1-2), 188–200. doi:10.1080/10496490903574831

Kim, D. Y., & Kim, H. Y. (2021). Influencer advertising on social media: The multiple inference model on influencer-product congruence and sponsorship disclosure. *Journal of Business Research*, *130*, 405–415. doi:10.1016/j.jbusres.2020.02.020

Kim, J.-E., Lloyd, S., & Cervellon, M.-C. (2016). Narrative-transportation storylines in luxury brand advertising: Motivating consumer engagement. *Journal of Business Research*, *69*(1), 304–313. doi:10.1016/j.jbusres.2015.08.002

Kim, S., Greenwell, T. C., Andrew, D. P., Lee, J., & Mahony, D. F. (2008). An analysis of spectator motives in an individual combat sport: A study of mixed martial arts fans. *Sport Marketing Quarterly*, *17*(2), 109–119. https://oaks.kent.edu/flapubs/17

Kim, S., Morgan, A., & Assaker, G. (2021). Examining the relationship between sport spectator motivation, involvement, and loyalty: A structural model in the context of Australian Rules football. *Sport in Society*, *24*(6), 1006–1032. doi:10.1080/17430437.2020.1720658

King, B. G. (2008). A political mediation model of corporate response to social movement activism. *Administrative Science Quarterly*, *53*(3), 395–421. doi:10.2189/asqu.53.3.395

Kirilina, E., Jelzow, A., Heine, A., Niessing, M., Wabnitz, H., Brühl, R., Ittermann, B., Jacobs, A. M., & Tachtsidis, I. (2012). The physiological origin of task-evoked systemic artefacts in functional near infrared spectroscopy. *NeuroImage*, *61*(1), 70–81. doi:10.1016/j.neuroimage.2012.02.074 PMID:22426347

Klein, N. (2002). *No Logo. O poder das marcas.* Relógio d'Água.

Korschun, D. (2021). Brand Activism Is Here to Stay: Here's Why. *NIM Marketing Intelligence Review*, *13*(2), 11–17. doi:10.2478/nimmir-2021-0011

Koschate-Fischer, N., & Gartner, S. (2015). Brand Trust: Scale Development and Validation. *Schmalenbach Business Review*, *67*(2), 171–195. doi:10.1007/BF03396873

Kose, M. R., Ahirwal, M. K., & Kumar, A. (2021). A new approach for emotions recognition through EOG and EMG signals. *Signal, Image and Video Processing*, *15*(8), 1863–1871. doi:10.100711760-021-01942-1

Kotler, P., Kartajaya, H., & Setiawan, I. (2017). *Marketing 4.0: Moving from traditional to digital*. Wiley.

Kozinets, R. V. (2022). Algorithmic branding through platform assemblages: Core conceptions and research directions for a new era of marketing and service management. *Journal of Service Management*, *33*(3), 437–452. doi:10.1108/JOSM-07-2021-0263

Kozinets, R. V., & Jenkins, H. (2022). Consumer movements, brand activism, and the participatory politics of media: A conversation. *Journal of Consumer Culture*, *22*(1), 264–282. doi:10.1177/14695405211013993

Krampe, C., Gier, N. R., & Kenning, P. (2018). The application of mobile fNIRS in marketing research—Detecting the "first-choice-brand" effect. *Frontiers in Human Neuroscience*, *12*, 433. doi:10.3389/fnhum.2018.00433 PMID:30443210

Krugman, H. E. (1965). The impact of television advertising: Learning without involvement. *Public Opinion Quarterly*, *29*(3), 349–356. doi:10.1086/267335

Ktari, J., Frikha, T., Chaabane, F., Hamdi, M., & Hamam, H. (2022). Agricultural Lightweight Embedded Blockchain System: A Case Study in Olive Oil. *Electronics (Switzerland)*, *11*(20), 3394. doi:10.3390/electronics11203394

Küçün, N. T., & Güler, E. G. (2021). Examination of Consumer Purchase Decisions via Neuromarketing Methods: A Social Psychology Approach. *Prizren Social Science Journal*, *5*(2), 14–29. doi:10.32936/pssj.v5i2.245

Kumar, N. (2020). Study the impact of brand activism and political activism on marketing trends. *European Journal of Molecular & Clinical Medicine*, *7*(10), 2010–2021.

Kwon, J.-H., Jung, S.-H., Choi, H.-J., & Kim, J. (2021). Antecedent factors that affect restaurant brand trust and brand loyalty: Focusing on US and Korean consumers. *Journal of Product and Brand Management*, *30*(7), 990–1015. doi:10.1108/JPBM-02-2020-2763

LaBarbera, P. A., & Tucciarone, J. D. (1995). GSR reconsidered: A behavior-based approach to evaluating and improving the sales potency of advertising. *Journal of Advertising Research*, *35*(5), 33–54.

Lane, K., & Levy, S. J. (2019). Marketing in the Digital Age: A Moveable Feast of Information. Marketing in a Digital World (Review of Marketing Research, Vol. 16), Emerald Publishing Limited, Bingley. doi:10.1108/S1548-643520190000016004

Latino, M. E., Menegoli, M., Lazoi, M., & Corallo, A. (2022). Voluntary traceability in food supply chain: A framework leading its implementation in Agriculture 4.0. *Technological Forecasting and Social Change*, *178*, 121564. doi:10.1016/j.techfore.2022.121564

Leão, P., & da Silva, M. M. (2021). Impacts of digital transformation on firms' competitive advantages: A systematic literature review. *Strategic Change*, *30*(5), 421–441. doi:10.1002/jsc.2459

Lee, J. M., An, Y. E., Bak, E., & Pan, S. (2022). Improvement of Negative Emotion Recognition in Visible Images Enhanced by Thermal Imaging. *Sustainability*, *14*(22), 15200. doi:10.3390u142215200

Lee, N., Brandes, L., Chamberlain, L., & Senior, C. (2017). This is your brain on neuromarketing: Reflections on a decade of research. *Journal of Marketing Management*, *33*(11-12), 878–892. doi:10.1080/0267257X.2017.1327249

Lemanski, J., & Villegas, J. (2018). Vaccine promotion: Impact of risk level on attitudes. *International Journal of Pharmaceutical and Healthcare Marketing*, *12*(2), 181–197. doi:10.1108/IJPHM-04-2017-0018

Leslie-Walker, A., & Mulvenna, C. (2022). The Football Association's Women's Super League and female soccer fans: Fan engagement and the importance of supporter clubs. *Soccer and Society*, *23*(3), 314–327. doi:10.1080/14660970.2022.2037218

Li, Y., Song, X. & Zhou, M. (2022). Impacts of brand digitalization on brand market performance: the mediating role of brand competence and brand warmth. *Journal of Research in Interactive Marketing*, 1-18. . doi:10.1108/JRIM-03-2022-0107

Liao, S. H., Chen, Y. J., & Hsieh, H. H. (2011). Mining customer knowledge for direct selling and marketing. *Expert Systems with Applications*, *38*(5), 6059–6069. doi:10.1016/j.eswa.2010.11.007

Liberatore, L., Casolani, N., & Murmura, F. (2018). What's behind organic certification of extra-virgin olive oil? A response from Italian consumers. *Journal of Food Products Marketing*, *24*(8), 946–959. doi:10.1080/10454446.2018.1426513

Likert, R. (1932). A technique for the measurement of attitudes. *Archives de Psychologie*.

Lim, H., & Childs, M. (2020a). Visual storytelling on Instagram: Branded photo narrative and the role of telepresence. *Journal of Research in Interactive Marketing*, *14*(1), 33–50. doi:10.1108/JRIM-09-2018-0115

Lin, Y. H. (2015). Innovative brand experience's influence on brand equity and brand satisfaction. *Journal of Business Research*, *68*(11), 2254–2259. doi:10.1016/j.jbusres.2015.06.007

Lipiäinen, H. S. M., & Karjaluoto, H. (2015). Industrial branding in the digital age. *Journal of Business and Industrial Marketing*, *30*(6), 733–741. doi:10.1108/JBIM-04-2013-0089

Lipovetsky, G. & Serroy, J. (2010). *A Cultura-Mundo. Resposta a uma sociedade desorientada.* Lisboa: Edições.

Lipovetsky, Gilles (2022). A sagração da Autenticidade. Edições 70.

Lisienkova, T., N., L., K., & R., K. (2022). A Model for Digital Innovation Assessment and Selection. *IV International Scientific Conference "INTERAGROMASH 2021".* Springer. 10.1007/978-3-030-81619-3_93

López, M. & Francisco, J. (2020). Influencer marketing: brand control, commercial orientation and post credibility. *Journal of Marketing Management 36.*

Loureiro, S. M., Bilro, R. G., & Japutra, A. (2019). Correia, R.G.Bilro, (2019),"The effect of consumer-generated media stimuli on emotions and consumer brand engagement. *Journal of Product and Brand Management, 29*(3), 387–408. doi:10.1108/JPBM-11-2018-2120

Lozano-Castellón, J., López-Yerena, A., Domínguez-López, I., Siscart-Serra, A., Fraga, N., Sámano, S., López-Sabater, C., Lamuela-Raventós, R. M., Vallverdú-Queralt, A., & Pérez, M. (2022). Extra virgin olive oil: A comprehensive review of efforts to ensure its authenticity, traceability, and safety. *Comprehensive Reviews in Food Science and Food Safety, 21*(3), 2639–2664. doi:10.1111/1541-4337.12949 PMID:35368142

Luna-Nevarez, C. (2021). Neuromarketing, ethics, and regulation: An exploratory analysis of consumer opinions and sentiment on blogs and social media. *Journal of Consumer Policy, 44*(4), 559–583. doi:10.100710603-021-09496-y

Macey, J., Tyrväinen, V., Pirkkalainen, H., & Hamari, J. (2022). Does eSports spectating influence game consumption? *Behaviour & Information Technology, 41*(1), 181–197. doi:10.1080/0144 929X.2020.1797876

Macit, C., Taner, N., Mercanoglu, G., & Mercanoglu, F. (2016). Brand Loyalty as a Strategy for the Competition with Generic Drugs: Physicians Perspective. *Journal of Developing Drugs, 5*(3). doi:10.4172/2329-6631.1000159

Maffei, A., & Angrilli, A. (2019). Spontaneous blink rate as an index of attention and emotion during film clips viewing. *Physiology & Behavior, 204*, 256–263. doi:10.1016/j.physbeh.2019.02.037 PMID:30822434

Mahmoudian, A., Sadeghi Boroujerdi, S., Mohammadi, S., Delshab, V., & Pyun, D. Y. (2021). Testing the impact of athlete brand image attributes on fan loyalty. *Journal of Business and Industrial Marketing, 36*(2), 244–255. doi:10.1108/JBIM-10-2019-0464

Majeed, M., Asare, C., Fatawu, A., & Abubakari, A. (2022). An analysis of the effects of customer satisfaction and engagement on social media on repurchase intention in the hospitality industry. *Cogent Business and Management, 9*(1), 2028331. doi:10.1080/23311975.2022.2028331

Makri, K., Papadas, K.-K., & Schlegelmilch, B. B. (2019). Global-local consumer identities as drivers of global digital brand usage. *International Marketing Review, 36*(5), 702–725. doi:10.1108/IMR-03-2018-0104

Manfredi-Sánchez, J. L. (2019). El activismo político de las marcas. *Comunicación y Sociedad (Guadalajara), 32*(4), 343–359. doi:10.15581/003.32.4.343-359

Mansor, A. A., Isa, S. M., & Noor, S. S. M. (2021). P300 and decision-making in neuromarketing. *Neuroscience Research Notes, 4*(3), 21–26. doi:10.31117/neuroscirn.v4i3.83

Marozzo, V., Vargas-Sánchez -Tindara, A., Augusto, A., & Amico, D. (2022). Investigating the importance of product traceability in the relationship between product authenticity and consumer willingness to pay 1. *Italian Journal of Management, 40.*

Martini, D., & Menozzi, D. (2021). Food labeling: Analysis, understanding, and perception. *Nutrients, 13*(1), 1–5. doi:10.3390/nu13010268 PMID:33477758

Marx, R. W., Blumenfeld, P. C., Krajcik, J. S., & Soloway, E. (1998). New technologies for teacher professional development. *Teaching and Teacher Education, 14*(1), 33–52. doi:10.1016/S0742-051X(98)00059-6

Maughan, L., Gutnikov, S., & Stevens, R. (2007). Like more, look more. Look more, like more: The evidence from eye-tracking. *Journal of Brand Management, 14*(4), 335–342. doi:10.1057/palgrave.bm.2550074

McCarthy, J. (2019, September 03). Big pharma sinks to the bottom of U.S. industry rankings. *Gallup News*. https://news.gallup.com/poll/266060/big-pharma-sinks-bottom-industry-rankings.aspx

McKewon, E. (2012). Talking points ammo: The use of neoliberal think tank fantasy themes to delegitimise scientific knowledge of climate change in Australian newspapers. *Journalism Studies, 13*(2), 277–297. doi:10.1080/1461670X.2011.646403

Meenaghan, T. (2001). Understanding sponsorship effects. *Psychology and Marketing, 18*(2), 95–122. doi:10.1002/1520-6793(200102)18:2<95::AID-MAR1001>3.0.CO;2-H

Meister, A. R. (2019). The Power of Apology: How Crisis Communication Practices Impact Brand Reputation. [Thesis].

Mellens, M., Dekimpe, M., & Steenkamp, J. (1996). A review of brand-loyalty measures in marketing. *Tijdschrift Voor Economie En Management, 4*, 507–533.

Menon, S., & Kahn, B. E. (2003). Corporate sponsorships of philanthropic activities: When do they impact perception of sponsor brand? *Journal of Consumer Psychology, 13*(3), 316–327. doi:10.1207/S15327663JCP1303_12

Menozzi, D. (2014). Extra-virgin olive oil production sustainability in northern Italy: A preliminary study. *British Food Journal, 116*(12), 1942–1959. doi:10.1108/BFJ-06-2013-0141

Mergel, I., Edelmann, N., & Haug, N. (2019). Defining digital transformation: Results from expert interviews. *Government Information Quarterly, 36*(4), 101385. doi:10.1016/j.giq.2019.06.002

Meyerding, S. G., & Risius, A. (2018). Reading minds: Mobile functional near-infrared spectroscopy as a new neuroimaging method for economic and marketing research—A feasibility study. *Journal of Neuroscience, Psychology, and Economics*, *11*(4), 197–212. doi:10.1037/npe0000090

Mian, A., & Khan, S. (2020). Coronavirus: The spread of misinformation. *BMC Medicine*, *18*(1), 89. doi:10.118612916-020-01556-3 PMID:32188445

Mians, J., & Majid, U. (2022). WSL clubs see ticket demand surge after Lionesses' Euro 2022 win. *The Guardian*. https://www.theguardian.com/football/2022/aug/03/wsl-clubs-see-ticket-demand-surge-after-lionesses-euro-22-win

Migacz, S. J., Zou, S., & Petrick, J. F. (2017). The "Terminal" Effects of Service Failure on Airlines: Examining Service Recovery with Justice Theory. *Journal of Travel Research*, *57*(1), 83–98. doi:10.1177/0047287516684979

Miguel, A., & Miranda, S. (2022). The role of social media in the proliferation and promotion of Brand Activism. *Comunicação Pública, 17*.

Mills, A. J., & Robson, K. (2020). Brand management in the era of fake news: Narrative response as a strategy to insulate brand value. *Journal of Product and Brand Management*, *29*(2), 159–167. doi:10.1108/JPBM-12-2018-2150

MIPAF. (2016). *Piano di settore olivicolo-oleario*. MIPAF.

Mirzaei, A., Wilkie, D. C., & Siuki, H. (2022). Woke brand activism authenticity or the lack of it. *Journal of Business Research*, *139*, 1–12. doi:10.1016/j.jbusres.2021.09.044

Monfared, R. (2016). Blockchain ready manufacturing supply chain using distributed ledger. In *Accepted to the International Journal of Research in Engineering and Technology-IJRET* (Issue 09). https://esatjournals.net/ijret/2016v05/i09/IJRET20160509001.pdfMetadataRecord:https://dspace.lboro.ac.uk/2134/22625

Montgomery, C., & Wernerfelt, B. (1992). Risk Reduction and umbrella branding. *The Journal of Business*, *65*(1), 31–50. doi:10.1086/296556

Moor, L. (2008). Branding consultants as cultural intermediaries. *The Sociological Review*, *56*(3), 408–428. doi:10.1111/j.1467-954X.2008.00797.x

Moorman, C. (2020). Commentary: Brand activism in a political world. *Journal of Public Policy & Marketing*, *39*(4), 388–392. doi:10.1177/0743915620945260

Morgan, R. M., & Hunt, S. D. (1994). The commitment-trust theory of relationship marketing. *Journal of Marketing*, *58*(3), 20–38. doi:10.1177/002224299405800302

Moses, E., & Clark, K. R. (2020). The Neuromarketing Revolution: Bringing Science and Technology to Marketing Insight. In Anthropological Approaches to Understanding Consumption Patterns and Consumer Behavior (pp. 449-464). IGI Global.

Moya, I., García-Madariaga, J., & Blasco, M. F. (2020). What can Neuromarketing tell us about food packaging? *Foods*, *9*(12), 1856. doi:10.3390/foods9121856 PMID:33322684

Mozdzenski, L. (2019). A publicidade-documentário e a construção discursiva do efeito de real em prol da causa LGBTQ. *Revista Ícone, Recife*, *17*(2), 107–124. doi:10.34176/icone.v17i2.238965

Muhammad, H. (2019). Gender differences and aggression: A comparative study of college and university sport players. *Humanities and Social Sciences*, *26*(2), 1–16.

Mukherjee, S., & Althuizen, N. (2020). Brand activism: Does courting controversy help or hurt a brand? *International Journal of Research in Marketing*, *37*(4), 772–788. doi:10.1016/j.ijresmar.2020.02.008

Mumcu, C., Lough, N., & Barnes, J. C. (2016). Examination of women's sports fans' attitudes and consumption intentions. *Journal of Applied Sport Management*, *8*(4), 25–43. doi:10.18666/JASM-2016-V8-I4-7221

Mutz, M., & Meier, H. E. (2016). Successful, sexy, popular: Athletic performance and physical attractiveness as determinants of public interest in male and female soccer players. *International Review for the Sociology of Sport*, *51*(5), 567–580. doi:10.1177/1012690214545900

Nakasone, A., Prendinger, H., & Ishizuka, M. (2005, September). Emotion recognition from electromyography and skin conductance. In *Proc. of the 5th international workshop on biosignal interpretation* (pp. 219-222). Citeseer.

Neureiter, M., & Bhattacharya, C. B. (2021). Why do boycotts sometimes increase sales? Consumer activism in the age of political polarization. *Business Horizons*, *64*(5), 611–620. doi:10.1016/j.bushor.2021.02.025

Niculescu, A., Dumitriu, D., Purdescu, C., & Popescu, M. A. M. (2019). Enhancing Brand Value of Modern Organizations through Digital Marketing Tools and Techniques: A Study on Top Ten Romanian Companies. *TEM Journal*, *8*(1), 171.

Nunnally, J. C. (1994). *Psychometric Theory* (2nd ed.). McGraw-Hill.

Nyadzayo, M., & Khajehzadeh, S. (2016). The antecedents of customer loyalty: A moderated mediation model of customer relationship management quality and brand image. *Journal of Retailing and Consumer Services*, *30*, 262–270. doi:10.1016/j.jretconser.2016.02.002

Oliver, R. L. (1999). Whence consumer loyalty? *Journal of Marketing*, *63*(4, suppl1), 33–44. doi:10.1177/00222429990634s105

Olympics. (2019). *Best of team USA women's football at the Olympics: Top moments*. [Video]. Youtube. https://www.youtube.com/watch?v=X2ByJNAsct4

OPAS. (2020). *Folha informativa sobre COVID-19. Histórico da pandemia de COVID-19*. OPAS. https://www.paho.org/pt/covid19/historico-da-pandemia-covid-19

Overby, J. W., Woodruff, R. B., & Gardial, S. F. (2005). The influence of culture upon consumers' desired value perceptions: A research agenda. *Marketing Theory*, 5(2), 139–163. doi:10.1177/1470593105052468

Ozkara, B. Y., & Bagozzi, R. (2021). The use of event related potentials brain methods in the study of conscious and unconscious consumer decision making processes. *Journal of Retailing and Consumer Services*, 58, 102202. doi:10.1016/j.jretconser.2020.102202

Pahus, L., Suehs, C. M., Halimi, L., Bourdin, A., Chanez, P., Jaffuel, D., Marciano, J., Gamez, A.-S., Vachier, I., & Molinari, N. (2020). Patient distrust in pharmaceutical companies: An explanation for women under-representation in respiratory clinical trials? *BMC Medical Ethics*, 21(1), 72. doi:10.118612910-020-00509-y PMID:32791969

Paris, C. (2022). *Achieving Brand Authenticity in the Age of Cancel Culture: Why Brands Can No Longer Be Neutral Without Being Seen as Complicit.* [Theses, University of Arkansas]. https://scholarworks.uark.edu/mktguht/54

Park, M., Im, H., & Kim, H. Y. (2020). "You are too friendly!" The negative effects of social media marketing on value perceptions of luxury fashion brands. *Journal of Business Research*, 117, 529–542. doi:10.1016/j.jbusres.2018.07.026

Parra-López, C., Reina-Usuga, L., Carmona-Torres, C., Sayadi, S., & Klerkx, L. (2021). Digital transformation of the agrifood system: Quantifying the conditioning factors to inform policy planning in the olive sector. *Land Use Policy*, 108, 105537. doi:10.1016/j.landusepol.2021.105537

Parsons, A. G., & Schumacher, C. (2012). Advertising regulation and market drivers. *European Journal of Marketing*, 46(11/12), 1539–1558. doi:10.1108/03090561211259970

Pascual, P. A. C. (2009). Ethical controversy over information and communication technology. In *Handbook of Research on Technoethics* (pp. 222–231). IGI Global. doi:10.4018/978-1-60566-022-6.ch015

Peloza, J., & Shang, J. (2011). How can corporate social responsibility activities create value for stakeholders? A systematic review. *Journal of the Academy of Marketing Science*, 39(1), 117–135. doi:10.100711747-010-0213-6

Pessemier, E. A. (1959). A New Way to Determine Buying Decisions. *Journal of Marketing*, 24(2), 41–46. doi:10.1177/002224295902400208

Pieters, R., Rosbergen, E., & Wedel, M. (1999). Visual attention to repeated print advertising: A test of scanpath theory. *JMR, Journal of Marketing Research*, 36(4), 424–438. doi:10.1177/002224379903600403

Pine, B. J., & Gilmore, J. H. (2019). *The experience economy: Competing for customer time, attention, and money.* Harvard Business Review Press.

Pinkleton, B. (1997). The effects of negative comparative political advertising on candidate evaluations and advertising evaluations: An exploration. *Journal of Advertising*, 26(1), 19–29. doi:10.1080/00913367.1997.10673515

Plessis, D., Sake, J. K., Halling, K., Morgan, J., Georgieva, A., & Bertelsen, N. (2017). Patient centricity and pharmaceutical companies: Is it feasible? *Therapeutic Innovation & Regulatory Science*, *51*(4), 460–467. doi:10.1177/2168479017696268 PMID:30227057

Polenzani, B., Riganelli, C., & Marchini, A. (2020). Sustainability perception of local extra virgin olive oil and consumers' attitude: A new Italian perspective. *Sustainability (Switzerland)*, *12*(3), 920. Advance online publication. doi:10.3390u12030920

Poon, P., & Albaum, G. (2019). Consumer trust in internet marketing and direct selling in china. *Journal of Relationship Marketing*, *18*(3), 216–232. doi:10.1080/15332667.2019.1589244

Power, M. (2019). Infrastructures of traceability. *Thinking Infrastructures*, *62*, 115–130. doi:10.1108/S0733-558X20190000062007

Pozharliev, R., Verbeke, W. J., Van Strien, J. W., & Bagozzi, R. P. (2015). Merely being with you increases my attention to luxury products: Using EEG to understand consumers' emotional experience with luxury branded products. *JMR, Journal of Marketing Research*, *52*(4), 546–558. doi:10.1509/jmr.13.0560

Press, J., Bellis, P., Buganza, T., & Magnanini, S. (Rami) Shani, A.B., Trabucchi, D., Verganti, R. & Zasa, F.P. (2021). Innovation in the Digital Era. IDeaLs (Innovation and Design as Leadership). Emerald Publishing Limited, Bingley, 13-34. doi:10.1108/978-1-80071-833-320211002

Pulizzi, J. (2012). The Rise of Storytelling as the New Marketing. *The Rise of Storytelling as the New Marketing*, *28*(2), 116–123. doi:10.100712109-012-9264-5

Quintanilla, C. (2021, May 05). *Consumer and brand perception in covid-19 vaccines*. CE Noticias Financieras.

Rahmanian, E. (2021), Consumption narratives: contributions, methods, findings and agenda for future research, *Spanish Journal of Marketing - ESIC*, *25*(1), 46-84. . doi:10.1108/SJME-10-2020-0179

Rahman, M. (2019). 21st century skill'problem solving': Defining the concept. Rahman, MM (2019). 21st Century Skill "Problem Solving": Defining the Concept. *Asian Journal of Interdisciplinary Research*, *2*(1), 64–74.

Rahman, M., Masum, M., Wajed, S., & Talukder, A. (2022). A comprehensive review on COVID-19 vaccines: Development, effectiveness, adverse effects, distribution and challenges. *VirusDis*, *33*(1), 1–22. doi:10.100713337-022-00755-1 PMID:35127995

Ramadhani, I. S., & Indradjati, P. N. (2023). Toward contemporary city branding in the digital era: conceptualizing the acceptability of city branding on social media. Open House International. doi:10.1108/OHI-08-2022-0213

Rao, S. (2002). Pharmaceutical marketing in a new age. *Marketing Health Services*, *22*(1), 6–12. PMID:11881547

Rao, V. R., & McLaughlin, E. W. (1989). Modeling the decision to add new products by channel intermediaries. *Journal of Marketing*, *53*(1), 80–88. doi:10.1177/002224298905300107

Rattanyu, K., & Mizukawa, M. (2011). Emotion recognition based on ecg signals for service robots in the intelligent space during daily life. *J. Adv. Comput. Intell. Intell. Inform.*, *15*(5), 582–591. doi:10.20965/jaciii.2011.p0582

Rees, S. (2022). Authentic Sports Branding in the Digital Age. Heřmanová, M., Skey, M. & Thurnell-Read, T. (Ed.) Cultures of Authenticity. Emerald Publishing Limited, Bingley. doi:10.1108/978-1-80117-936-220221009

Reichheld, F. (1996). *The Loyalty Effect: The Hidden Force Behind Growth, Profits and Lasting Value*. Harvard Business School Press.

Reportlinker (2021). *COVID-19 Vaccine Market - Global Outlook and Forecast 2021-2024.* Aritzon. https://www.reportlinker.com/p06036826/?utm_source=GNW

Reuters. (2021). *Record viewership for 2021 NWSL finale*. Reuters. https://www.reuters.com/lifestyle/sports/record-viewership-2021-nwsl-finale-2021-11-23/

Rimm, D. C., & Litvak, S. B. (1969). Self-verbalization and emotional arousal. *Journal of Abnormal Psychology*, *74*(2), 181–187. doi:10.1037/h0027116 PMID:5783231

Ripoll Gonzalez, L., & Gale, F. (2023). Sustainable city branding narratives: A critical appraisal of processes and outcomes. *Journal of Place Management and Development*, *16*(1), 20–44. doi:10.1108/JPMD-09-2021-0093

Ritter, T., & Pedersen, C. L. (2020). Digitization capability and the digitalization of business models in business-to-business firms: Past, present, and future. *Industrial Marketing Management*, *86*, 180–190. doi:10.1016/j.indmarman.2019.11.019

Robbins, R. H., & Dowty, R. (2008). *Global problems and the culture of capitalism*. Pearson/Allyn & Bacon.

Rooj, S., Routray, A., & Mandal, M. K. (2023). Feature based analysis of thermal images for emotion recognition. *Engineering Applications of Artificial Intelligence*, *120*, 105809. doi:10.1016/j.engappai.2022.105809

Rosa, P. (2015). What do your eyes say? Bridging eye movements to consumer behavior. *International Journal of Psychological Research*, *8*(2), 90–103. doi:10.21500/20112084.1513

Rosen, H. (2022). *The problem with women's sports | Haley Rosen*. TEDxBoston. https://www.youtube.com/watch?v=vG6P9gfgO6g

Rotsios, K., Konstantoglou, A., Folinas, D., Fotiadis, T., Hatzithomas, L., & Boutsouki, C. (2022). Evaluating the Use of QR Codes on Food Products. *Sustainability (Switzerland)*, *14*(8), 4437. doi:10.3390u14084437

Royo-Vela, M., & Varga, Á. (2022). Unveiling Neuromarketing and Its Research Methodology. *Encyclopedia*, *2*(2), 729–751. doi:10.3390/encyclopedia2020051

Ruão, T. (2005). Clifton, Rita; Simmons, John (2005) O Mundo das Marcas, Lisboa: Actual Editora. *Comunicação e Sociedade*, *8*, 323–327. doi:10.17231/comsoc.8(2005).1204

Ruão, T. (2016). *A Organização Comunicativa: Teoria e Prática em Comunicação Organizacional.* CS Edições.

Rubin, A. (1981). The interaction of television uses and gratifications. *Journal of Broadcasting*, *27*, 37–51. doi:10.1080/08838158309386471

Ryall, E. (2015). Good games and penalty shoot-outs. *Sport, Ethics and Philosophy*, *9*(2), 205–213. doi:10.1080/17511321.2015.1020854

Saatchi, S. S., Houghton, R. A., Dos Santos Alvalá, R. C., Soares, J. V., & Yu, Y. (2007). Distribution of aboveground live biomass in the Amazon basin. *Global Change Biology*, *13*(4), 816–837. doi:10.1111/j.1365-2486.2007.01323.x

Sabharwal, D. (2017). Determinants of Brand Reliability: A Study of the Familiarity-Assurance-Loyalty. *IJARIIE*, *3*(2), 2755–2762.

Samarah, T., Bayram, P., Aljuhmani, H., & Elrehail, H. (2022). The role of brand interactivity and involvement in driving social media consumer brand engagement and brand loyalty: The mediating effect of brand trust. *Journal of Research in Interactive Marketing*, *16*(4), 648–664. doi:10.1108/JRIM-03-2021-0072

Sanderson, J. (2011). *It's a whole new ballgame: How social media is changing sports.* Hampton Press.

Sarfraz, M., Hamid, S., Rawstorne, P., Ali, M., & Jayasuriya, R. (2021). Role of social network in decision making for increasing uptake and continuing use of long acting reversible (LARC) methods in Pakistan. *Reproductive Health*, *18*(1), 96. doi:10.118612978-021-01149-0 PMID:34001169

Sarkar, P., & Etemad, A. (2020, May). Self-supervised learning for ecg-based emotion recognition. In *ICASSP 2020-2020 IEEE International Conference on Acoustics, Speech and Signal Processing (ICASSP)* (pp. 3217-3221). IEEE. 10.1109/ICASSP40776.2020.9053985

Sato, W., Fujimura, T., Kochiyama, T., & Suzuki, N. (2013). Relationships among facial mimicry, emotional experience, and emotion recognition. *PLoS One*, *8*(3), e57889. doi:10.1371/journal.pone.0057889 PMID:23536774

Savelli, E. (2022). Neuromarketing: ethical dilemma and consumers' perception. In *21th International Marketing Trends Conference* (pp. 1-7). AE Mark.

Schad, T. (2022). 'Where the heck are the women?' Why women's sports could see financial boon in future TV deals. *USA Today*. https://eu.usatoday.com/story/sports/2022/07/12/womens-sports-tv-financial-boon-coming/7810802001/

Schmitt, B. (1999). *Experiential marketing: How to get customers to sense, feel, think, act, relate to your company and brands*. Free Press.

Schuiling, I., & Moss, G. (2004). How different are branding strategies in the pharmaceutical industry and the fast-moving consumer goods sector? *Journal of Brand Management, 11*(5), 366–380. doi:10.1057/palgrave.bm.2540182

Schwägele, F. (2005). Traceability from a European perspective. *Meat Science, 71*(1), 164–173. doi:10.1016/j.meatsci.2005.03.002 PMID:22064062

Scottish Government. (2019). *Unveiling a plaque at the Hibs Supporters' Club to commemorate the first women's international football match in 1881*. Scootish Government. https://twitter.com/scotgovhealth/status/1201846754603347968

Shagass, C., Roemer, R. A., & Amadeo, M. (1976). Eye-tracking performance and engagement of attention. *Archives of General Psychiatry, 33*(1), 121–125. doi:10.1001/archpsyc.1976.01770010077015 PMID:1247358

Sharma, K., Koirala, A., Nicolopoulos, K., & Chiu, C. (2020). Coronavirus goes viral: Quantifying the COVID-19 misinformation epidemic on Twitter. *Cureus, 12*(3). doi:10.7759/cureus.7255 PMID:32337139

Sharma, K., Koirala, A., Nicolopoulos, K., Chiu, C., Wood, N., & Britton, P. N. (2021). Vaccines for COVID-19: Where do we stand in 2021? *Paediatric Respiratory Reviews, 39*, 22–31. doi:10.1016/j.prrv.2021.07.001 PMID:34362666

Sharma, Y., Silal, P., Kumar, J., & Singh, R. (2022). From pandemic to Prada: Examining online luxury-brand self-narrative. *Marketing Intelligence & Planning, 40*(4), 527–541. doi:10.1108/MIP-05-2021-0153

Shavelson, R. J. (1973). What is the basic teaching skill? *Journal of Teacher Education, 24*(2), 144–151. doi:10.1177/002248717302400213

Shetty, A. S., Venkataramaiah, N. B., & Anand, K. (2019). Brand activism and millennials: An empirical investigation into the perception of millennials towards brand activism. *Problems and Perspectives in Management, 17*(4), 163–175. doi:10.21511/ppm.17(4).2019.14

Shi, X., Lin, Z., Liu, J., & Hui, Y. K. (2018). p, (2018), "Consumer loyalty toward smartphone brands: The determining roles of deliberate inertia and cognitive lock-in. *Information & Management, 55*(7), 866–876. doi:10.1016/j.im.2018.03.013

Shukla, S. (2019). Neuromarketing: A change in marketing tools and techniques. *International Journal of Business Forecasting and Marketing Intelligence, 5*(3), 267–284. doi:10.1504/IJBFMI.2019.104044

Sibai, O., Mimoun, L., & Boukis, A. (2021). Authenticating brand activism: Negotiating the boundaries of free speech to make a change. *Psychology and Marketing, 38*(10), 1651–1669. doi:10.1002/mar.21477

Simkovitch, A. (2019). *Political Consumerism and Branding: An Analysis of the Exploitation of Political Movements for Brand Equity and Profit. Honors College Theses*. Ace University.

Singh, S. (2020). Impact of neuromarketing applications on consumers. *Journal of Business and Management*, *26*(2), 33–52.

Singh, Y., Eisenberg, M., & Sood, N. (2023). Factors Associated with Public Trust in Pharmaceutical Manufacturers. *Public Health*, *6*(3), e233002. doi:10.1001/jamanetworkopen.2023.3002 PMID:36917113

Sivarajah, R. T., Curci, N. E., Johnson, E. M., Lam, D. L., Lee, J. T., & Richardson, M. L. (2019). A review of innovative teaching methods. *Academic Radiology*, *26*(1), 101–113. doi:10.1016/j. acra.2018.03.025 PMID:30929697

Skillen, F., Byrne, H., Carrier, J., & James, G. (2022). 'The game of football is quite unsuitable for females and ought not to be encouraged': A comparative analysis of the 1921 English Football Association ban on women's football in Britain and Ireland. *Sport in History*, *42*(1), 49–75. doi:10.1080/17460263.2021.2025415

Sky Sports. (2021). WSL: Barclays extends FA and Premier League partnership and will sponsor FA Women's Championship. *Sky Sports*. https://www.skysports.com/football/news/28508/12496102/wsl-barclays-extends-fa-and-premier-league-partnership-and-will-sponsor-fa-womens-championship

Sokolova, K., & Kefi, H. (2020, March). Instagram and YouTube bloggers promote it, why should I buy? How credibility and parasocial interaction influence purchase intentions. *Journal of Retailing and Consumer Services*, *53*, 101742. doi:10.1016/j.jretconser.2019.01.011

Somppi, S. (2017, November 16). *RESEARCH: Instagram Influencer Marketing in Finland*. Annalect. https://www.annalect.fi/research-instagram-influencer-marketing-finland/

Song, T., Zheng, W., Song, P., & Cui, Z. (2018). EEG emotion recognition using dynamical graph convolutional neural networks. *IEEE Transactions on Affective Computing*, *11*(3), 532–541. doi:10.1109/TAFFC.2018.2817622

Spiteri, M., & Chang Rundgren, S. N. (2020). Literature review on the factors affecting primary teachers' use of digital technology. Technology. *Knowledge and Learning*, *25*(1), 115–128. doi:10.100710758-018-9376-x

Srivastava, N., Dash, S., & Mookerjee, A. (2016). Determinants of brand trust in high inherent risk products: The moderating role of education and working status. *Marketing Intelligence & Planning*, *34*(3), 394–420. doi:10.1108/MIP-01-2015-0004

Stafford, J. E., Birdwell, A. E., & Van Tassel, C. E. (1970). Integrated advertising: White backlash. *Journal of Advertising Research*, *10*, 15–20.

Statista. (2022, June 15). *Latvia number of social media users 2017-2026*. Statista. https://www.statista.com/statistics/568969/predicted-number-of- social-network-users-in-latvia/

Stipp, H. (2015). The Evolution Of Neuromarketing Research: From Novelty To Mainstream. *Journal of Advertising Research*, *55*(2), 120–122. doi:10.2501/JAR-55-2-120-122

Stolle, D., Hooghe, M., & Micheletti, M. (2005). Politics in the Supermarket: Political Consumerism as a Form of Political Participation. *International Political Science Review*, *26*(3), 245–269. doi:10.1177/0192512105053784

Stolle, D., & Micheletti, M. (2013). *Political consumerism: global responsibility in action.* Cambridge University Press. doi:10.1017/CBO9780511844553

Sunstein, C., & Vermeule, A. (2009). Conspiracy theories: Causes and cures. *Journal of Political Philosophy*, *17*(2), 202–227. doi:10.1111/j.1467-9760.2008.00325.x

Sutera, D. (2013). *Sports fans 2.0: How fans are using social media to get closer to the game.* Scarecrow Press.

Švarc, J., Lažnjak, J., & Dabić, M. (2020). The role of national intellectual capital in the digital transformation of EU countries. Another digital divide? *Journal of Intellectual Capital*. . doi:10.1108/JIC-02-2020-0024

Szilagyi, P., Thomas, K., Shah, M., Vizueta, N., Cui, Y., Vangala, S., & Kapteyn, A. (2021). The role of trust in the likelihood of receiving a COVID-19 vaccine: Results from a national survey. *Preventive Medicine*, *153*, 106727. doi:10.1016/j.ypmed.2021.106727 PMID:34280405

Tafesse, W., & Wood, B. P. (2021). Followers' engagement with instagram influencers: The role of influencers' content and engagement strategy. *Journal of Retailing and Consumer Services*, *58*, 102303. doi:10.1016/j.jretconser.2020.102303

Taylor, C. R. (2017). How to avoid marketing disasters: Back to the basic communications model, but with some updates illustrating the importance of e-word-of-mouth research. *International Journal of Advertising*, *36*(4), 515–519. doi:10.1080/02650487.2017.1323406

Tharatipyakul, A., & Pongnumkul, S. (2021). User Interface of Blockchain-Based Agri-Food Traceability Applications: A Review. *IEEE Access : Practical Innovations, Open Solutions*, *9*, 82909–82929. doi:10.1109/ACCESS.2021.3085982

The Economist. (2019). Competition between sports for fans' money and attention is increasingly fierce. *The Economist.* https://www.economist.com/international/2019/10/05/competition-between-sports-for-fans-money-and-attention-is-increasingly-fierce

Theodoridis, P. K., & Zacharatos, T. (2022). Food waste during Covid- 19 lockdown period and consumer behaviour – The case of Greece. *Socio-Economic Planning Sciences*, *83*, 101338. doi:10.1016/j.seps.2022.101338

Thorson, E., & Lang, A. (1992). . The Effects Of Television Videographics And Lecture Familiarity On Adult Cardiac Orienting Responses And Memory. *Communication Research*, 346-369.

Tian, Y., Babcock, R., Taylor, C., & Ji, Y. (2018). A new live video streaming approach based on Amazon S3 pricing model. In *2018 IEEE 8th Annual computing and communication workshop and conference (CCWC)* (pp. 321-328). IEEE. 10.1109/CCWC.2018.8301615

Tirandazi, P., Bamakan, S. M. H., & Toghroljerdi, A. (2022). A review of studies on internet of everything as an enabler of neuromarketing methods and techniques. *The Journal of Supercomputing*, 1–42.

Tonacci, A., Dellabate, A., Dieni, A., Bachi, L., Sansone, F., Conte, R., & Billeci, L. (2020). Can Machine Learning Predict Stress Reduction Based on Wearable Sensors' Data Following Relaxation at Workplace? A Pilot Study. *Processes (Basel, Switzerland)*, 8(4), 448. doi:10.3390/pr8040448

Trail, G. (2012). *Manual for the Motivation Scale for Sport Consumption (MSSC)*. Sports Research Consultants. https://sportconsumerresearchconsultants.yolasite.com/resources/MSSC%20Manual%20-%202012.pdf

Trail, G. T., Robinson, M., Dick, R., & Gillentine, A. (2003). Motives and points of attachment: Fans versus spectators in intercollegiate athletics. *Sport Marketing Quarterly*, 12, 217–227.

Trail, G., & James, J. D. (2001). The Motivation Scale for Sport Consumption: Assessment of the scale's psychometric properties. *Journal of Sport Behavior*, 24(1), 108–128.

Treviño, T., & Pineda Garelli, J. L. (2019). Understanding digital moms: Motivations to interact with brands on social networking sites. *Qualitative Market Research*, 22(1), 70–87. doi:10.1108/QMR-01-2017-0013

UEFA. (2022a). *UEFA Women's EURO 2022 becomes most watched Women's EURO in history*. UEFA. https://www.uefa.com/insideuefa/news/0277-15b76971bb48-092500679b6d-1000--uefa-women-s-euro-2022-becomes-most-watched-women-s-euro-in-his/

UEFA. (2022b). *The business case for women's football*. UEFA. https://editorial.uefa.com/resources/0278-15e121074702-c9be7dcd0a29-1000/business_case_for_women_s_football-_external_report_1_.pdf

Urigüen, J. A., & Garcia-Zapirain, B. (2015). EEG artifact removal—state-of-the-art and guidelines. Journal of neural engineering, 12(3), .

USC Annenberg Center for Public Relations. (2022). The future of Corporate Activism. *Global Communication Report*. USC Annenberg. https://annenberg.usc.edu/research/center-public-relations/global-communication-report

Van der Waldt, D. M., van Loggerenberg, M., & Wehmeyer, L. (2011, August 12). Celebrity endorsements versus created spokespersons in advertising: A survey among students. *Suid-Afrikaanse Tydskrif vir Ekonomiese en Bestuurswetenskappe*, 12(1), 100–114. doi:10.4102ajems.v12i1.263

van Deth, J. W. (2014). A conceptual map of political participation. *Acta Politica*, 49(3), 349–367. doi:10.1057/ap.2014.6

Van Rijswijk, W., & Frewer, L. J. (2008). Consumer perceptions of food quality and safety and their relation to traceability. *British Food Journal*, *110*(10), 1034–1046. doi:10.1108/00070700810906642

Vázquez, A. N. (2014). "Consumocracia". El consumo político como forma de participación de la ciudadanía. *Política y Sociedad*, *51*(1), 121–146.

ve Kossylyn, Z. (1998). *Neuroimaging as a Marketing tool*. US6099319A. Google. https://patents. google.com/patent/US6099319A/

Vecchiato, G., Astolfi, L., Fallani, F. D. V., Toppi, J., Aloise, F., Cincotti, F., & Babiloni, F. (2011). Understanding cerebral activations in neuromarketing: A neuroelectrical perspective. In *International Conference on Bio-Inspired Systems and Signal Processing, BIOSIGNALS 2011* (pp. 91-97). Research Gate.

Venciute, D., Kazukauskaite, M., Correia, R., Kuslys, M., & Vaiciukynas, E. (2023). The effect of cause-related marketing on the green consumption attitude–behaviour gap in the cosmetics industry. *Journal of Contemporary Marketing Science*, *6*(1), 22–45. doi:10.1108/JCMARS-08-2022-0019

Villringer, A., Planck, J., Hock, C., Schleinkofer, L., & Dirnagl, U. (1993). Near infrared spectroscopy (NIRS): A new tool to study hemodynamic changes during activation of brain function in human adults. *Neuroscience Letters*, *154*(1), 101–104. doi:10.1016/0304-3940(93)90181-J PMID:8361619

Violino, S., Pallottino, F., Sperandio, G., Figorilli, S., Antonucci, F., Ioannoni, V., Fappiano, D., & Costa, C. (2019). Are the innovative electronic labels for extra virgin olive oil sustainable, traceable, and accepted by consumers? *Foods*, *8*(11), 529. doi:10.3390/foods8110529 PMID:31731433

Violino, S., Pallottino, F., Sperandio, G., Figorilli, S., Ortenzi, L., Tocci, F., Vasta, S., Imperi, G., & Costa, C. (2020). A full technological traceability system for extra virgin olive oil. *Foods*, *9*(5), 624. doi:10.3390/foods9050624 PMID:32414115

Vredenburg, J., Kapitan, S., Spry, A., & Kemper, J. A. (2020). Brands taking a stand: Authentic brand activism or woke washing? *Journal of Public Policy & Marketing*, *39*(4), 444–460. doi:10.1177/0743915620947359

Wang, C. A., Baird, T., Huang, J., Coutinho, J. D., Brien, D. C., & Munoz, D. P. (2018). Arousal effects on pupil size, heart rate, and skin conductance in an emotional face task. *Frontiers in Neurology*, *9*, 1029. doi:10.3389/fneur.2018.01029 PMID:30559707

Wang, C., Jong, E., Faure, J., Ellington, J., Chen, C., & Chang, C. (2022). A matter of trust: A qualitative comparison of the determinants of COVID-19 vaccine hesitancy in Taiwan, the United States, the Netherlands, and Haiti. *Human Vaccines & Immunotherapeutics*, *18*(7), 2050121. doi:10.1080/21645515.2022.2050121 PMID:35349382

Wang, E. S. (2019). Tse. (2019) "Effects of brand awareness and social norms on user-perceived cyber privacy risk. *International Journal of Electronic Commerce*, *23*(2), 272–293. doi:10.1080/10864415.2018.1564553

Wang, R. T., Zhang, J. J., & Tsuji, Y. (2011). Examining fan motives and loyalty for the Chinese Professional Baseball League of Taiwan. *Sport Management Review*, *14*(4), 347–360. doi:10.1016/j.smr.2010.12.001

Wann, D. L. (1995). Preliminary validation of the sport fan motivation scale. *Journal of Sport and Social Issues*, *19*(4), 377–396. doi:10.1177/019372395019004004

Wann, D. L., & James, J. D. (2019). *Sport fans: The psychology and social impact of fandom* (2nd ed.). Routledge.

Wedel, M. (2013). *Attention research in marketing: A review of eye tracking studies*. Robert H. Smith School Research Paper No. RHS, 2460289.

Wedel, M., & Pieters, R. (2017). A review of eye-tracking research in marketing. *Review of marketing research,* 123-147.

Wells, W., Burnett, J., & Moriarty, S. (2000). Advertising: Principles and Practice, 5th edition, Pearson World Business Council for Sustainable Development (WBCSD).

Williams, J. (2003). *A game for rough girls? A history of women's football in Britain*. Routledge.

Williams, J. (2011). *Women's Football, Europe and professionalization 1971-2011*. International Centre for Sports History and Culture.

Won, J. U., & Kitamura, K. (2006). Motivational factors affecting sports consumption behavior of K-league and J-league spectators. *International Journal of Sport and Health Science*, *4*, 233–251. doi:10.5432/ijshs.4.233

Wood, L. (2000). Brands and brand equity: Definition and management. *Management Decision*, *38*(9), 662–669. doi:10.1108/00251740010379100

Xiao, M. (2020). Factors influencing eSports viewership: An approach based on the theory of reasoned action. *Communication & Sport*, *8*(1), 92–122. doi:10.1177/2167479518819482

Xu, S., Ni, Q., & Du, Q. (2019). The effectiveness of virtual reality in safety training: Measurement of emotional arousal with electromyography. In *ISARC. Proceedings of the International Symposium on Automation and Robotics in Construction* (Vol. 36, pp. 20-25). IAARC Publications.

Xue, W., Ma, D., & Hu, J. (2022). Recycling Model Selection for Electronic Products Considering Platform Power and Blockchain Empowerment. *Sustainability 14*.

Xue, L., Weiwei, G., Zettan, F., Peng, X., & Weiguang, L. (2007). Traceability and IT: Implications for the future international competitiveness and structure of China's vegetable sector. *New Zealand Journal of Agricultural Research*, *50*(5), 911–917. doi:10.1080/00288230709510367

Yin, S., Li, Y., Xu, Y., Chen, M., & Wang, Y. (2017). Consumer preference and willingness to pay for the traceability information attribute of infant milk formula: Evidence from a choice experiment in China. *British Food Journal*, *119*(6), 1276–1288. doi:10.1108/BFJ-11-2016-0555

Yung, R., & Khoo-Lattimore, C. (2019). New realities: A systematic literature review on virtual reality and augmented reality in tourism research. *Current Issues in Tourism, 22*(17), 2056–2081. doi:10.1080/13683500.2017.1417359

Yu, X., & Yuan, C. (2019). How consumers' brand experience in social media can improve brand perception and customer equity. *Asia Pacific Journal of Marketing and Logistics, 31*(5), 1233–1251. doi:10.1108/APJML-01-2018-0034

Zamani, J., & Naieni, A. B. (2020). *Best feature extraction and classification algorithms for EEG signals in neuromarketing*. Frontiers in Biome.

Zhang, X., & Yuan, S. M. (2018). An eye tracking analysis for video advertising: Relationship between advertisement elements and effectiveness. *IEEE Access : Practical Innovations, Open Solutions, 6*, 10699–10707. doi:10.1109/ACCESS.2018.2802206

Zietek, N. (2016). *Influencer Marketing: the characteristics and components of fashion influencer marketing*.

Zurawicki, L. (2010). Neuromarketing: Exploring the Brain of the Consumer. Springer, and London, UK.

About the Contributors

Ricardo Fontes Correia started an academic career in 2003, and is Associated Professor at the Polytechnic Institute of Bragança (Portugal), where he is the head of the Master programme in Tourism Marketing, and visiting Professor at ISM University of Management and Economics (Lithuania). Ricardo has served as an external consultant in programs such as the European Union Agris Program and Interreg and as consultant for Deloitte & Touche. We should also emphasize his regular participation in research programs, conferences and international scientific meetings, as well as the publication of several chapters in books and articles in international journals.

Dominyka Venciute as contributor: her short bio that should be added is the following: Dr. Dominyka Venciute is Senior Assistant Professor and Postdoctoral Researcher at the ISM University of Management and Economics where she teaches Marketing Principles, Social Media Marketing and Integrated Marketing Communications. Besides her activities in academia, she runs a personal branding and marketing consultancy that aims to help professionals and organizations unleash the power of their personal and corporate brands.

Bruno Barbosa Sousa is Adjunct Professor of Marketing at Polytechnic Institute of Cávado and Ave (IPCA), Portugal and PhD in Marketing and Strategy in Universidade do Minho, Portugal. Head of Masters Program - Tourism Management and Marketing Tourism (IPCA); CiTUR – Center for Tourism Research, Development and Innovation and UNIAG research member. He has published in the Journal of Enterprising Communities, Tourism Management Perspectives, Current Issues in Tourism, Journal of Organizational Change Management, World Review of Entrepreneurship, Management and Sust. Development, among others.

Sefa Asortse, is currently working on his thesis relating to supply chain and logistic management as a Phd student in the department of management, Faculty of Business Administration, University of Nigeria, Enugu Campus. He is a certified electrical engineer with vast knowledge in rural electrification. His professional work involves management of people, resources, technology built on green principles and ensuring electricity is delivered to rural community along the power supply chain. He is a research assistance and has experience in green human resources management and entrepreneurship development. He is gradually developing scholarly skills in general management, digital visibility for business sustainability marketing and supply chain and logistic management in particular.

Ana Canavarro is assistant professor at IPAM Porto, collaborated with several university institutions over the years. She has 13 years of shopping center management experience. Bachelor in Law, from the University of Porto, she is also post-graduated in Marketing Management and Business Management. She is PhD in Political Science, Citizenship and International Relations. She is still specialist title in Marketing and Advertising.

Edna Denga is a graduate student at the American University of Nigeria.

Alexandre Duarte has a PhD in Communication Sciences from University of Minho, a Master degree in Communication & Image and a Bachelor in Marketing & Advertising by IADE. Alexandre is an Assistant Professor in Universidade NOVA de Lisboa, invited Professor in Universidade Católica Portuguesa and researcher of the R&D Unit ICNOVA. Throughout his career, Alexandre had the opportunity to work for several multinational advertising agencies such as TBWA, Saatchi & Saatchi, Ogilvy, W/Portugal, W/Brazil, Lowe&Partners, or BrandiaCentral as a Senior Creative Copywriter. Author of many seminars on communication, regularly participates in different conferences and lectures in both business and academic contexts. Between 2012 and 2014, was the Tutor of the EUROBEST Young Marketers Academy and in the beginning of 2014, was appointed CEO of RESTART, an Institute of Creativity, Arts and New Technologies. In 2018 was invited to teach in the Universidade Católica Portuguesa, where now Coordinates the Post-Graduation Courses in Advertising&Creativity and Service Design and, in 2019 was re-elected member of the Directors Board of EDCOM - European Institute for Commercial Communications Education.

Ruta Fontes is a PhD Student in Tourism at Aveiro University, Portugal.

Nihan Tomris Küçün graduated from Uludağ University, Faculty of Arts and Science in 2008. In 2011, she completed the Master of Science in Marketing program at Eskisehir Osmangazi University Institute of Social Sciences and then completed the Business Administration PhD program at Trakya University. The author focuses on neuromarketing and customer behavior in her academic studies. She has been working as a post-doctoral researcher at Eskisehir Osmangazi University BILDAM Cognitive and Behavioural Research and Applications Centre since 2020.

Sebastiano Mereu is a Researcher for the Sports Business Research Academy, as well as Lecturer of Digital Marketing and Branding at BHMS Business & Hotel Management School and Kalaidos University of Applied Sciences in Switzerland. His main research interests include second-screening and spectator sports, uses and gratifications of watching unscripted shows, metaverse adoption, retro marketing and apparel promotion, driving social media engagement, intentions to watch women's sports, and more. He also works as a Digital Marketing and Communications Specialist for the Swiss National Museum. Dr. Mereu holds a Doctor of Business Administration degree and a Master of Science in Marketing degree from Heriot-Watt University, UK, and a Bachelor of Science (Hons.) in International Management degree from FHNW University of Applied Sciences Northwestern Switzerland.

Liu MingHui, Assistant Professor of Guangzhou College of Technology and Business, China. Research direction for tourism transportation, intelligent transportation operation and engineering.

Ana Pinto Borges has a PhD in Economics, Faculty of Economics, University of Porto, in 2009. Since 2010 is Coordinating Professor at ISAG - European Business School. Scientific Coordinator of Research Center in Business Sciences and Tourism (CICET – FCVC) since 2021 and coordinated the ISAG Research Center between 2015 and 2021. Author of several publications of papers and book chapters indexed to the main bibliographic databases (WoS - Clarivate Analytics and Scopus). She also publishes books of international distribution, namely "New Techniques for Brand Management in the Healthcare Sector", "Building Consumer-Brand Relationship in Luxury Brand Management" and "Gastronomy, Hospitality, and the Future of the Restaurant Industry". Participation in presentations in various national and international congresses and member of the scientific committees in academic events. Editor and one of the founding members of the European Journal of Applied Business and Management (EJABM). She supervised several final master's and doctoral works. Former Accenture consultant in the financial area. Economist at the Health Regulatory Entity since 2010 with the main function of carrying out sectoral studies and issuing opinions in the scope of access, quality and competition in the health sector.

Mariagrazia Provenzano is a PhD student.

Maria Randers is graduated in International Business and Communication at ISM University of Management and Economics, Lithuania.

Paula Rodrigues holds a Ph.D. in Management, in the Faculty of Economics at the University of Porto, Portugal. She is an Associate Professor in Brand Management at the School of Economics and Management, Lusíada University - North, Portugal. Since 1995, she teaches Brand Management, Consumer Behaviour, Econometrics, statistics, and Quantitative Methods at the Universidade Lusíada - Norte. She has published several scientific papers, chapters, and books. Her on-going research projects concern consumer-brand relationships in the field of luxury, tourism and hospitality, and consumer goods.

Cecilia Silvestri is Researcher of Commodity Science at the Department of Economics and Management (DEIM) at the University of Tuscia, Viterbo (Italy) where she held the course Quality and Customer Relationships. She had her PhD in 2011 in "Economics and local development" at the University of Tuscia. Consistent with carried out studies, her research has developed along the following guidelines: (i) Quality of goods, products and services. Studies and research on the quality according to the approaches of "Total Quality Management" and standards "ISO 9000", (ii) The relationship between quality and consumers, with particular reference to satisfaction and loyalty, (iii) Quality and innovation in the agro -food, (iv) Innovation and technology transfer, with particular attention to the role of technological innovation for territorial development.

Narasimha Rao Vajjhala is working as an Associate Professor and the Chair of the Information Systems department at the School of IT and Computing at the American University of Nigeria. He had previously worked at the Faculty of Engineering and Architecture at the University of New York Tirana, Albania. He is a senior member of ACM and IEEE. He is the Editor-in-Chief (EiC) of the International Journal of Risk and Contingency Management (IJRCM). He is also a member of the Risk Management Society (RIMS), and the Project Management Institute (PMI). He has over 20 years of experience teaching programming and database-related courses at both graduate and undergraduate levels in Europe and Africa. He has also worked as a consultant in technology firms in Europe and has experience participating in EU-funded projects. He has completed a Doctorate in Information Systems and Technology (United States); holds a Master of Science in Computer Science and Applications (India), and a Master of Business Administration with a specialization in Information Systems (Switzerland).

Elvira Vieira holds a PhD in Applied Economics from the University of Santiago de Compostela (Spain) is currently the Dean of ISAG-EBS (Porto, Portugal), where is also a Coordinating Professor and Researcher. President of the Board of Directors of the Consuelo Vieira da Costa Foundation (FCVC), Scientific Coordinator and Researcher in its Research Centre in Business Sciences and Tourism (CICET-FCVC). Adjunct Professor at the Polytechnic Institute of Viana do Castelo (IPVC) and Researcher at UNIAG – Applied Management Research Unit. She is the author of several indexed articles, papers, book chapters and 2 books, in the areas of Economics and Management, Business Sciences, and Tourism.

Liu Xinyu primary research interests encompass influencer communication, new media, and media integration. Currently pursuing a master's degree in communication studies at the Universidade católica portuguesa, previously earned a bachelor's degree in Portuguese studies from the University of Macau. Liu Xinyu's academic journey is enhanced by her hands-on experience through internships, where she focused on influencers and short videos. This practical exposure has propelled her to take a proactive stance toward deeply exploring this topic within the academic realm. She actively seeks opportunities to engage in and contribute to scholarly discussions centered around influencers.

Index

A

advertising 1-2, 7, 10, 12-13, 15-17, 45, 61-62, 64-66, 72-73, 78, 83, 85-86, 147, 151, 155, 160, 162, 175, 177, 185, 187, 191, 197-198, 203-211

agencies 1-2, 4-5, 10, 15-17, 86

B

Baltic states 4-5, 10, 15, 17

Brand Activertising 198, 204

Brand Activism 198, 200, 202-203, 205, 209

Brand Management 26, 171, 173-174, 177, 180, 193, 202

brand market 147, 150, 163-164

Brand Narrative 45-63, 65-67, 70, 174

Brand Story 51, 53, 67, 185

Branding 26, 37, 46, 48, 52, 57, 61, 171-189, 191-193, 197

Brands 3, 17, 21-23, 25-28, 30-31, 37, 45-47, 49-65, 67, 70-71, 84-86, 88-89, 114-115, 146-148, 150-152, 160-163, 171-193, 199-203, 205, 207-210

C

consumer behavior 18, 71-73, 78-79, 82-84, 88-89

consumer neuroscience 88

consumer perception 84, 123, 137-138, 140

credibility 1-4, 10-11, 15-18, 23, 28, 45, 50, 99, 137, 151, 153, 162, 180-181, 184, 188, 211

D

Digital age 59, 62, 65-66, 172-173, 175, 177, 191-193

Digital Branding 171-175, 180, 182, 184, 187, 189, 197

Digital Era 46, 171-173, 176-177, 179-180, 182, 187, 189-193, 197

Digital Marketing 46, 172-174, 176-177, 179, 183, 185, 187-190, 193

Digital technology 138, 177, 189

Digital tools 49, 88, 123, 132, 137-138

Digital transformation 123, 126

Digitalization 89, 173, 177, 191, 193

E

EEG 74, 78, 82-84

EMG 74, 77, 82-84

emotion recognition 77-79, 82

EVOO oil 124-125, 128, 130, 133-139

eye tracking 73, 75, 82-84

F

fMRI 72, 78-79, 82-84

fNIRS 79, 82

food 123, 125-128, 133, 135-137

G

GSR 73, 76, 82-84

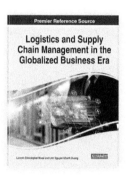

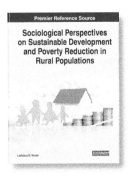

Printed in the USA
CPSIA information can be obtained
at www.ICGtesting.com
LVHW080809310724
786978LV00005B/291

9 781668 483510